About the Book

Food safety is a scientific discipline describing handling, preparation, and storage of food in ways that prevent foodborne illness. This includes a number of routines that should be followed to avoid potentially severe health hazards. The tracks within this line of thought are safety between industry and the market and then between the market and the consumer. In considering industry to market practices, food safety considerations include the origins of food including the practices relating to food labeling, food hygiene, food additives and pesticide residues, as well as policies on biotechnology and food and guidelines for the management of governmental import and export inspection and certification systems for foods.

About the Author

Dr. Nisha Tripati, MBBS currently Pusing MD in the department of Community Medicine SKIMS, Srinagar. She has done MBBS from National University of Singapore,and currently Assistant Professor in department of Food and Sciecne, Thereafter she worked as Assistant Professor In various Department of Emergency Medicine and Orthopaedics from MAMC, New delhi .She also worked as Assistant Surgeon in Department of Urology in Lucknow. She has attented various conferences, Scientific Sessions and Conventions at State level and National Level and has Actively Participated in Health camps and awareness programme organized by department of community medicine SKIMS.

Essential Oils in Food Safety Preservation, Flavor for vacuum and seal

Dr. Nisha Tripati

AMIGA PRESS INC.
DELHI (INDIA)

AMIGA PRESS INC.
H.O.: 28-A, Indra Park,
Chander Nagar, Delhi-110051 (India)
Tel.: 011-22504028, +91-98736-57000
E-mail: amigapress@gmail.com
amigaeditorial@gmail.com
amigapub@gmail.com
info@amigapress.co.in
Website : www.amigapress.co.in

This edition is published by Amiga Press Inc.

ISBN: 978-93-87295-26-1

First Published 2019

Printed and bound by Amiga Press Inc.

Preface

Food safety is the utilization of various resources and strategies to ensure that all types of foods are properly stored, prepared, and preserved so they are safe for consumption. Practicing this level of food sanitation begins with the purchase or acquisition of different food items and ends with the proper storage of leftovers for future use. Many of the food safety methods used in restaurants can also be employed at home.

Food safety is a scientific discipline describing handling, preparation, and storage of food in ways that prevent foodborne illness. This includes a number of routines that should be followed to avoid potentially severe health hazards. The tracks within this line of thought are safety between industry and the market and then between the market and the consumer. In considering industry to market practices, food safety considerations include the origins of food including the practices relating to food labeling, food hygiene, food additives and pesticide residues, as well as policies on biotechnology and food and guidelines for the management of governmental import and export inspection and certification systems for foods.

Food preservation refers to the process of treating and handling food to slow down spoilage. Food preservation is attained through various methods such as drying, exclusion of air, refrigeration and use of preservatives so as to increase the lifespan of the food in context. Food preservation provides an unfavorable condition for growth of bacteria and microorganisms that lead to food spoilage.

Food preservative technologies are accepted differently by consumers. Many processes designed to preserve food will involve a number of food preservation methods. Preserving fruit by turning it into jam, for example, involves boiling (to reduce the fruit's moisture content and to kill bacteria, yeasts, etc.), sugaring (to prevent their re-growth) and sealing within an airtight jar (to prevent recontamination). There are many traditional methods of preserving food that lhnit the energy inputs and reduce carbon footprint.

The book is also useful to the teachers and professionals for understanding important aspects ofFood Safety and Preservation.

-Author

Contents

Chapter-1

Introduction to Food

Food is any substance, usually composed of carbohydrates, fats, proteins and water, that can be eaten or drunk by an animal, including humans, for nutrition or pleasure. Items considered as food may be sourced from plants, animals or other categories such as fungus or fermented products like alcohol.

Although many human cultures sought food items through hunting and gathering, today most cultures use farming, ranching, and fishing, with hunting, foraging and other methods of a local nature included but playing a minor role. Most traditions have a recognizable cuisine, a specific set of cooking traditions, preferences, and practices, the study of which is known as gastronomy.

Many cultures have diversified their foods by means of preparation, cooking methods and manufacturing. This also includes a complex food trade which helps the cultures to economically survive by way of food, not just by consumption. Many cultures study the dietary analysis of food habits.

While humans are omnivores, religion and social constructs such as morality often affect which foods they will consume. Food safety is also a concern with food-borne illness claiming many lives each year. In many languages, food is often used metaphorically or figuratively, as in "food for thought".

The term *food* also includes liquid drinks. Food is the main source of energy and of nutrition for animals, and is usually of animal or plant origin. There are 4 (four) basic food energy sources: fats, proteins, carbohydrates and alcohol. Humans are omnivorous animals that can consume both plant and animal products.

We changed from *gatherers* to *hunter gatherers*. After the experience of the Ice Age it is probable that humans wanted to create some feeling of security by controlling what plants were growing and which animals were available.

This led to agriculture, which has continually improved and altered the way in which food is obtained.

TYPES OF FOOD

Fats

In biochemistry, fat is a generic term for a class of lipids. Fats are produced by organic processes in animals and plants. All fats are insoluble in water and have a density significantly below that of water (i.e., they float on water). Fats that are liquid at room temperature are often referred to as oil.

Most fats are composed primarily of triglycerides; some monoglycerides and diglycerides are mixed in, produced by incomplete esterification. These are extracted and used as an ingredient. Products with a lot of saturated fats tend to be solid at room temperature, while products containing unsaturated fats, which include monounsaturated fats and polyunsaturated fats, tend to be liquid at room temperature.

Predominantly saturated fats (solid at room temperature) include all animal fats (e.g., milk fat, lard, tallow), as well as palm oil, coconut oil, cocoa fat and hydrogenated vegetable oil (shortening).

All other vegetable fats, such as those coming from olive, peanut, maize (corn oil), cottonseed, sunflower, safflower, and soybean, are predominantly unsaturated and remain liquid at room temperature.

However, both vegetable and animal fats contain saturated and unsaturated fats. Some oils (such as olive oil) contain in majority monounsaturated fats, while others present quite a high percentage of polyunsaturated fats (sunflower, rape).

Myristic Acid	Palmitic Acid	Stearic Acid	Linoleic Acid
Oleic Acid Choline	Arachidonic	Omega-3	Phosphatidyl Acid
Omega-6	Cholesterol	Trans Fatty Acids	

Proteins

A protein is a complex, high molecular weight organic compound that consists of amino acids joined by peptide bonds. Protein is essential to the structure and function of all living cells and viruses. Many proteins are enzymes or subunits of enzymes.

Other proteins play structural or mechanical roles, such as those that form the struts and joints of the "cytoskeleton". Proteins are also nutrient sources for organisms that do not produce their own energy from sunlight. Proteins differ from carbohydrates chiefly in that they contain much nitrogen and a little bit of sulphur, besides carbon, oxygen and hydrogen. Proteins are a primary constituent of living things.

In carnivores protein is one of the largest component of the diet. The metabolism of proteins by the body releases ammonia, an extremely toxic substance. It is then converted in the liver into urea, a much less toxic chemical, which is excreted in urine. Some animals convert it into uric acid instead.

Protein Nutrition in Humans

In terms of human nutritional needs, proteins come in two forms: complete proteins contain all eight of the amino acids that humans cannot produce themselves, while incomplete proteins lack or contain only a very small proportion of one or more. Humans' bodies can make use of all the amino acids they extract from food for synthesizing new proteins, but the inessential ones themselves need not be supplied by the diet, because our cells can make them themselves. When protein is listed on a nutrition label it only refers to the amount of complete proteins in the food, though the food may be very strong in a subset of the essential amino acids. Animal-derived foods contain all of those amino acids, while plants are typically stronger in some acids than others. Complete proteins can be made in an all vegan diet by eating a sufficient variety of foods and by getting enough calories. It was once thought that in order to get the complete proteins vegans needed to do protein combining by getting all amino acids in the same meal (the most common example is eating beans with rice) but nutritionists now know that the benefits of protein combining can be achieved over the longer period of the day.

Ovo-lacto vegetarians usually do not have this problem, since egg's white and cow's milk contain all essential amino acids. Peanuts, soy milk, nuts, seeds, green peas, Legumes, the alga spirulina and some grains are some of the richest sources of plant protein. All eight essential amino acids must be part of one diet in order to survive and are needed in a fixed ratio. A shortage if any one of these amino acids will constrain the body's ability to make the proteins it needs to function. Different foods contain different ratios of the essential amino acids. By mixing foods that are rich in some amino acids with foods that are rich in others, one can acquire all the needed amino acids in sufficient quantities.

Omnivores typically eat a sufficient variety of foods that this is not an issue, however, vegetarians and especially vegans should be careful to eat appropriate combinations of foods (e.g., nuts and green vegetables) so as to get all the essential amino acids in sufficient quantities that the body may produce all the proteins that it needs. Protein deficiency can lead to symptoms such as fatigue, insulin resistance, hair loss, loss of hair pigment (hair that should be black becomes reddish), loss of muscle mass (proteins repair muscle tissue), low body temperature, and hormonal irregularities. Severe protein deficiency is fatal. Excess protein can cause problems as well, such as causing the immune system to overreact, liver dysfunction from increased toxic residues, possibly bone loss due to increased acidity in the blood, and foundering (foot problems) in horses. Proteins can often figure in allergies and allergic reactions to certain foods. This is because the structure of each form of protein is slightly different, and some may trigger a response from the immune system while others are perfectly safe. Many people are allergic to casein, the protein in milk; gluten, the protein in wheat and other grains; the particular proteins found in peanuts; or those in shellfish or other seafoods. It is extremely unusual for the same person to adversely react to more than two different types of proteins.

Table: Amino Acids

Alanine	Arginine	Asparagine	Aspartic Acid
Cysteine	Glutamic Acid	Glycine	Histidine
Isoleucine	Leucine	Lysine	Methionine
Phenylalanine	Proline	Serine	Tryptophan
Tyrosine	Valine		

Carbohydrates

Carbohydrates (literally hydrates of carbon) are chemical compounds which act as the primary biological means of storing or consuming energy; other forms being via fat and protein. Relatively complex carboyhydrates are known as polysaccharides.

The simplest carbohydrates are monosaccharides, which are small straight-chain aldehydes and ketones with many hydroxyl groups added, usually one on each carbon except the functional group. Other carbohydrates are composed of monosaccharide units, and break down under hydrolysis. These may be classified as disaccharides, oligosaccharides, or polysaccharides, depending on whether they have two, several, or many monosaccharide units.

Food Phenolics

Phenolic food compounds (also known as aromatic food compounds) occur naturally in all foods: they give the food colour and flavour and help to prevent premature decomposition. Any substance is taken into the body for the purpose of providing nourishment. However, factors such as satisfying social needs, achieving psychological ends, and satisfying hunger, more than nutritional needs, govern the selection and consumption of foods.

When foods are selected carefully, they can provide all of the essential nutrients needed for normal functioning of the human body. In this context, food is necessary to provide energy, to provide structural components for building and repairing body tissues, and to regulate body processes.

There are essential nutrients (carbohydrates, fats, proteins, minerals, vitamins, and water) that have specific functions in the human body. When the energy-yielding nutrients, that is, carbohydrates, fats, and proteins, are oxidized in the body, energy is captured in a chemical compound known as adenosine triphosphate (ATP), which will then release the energy slowly so that it can be used for physical activity (work), heat production, and metabolic processes.

Enzymes, vitamins, and minerals, as well as water, are needed in order for these oxidation reactions to take place. Energy requirements are expressed in terms of kilocalories (kcal), calories (cal), or kilojoules (kJ). Fats and carbohydrates contain only the elements carbon, oxygen, and hydrogen. Since fats contain less oxygen than carbohydrates, they have greater potential for oxidation and thus provide more energy per gram than carbohydrates. Proteins also contain nitrogen, but this does not contribute substantially to the energy value.

The physiological fuel value, or the amount of energy generated in the body, of 1 gramme of protein is 4 kcal (17 kJ); carbohydrate, 4 kcal (17 kJ); fat, 9 kcal (38 kJ). Although it is unlikely that any individual food or combination of foods can provide complete disease protection, risk of chronic disease can be reduced by increased consumption of plant-based foods and decreased consumption of fats.

IMPORTANT FOOD ISSUES

FOOD SAFETY, QUALITY AND CONSUMER PROTECTION

The terms food safety and food quality can sometimes be confusing. Food safety refers to all those hazards, whether chronic or acute, that may make food injurious to the health of the consumer. It is not negotiable. Quality includes all other attributes that influence a product's value to the consumer. This includes negative attributes such as spoilage, contamination with filth, discoloration, off-odours and positive attributes such as the origin, colour, flavour, texture and processing method of the food. This distinction between safety and quality has implications for public policy and influences the nature and content of the food control system most suited to meet predetermined national objectives. Food control is defined as:

- A mandatory regulatory activity of enforcement by national or local authorities to provide consumer protection and ensure that all foods during production, handling, storage, processing, and distribution are safe, wholesome and fit for human consumption; conform to safety and quality requirements; and are honestly and accurately labelled as prescribed by law.

The foremost responsibility of food control is to enforce the food law(s) protecting the consumer against unsafe, impure and fraudulently presented food by prohibiting the sale of food not of the nature, substance or quality demanded by the purchaser. Confidence in the safety and integrity of the food supply is an important requirement for consumers. Foodborne disease outbreaks involving agents such as *Escherichia coli*, Salmonella and chemical contaminants highlight problems with food safety and increase public anxiety that modern farming systems, food processing and marketing do not provide adequate safeguards for public health. Factors which contribute to potential hazards in foods include improper agricultural practices; poor hygiene at all stages of the food chain; lack of preventive controls in food processing and preparation operations; misuse of chemicals; contaminated raw materials, ingredients and water; inadequate or improper storage, etc.

Specific concerns about food hazards have usually focused on:

- Microbiological hazards;
- Pesticide residues;
- Misuse of food additives;
- Chemical contaminants, including biological toxins; and
- Adulteration.

The list has been further extended to cover genetically modified organisms, allergens, veterinary drugs residues and growth promoting hormones used in the production of animal products. Consumers expect protection from hazards occurring along the entire food chain, from primary producer through consumer.

Protection will only occur if all sectors in the chain operate in an integrated way, and food control systems address all stages of this chain. As no mandatory activity of this nature can achieve its objectives fully without the cooperation and active participation of all stakeholders e.g. farmers, industry, and consumers, the term Food Control System is used in these Guidelines to describe the integration of a mandatory regulatory approach with preventive and educational strategies that protect the whole food chain.

Thus an ideal food control system should include effective enforcement of mandatory requirements, along with training and education, community outreach programmes and promotion of voluntary compliance. The introduction of preventive approaches such as the Hazard Analysis Critical Control Point System, have resulted in industry taking greater responsibility for and control of food safety risks. Such an integrated approach facilitates improved consumer protection, effectively stimulates agriculture and the food processing industry, and promotes domestic and international food trade.

GLOBAL CONSIDERATIONS

International Trade

With an expanding world economy, liberalization of food trade, growing consumer demand, developments in food science and technology, and improvements in transport and communication, international trade in fresh and processed food will continue to increase. Access of countries to food export markets will continue to depend on their capacity to meet the regulatory requirements of importing countries. Creating and sustaining demand for their food products in world markets relies on building the trust and confidence of importers and consumers in the integrity of their food systems. With agricultural production the focal point of the economies of most developing countries, such food protection measures are essential.

CODEX ALIMENTARIUS COMMISSION

The Codex Alimentarius Commission is an intergovernmental body that coordinates food standards at the international level. Its main objectives are to protect the health of consume and ensure fair practices in food trade. The CAC has proved to be most successful in achieving international harmonization in food quality and safety requirements. It has formulated international standards for a wide range of food products and specific requirements covering pesticide residues, food additives, veterinary drug residues, hygiene, food contaminants, labelling, etc. These Codex recommendations are used by governments to determine and refine policies and programmes under their national food control system.

More recently, Codex has embarked on a series of activities based on risk assessment to address microbiological hazards in foods, an area previously unattended. Codex work has created worldwide awareness of food safety, quality and consumer protection issues, and has achieved international consensus on how to deal with them scientifically, through a risk-based approach. As a result, there has been a continuous appraisal of the principles of food safety and quality at the international level. There is increasing pressure for the adoption of these principles at the national level.

SPS and TBT Agreements

The conclusion of the Uruguay Round of Multilateral Trade Negotiations in Marrakech led to the establishment of the WTO on 1st January 1995, and to the coming into force of the Agreement on the Application of Sanitary and Phytosanitary Measures and the Agreement on Technical Barriers to Trade. Both these Agreements are relevant in understanding the requirements for food protection measures at the national level, and the rules under which food is traded internationally. The SPS Agreement confirms the right of WTO member countries to apply measures to protect human, animal and plant life and health. The Agreement covers all relevant laws, decrees, regulations; testing, inspection, certification and approval procedures; and packaging and labelling requirements directly related to food safety.

Member States are asked to apply only those measures for protection that are based on scientific principles, only to the extent necessary, and not in a manner which may constitute a disguised restriction on international trade. The Agreement encourages use of international standards, guidelines or recommendations where they exist, and identifies those from Codex to be consistent with provisions of SPS. Thus, the Codex standards serve as a benchmark for comparison of national sanitary and phytosanitary measures. While it is not compulsory for Member States to apply Codex Standards, it is in their best interests to harmonize their national food standards with those elaborated by Codex. The TBT Agreement requires that technical regulations on traditional quality factors, fraudulent practices, packaging, labelling, etc., imposed by countries will not be more restrictive on imported products than they are on products produced domestically. It also encourages use of international standards.

ELEMENTS OF A NATIONAL FOOD CONTROL SYSTEM

OBJECTIVES

The principal objectives of national food control systems are:

- Protecting public health by reducing the risk of foodborne illness;
- Protecting consumers from unsanitary, unwholesome, mislabelled or adulterated food; and
- Contributing to economic development by maintaining consumer confidence in the food system and providing a sound regulatory foundation for domestic and international trade in food.

SCOPE

Food control systems should cover all food produced, processed and marketed within the country, including imported food. Such systems should have a statutory basis and be mandatory in nature.

BUILDING BLOCKS

While the components and priorities of a food control system will vary from country to country, most systems will typically comprise the following components:

Food Law and Regulations

The development of relevant and enforceable food laws and regulations is an essential component of a modern food control system. Many countries have inadequate food legislation and this will impact on the effectiveness of all food control activities carried out in the country. Food law has traditionally enforcement tools for removing unsafe food from commerce and punishing responsible parties after the fact. It has generally not provided food control agencies with a clear mandate and authority to prevent food safety problems. The result has been food safety programmes that are reactive and enforcement- oriented rather than preventive and holistic in their approach to reducing the risk of foodborne illness. To the extent possible, modern food laws not only contain the necessary legal powers and prescriptions to ensure food safety, but also allow the competent food authority or authorities to build preventive approaches into the system.

In addition to legislation, governments need updated food standards. In recent years, many highly prescriptive standards have been replaced by horizontal standards that address the broad issues involved in achieving food safety objectives. While horizontal standards are a viable approach to delivering food safety goals, they require a food chain that is highly controlled and supplied with good data on food safety risks and risk management strategies and as such may not be feasible for many developing countries.

Similarly, many standards on food quality issues have been cancelled and replaced by labelling requirements. In preparing food regulations and standards, countries should take full advantage of Codex standards and food safety sessions learned in other countries. Taking into account the experiences in other countries while tailoring the information, concepts and requirements to the national context is the only sure way to develop a modern regulatory framework that will both satisfy national needs and meet the demands of the SPS Agreement and trading partners.

Food legislation should include the following aspects:

- It must provide a high level of health protection;
- It should include clear definitions to increase consistency and legal security;
- It should be based on high quality, transparent, and independent scientific advice following risk assessment, risk management and risk communication;
- It should include provision for the use of precaution and the adoption of provisional measures where an unacceptable level of risk to health has been identified and where full risk assessment could not be performed;
- It should include provisions for the right of consumers to have access to accurate and sufficient information;
- It should provide for tracing of food products and for their recall in case of problems;
- It should include clear provisions indicating that primary responsibility for food safety and quality rests with producers and processors;
- It should include obligation to ensure that only safe and fairly presented food is placed on the market;
- It should also recognise the country's international obligations particularly in relation to trade; and
- It should ensure transparency in the development of food law and access to information.

Food Control Management

Effective food control systems require policy and operational coordination at the national level. While the detail of such functions will be determined by the national legislation, they would include the establishment of a leadership function and administrative structures with clearly defined accountability for issues such as: the development and implementation of an integrated national food control strategy; operation of a national food control programme; securing funds and allocating resources; setting standards and regulations; participation in international food control related activities; developing emergency response procedures; carrying out risk analysis; etc. Core responsibilities include the establishment of regulatory measures, monitoring system performance, facilitating continuous improvement, and providing overall policy guidance.

Inspection Services

The administration and implementation of food laws require a qualified, trained, efficient and honest food inspection service. The food inspector is the key functionary who has day-to-day contact with the food industry, trade and often the public. The reputation and integrity of the food control system depends, to a very large extent, on their integrity and skill.

The responsibilities of the inspection services include:

- Inspecting premises and processes for compliance with hygienic and other requirements of standards and regulations;
- Evaluating HACCP plans and their implementation;
- Sampling food during harvest, processing, storage, transport, or sale to establish compliance, to contribute data for risk assessments and to identify offenders;
- Recognizing different forms of food decomposition by organoleptic assessment; identifying food which is unfit for human consumption; or food which is otherwise deceptively sold to the consumer; and taking the necessary remedial action;
- Recognizing, collecting and transmitting evidence when breaches of law occur, and appearing in court to assist prosecution;
- Encouraging voluntary compliance in particular by means of quality assurance procedures;
- Carrying out inspection, sampling and certification of food for import/export inspection purposes when so required;
- In Establishments working under safety assurance programmes such as HACCP, conduct risk based audits.

Proper training of food inspectors is a prerequisite for an efficient food control system. As current food systems are quite complex, the food inspector must be trained in food science and technology to understand the industrial processes, identify potential safety and quality problems, and have the skill and experience to inspect the premises, collect food samples and carry out an overall evaluation. The inspector must have a good understanding of the relevant food laws and regulations, their powers under those laws, and the obligations such laws impose on the food sector. They should also be conversant with procedures for collecting evidence, writing inspection reports, collecting samples and sending them to a laboratory for analysis. With gradual introduction of HACCP systems in the food industry, the inspector should be trained to handle HACCP audit responsibilities.

Clearly, there is a continuing need for training and upgrading the skills of existing inspectional staff and having a policy for human resource development, especially the development of inspectional specialists in specific technical areas. As human resources in some food control agencies in developing countries may be limited, environmental health inspectors are often also asked to work as food inspectors. This is not the ideal situation as they may lack the skills and knowledge to effectively evaluate and inspect food operations. If environmental health inspectors must be used, then they should be carefully supervised and provided with on-the-job training.

Laboratory Services: Food Monitoring and Epidemiological Data

Laboratories are an essential component of a food control system. The establishment of laboratories requires considerable capital investment and they are expensive to maintain and operate. Therefore careful planning is necessary to achieve optimum results. The number and location of the laboratories should be determined in relation to the objectives of the system and the volume of work.

If more than one laboratory is required, consideration should be given to apportioning the analytical work to achieve the most effective coverage of the food analyses to be performed and also to having a central reference laboratory equipped for sophisticated and reference analyses. All food analysis laboratories may not be under the control of one agency or ministry, and a number could be under the jurisdiction of the states, provinces and local authorities. The Food Control Management should, however, lay down the norms for food control laboratories and monitor their performance. The laboratories should have adequate facilities for physical, microbiological and chemical analyses. In addition to simple routine analysis, the laboratories can be equipped with more sophisticated instruments, apparatus and library facilities as required.

It is not only the type of equipment that determines the accuracy and reliability of analytical results but also the qualification and skill of the analyst and the reliability of the method used. The analytical results of a food control laboratory are often used as evidence in a court of law to determine compliance with regulations or standards of the country. It is therefore necessary that utmost care be taken to ensure the efficient and effective performance of the laboratory. The introduction of analytical quality assurance programmes and accreditation of the laboratory by an appropriate accreditation agency within the country or from outside, enables the laboratory to improve its performance and to ensure reliability, accuracy and repeatability of its results. Prescription of official methods of sampling and analysis also support this effort.

An important element of a national food control system is its integration in a national food safety system so that links between food contamination and foodborne diseases can be established and analysed. Access to reliable and current intelligence on the incidence of foodborne illness is critical. The laboratory facilities for this type of activity are generally situated outside the food control agencies. It is essential, however, that effective linkages are established between food control agencies and the public health system including epidemiologists and microbiologists. In this way information on foodborne diseases may be linked with food monitoring data, and lead to appropriate risk-based food control policies. This information includes annual incidence trends, identification of susceptible population groups, identification of hazardous foods, identification and tracing of causes of foodborne diseases, and the development of early warning systems for outbreaks and food contamination.

Information, Education, Communication and Training

An increasingly important role for food control systems is the delivery of information, education and advice to stakeholders across the farm-to-table continuum. These activities include the provision of balanced factual information to consumers; the provision of information packages and educational programmes for key officials and workers in the food industry; development of train-the-trainer programmes; and provision of reference literature to extension workers in the agriculture and health sectors. Food control agencies should address the specific training needs of their food inspectors and laboratory analysts as a high priority. These activities provide an important means of building food control expertise and skills in all interested parties, and thereby serve an essential preventive function.

CONSIDERATIONS OF FOOD SAFETY AND CONSUMER PROTECTION

Food safety is an essential public health issue for all countries. Foodborne food represent serious threats to the health of thousands of millions of people. Serious outbreaks of foodborne disease have been documented on every continent in the past decades, illustrating both the public health and social significance of these diseases.

Consumers everywhere view foodborne disease outbreaks with ever- increasing concern. Outbreaks are likely, however, to be only the most visible aspect of a much broader, more persistent problem. Foodborne diseases not only significantly affect people's health and well-being, but they also have economic consequences for individuals, families, communities, businesses and countries. These diseases impose a substantial burden on healthcare systems and markedly reduce economic productivity. Poor people tend to live from day-to-day, and loss of income due to foodborne illness perpetuates the cycle of poverty. The integration and consolidation of food industries and the globalization of the food trade are changing the patterns of food production and distribution. Food and feed are distributed over far greater distances than before, creating the conditions necessary for widespread outbreaks of foodborne illness. In a recent crisis, more than 1,500 farms in Europe received dioxincontaminated feed from a single source over a two-week period. Food produced from animals given this contaminated fodder found its way onto every continent within weeks.

The international spread of meat and bonemeal prepared from cattle affected by bovine spongiform encephalitis needs no further description. The full economic consequences of such incidents and the anxiety raised among consumers are still being assessed. Other factors account for the emergence of food safety as a public health issue. Increasing urbanization leads to greater requirements for transport, storage and preparation of food.

In developing countries, food is often prepared by street vendors. In developed countries, up to 50 per cent of the food budget may be spent on food prepared outside the home. All these changes lead to situations in which a single source of contamination can have widespread, even global consequences. The globalization of the food trade offers many benefits to consumers, as it results in a wider variety of high-quality foods that are accessible, affordable and safe, meeting consumer demand. The global food trade provides opportunities for food-exporting countries to earn foreign exchange, which is indispensable for the economic development of many countries.

However, these changes also present new challenges to safe food production and distribution and have been shown to have widespread repercussions on health. Food safety programmes are increasingly focusing on a farm-to-table approach as an effective means of reducing foodborne hazards. This holistic approach to the control of food-related risks involves consideration of every step in the chain, from raw material to food consumption. Hazards can enter the food chain on the farm and can continue to be introduced or exacerbated at any point in the chain. Although significant progress has been made in many countries in making food safer, thousands of millions of people become ill each year from eating contaminated food. The emergence of increased antimicrobial resistance in bacteria causing disease is aggravating this picture. The public is increasingly aware of the risks posed by pathogenic microorganisms and chemical substances in the food supply. The introduction of new technologies, including genetic engineering and irradiation, in this climate of concern about food safety is posing a special challenge. Some new technologies will increase agricultural production and make food safer, but their usefulness and safety must be demonstrated if they are to be accepted by consumers. Furthermore, the evaluation must be participatory, transparent and conducted using internationally agreed methods. Until recently, most systems for regulating food safety were based on legal definitions of unsafe food, enforcement programmes for the removal of unsafe food from the market and sanctions for the responsible parties after the fact.

These traditional systems cannot respond to existing and emerging challenges to food safety because they do not provide or stimulate a preventive approach. During the past decade, there was a transition to risk analysis based on better scientific knowledge of foodborne illness and its causes. This provides a preventive basis for regulatory measures for food safety at both national and international levels. The risk-based approach must be backed by information on the most appropriate and effective means to control foodborne hazards.

MICROBIOLOGICAL HAZARDS

The dangers of foodborne pathogenic microorganisms have been known for decades. The risk of milk-borne transmission of tuberculosis and salmonellosis was recognized early in the twentieth century, and control by pasteurization was an early intervention. Similarly, problems with botulism were managed by controlling the application of heat to low acid foods in hermetically sealed containers. Despite remarkable advances in food science and technology, foodborne illness is a rising cause of morbidity in all countries and the list of potential foodborne microbial pathogens keeps increasing.

Furthermore, foodborne illness is a major cause of preventable death and economic burden in most countries. Unfortunately, most countries have limited data on foodborne disease and its impact on public health. It is only recently that the burden of food contamination and foodborne disease have been systematically assessed and quantified. Studies on foodborne disease outbreaks in the USA, Australia, Germany, and India have confirmed the enormity of the problem with millions being affected or dying from foodborne diseases. The data indicates that up to 30 per cent of the population in industrialized countries may be affected by foodborne illness each year.

The Global incidence 1998 it was estimated that 2.2 million people, including 1.8 million children, died from diarrhoeal diseases. The economic cost associated with foodborne diseases caused by microorganisms has only recently been estimated. In the US, the costs of human illness due to seven specific pathogens have been estimated to range between US $6.5 billion to $34.9 billion. The medical costs and value of lives lost from five foodborne infections in England and Wales were estimated at UK £300-700 million annually in 1996.

The cost of an estimated 11,500 cases of food poisoning per day in Australia was calculated at AUD $2.6 billion annually. Yet on the basis of per capita income, the economic burden on people in India affected by an outbreak of Staphylococcus aureus food poisoning was found to be higher than in case of a similar outbreak in the US. Major outbreaks involving *E.coli* and Salmonella have highlighted problems with food safety and increased public anxiety that modern farming systems, food processing and marketing may not provide adequate safeguards for public health. While our understanding of the ecology of food poisoning organisms and the environment in which they may grow and survive has increased, our ability to control some of these organisms has declined.

This may be due in part to modified production practices, lack of control of hazards at the farm level, industry difficulties in controlling hazards during production, growing demand for fresh foods, the trend towards minimal processing of foodstuffs and longer shelf-life for many foodstuffs. For example, Salmonella persists as a major cause of food poisoning and its incidence is on the rise. *Salmonella typhimurium* is widely distributed in cattle herds and is resistant to several antibiotics. The incidence of this organism is on the increase, as is the number of antibiotic resistant isolates.

More than one third of people infected by this organism require hospitalization with approximately three per cent of cases being fatal. Enterohaemorrhagic *Escherichia coli* has emerged as a significant foodborne pathogen, and has been highly publicised through major outbreaks of disease. E.coli O157:H7 was first recognized as a pathogen in 1982, but progress to identify reservoirs and sources of the organism was initially hampered by a lack of sufficiently sensitive detection methods.

Other strains of enterohaemorrhagic *E.coli* pose a particular problem in that they are impossible to differentiate culturally from other flora in the gut. Identification requires advanced techniques. *E.coli* serves as an example of the limitation of the present knowledge and understanding of many pathogens and how they contaminate food. In the past few decades a range of microorganisms have emerged as potential causes of foodborne disease. Several relatively unknown bacteria have been identified as major causes of foodborne illness, e.g. *Campylobacter jejuni, Vibrio parahaemolyticus,* and *Yersinia enterocolitica* may cause foodborne illness. As microorganisms have the ability to adapt, modified modes of food production, preservation and packaging have resulted in altered food safety hazards.

For example, organisms such as Listeria monocytogenes, and to a lesser extent *Clostridium botulinum,* have emerged and re-emerged because of changes in the way high-risk foods are packaged and processed. A range of protozoa and viruses may also infect food, e.g. *Cryptosporidium parvum, Toxoplasma gondii, Clonorchis sinensis, Norwalk virus,* and hepatitis A. The effective prevention and control of these organisms requires widespread education and possibly new initiatives such as HACCP being introduced at primary production level.

CHEMICAL HAZARDS

Chemical hazards are also a significant source of foodborne illness, although the effect is often difficult to link to a particular food and may occur long after consumption. In particular, there have been long-standing concerns about the chemical safety of food due to misuse of pesticides during food production and storage, resulting in the occurrence of undesirable residues.

Similarly, heavy metal contaminants can enter food through soil or water or food contact material, as can other environmental contaminants such as PCBs. All can lead to acute or chronic illness. More recently, contamination from dioxins entering the animal feed supply has highlighted both the importance of controlling the whole food chain and the international concerns about food safety systems.

Misuse and illegal use of food additives create their own food safety problems. Phthalates in infant formulae, substances in food with oestrogenic activity, and veterinary drug residues, etc. have also heightened public concern. These problems are not confined to food produced on land. They also include algal toxins in fish and the widespread use of chemicals in fish farming. Mycotoxins are another group of highly toxic or carcinogenic chemical contaminants of biological origin produced by certain species of fungi. Five important mycotoxins are aflatoxins, ochratoxins, fumonisins, zearalenone, and trichothecenes. Crops such as peanuts, corn, pistachio, walnuts, copra are susceptible to mycotoxin contamination.

Aflatoxins are among the most studied mycotoxins, and the

relationship between aflatoxin ingestion and primary liver cancer is well established. Almost all plant products can serve as substrates for fungal growth, and subsequently mycotoxin contamination of human food and animal feed. Animal feed contaminated with mycotoxins can result in the carry-over of toxins through milk and meat to consumers.

While the importance of chemicals hazards is well recognized, our understanding of the effect of chemicals in food intolerances and allergies, endocrine system disruption, immunotoxicity, and certain forms of cancer are incomplete. Further research is necessary to determine the role of chemicals information is available on the exposure of the population to chemicals in food.

FOOD ADULTERATION

Consumers, particularly in developing countries, are often exposed to wilful adulteration of their food supply. This can lead to health hazards and to financial losses for the consumer. Adulteration of milk and milk products, honey, spices, edible oils, and the use of colours to mask product quality to cheat the consumer are quite common.

Although risks associated with adulteration are usually low, such episodes invoke public outrage and anger as it violates public trust in the integrity of the food supply. With 60-70 per cent of the income of middle class families in developing countries being spent on food, food adulteration can impact heavily on both the family budget and the health status of the family members.

GENETICALLY MODIFIED ORGANISMS AND NOVEL FOODS

Modern biotechnology, also referred to as genetic engineering or genetic manipulation, involves transfer of hereditary material from one organism to another in a way that cannot be achieved naturally *i.e.* through mating or cross breeding. Genetic engineering can now transfer the hereditary material across species boundaries. This can broaden the range of genetic changes that can be made to food and can expand the spectrum of possible food sources. The accelerating pace of developments in modern biotechnology has opened a new era in food production and this may have a tremendous impact on world food supply systems.

However, there are considerable differences of opinion among scientists about the safety, nutritional value and environmental effects of such foods. Overall, it is argued that the consequences of some gene transfer methods are less predictable when compared to those of traditional plant breeding methods and considerable scientific evidence will be needed to clear these foods from points of view of nutrition, food safety and impact on the environment.

The revolutionary nature of modern biotechnology and its likely impact on world food resources has created worldwide interest and debate among scientists, consumers and industry as well as among policy makers at national and international levels.

URBANIZATION, NUTRITION AND FOOD SECURITY

In 2020, the world population is projected to reach 7.6 billion, an increase of 31 per cent over the mid-1996 population of 5.8 billion. Approximately 98 per cent of the population growth occurring during this period will take place in developing countries. While urbanization is a global phenomenon, it has been estimated that between the years 1995 and 2020 the developing world's urban population will double, reaching 3.4 billion. Such population growth poses great challenges to world food security and food systems.

Further extension of improved agriculture and animal husbandry practices; use of measures to prevent and control pre- and post-harvest losses; more efficient food processing and distribution systems; introduction of new technologies including the application of biotechnology, and others will have to be exploited to increase food availability to meet the needs of growing populations. Growing urbanization and associated changes in the way food is produced and marketed have led to a lengthening of the food chain and potential for introducing or exacerbating foodborne hazards.

NUTRITIVE VALUE OF FOODS

The nutritional value of food that we eat greatly governs our health and therefore most of the activities that we do in our life. Our food is the only source of energy, minerals and vitamin for our body and is responsible for the efficient metabolism of the same. In order to get different types of nutrients in the right quantities, we should eat all types of food including fruits such as apricot, banana, apple, orange, mango, pomegranate, grapes, grapefruit, pear, plum, cherry, dates, pineapple, blueberry, kiwi, lemon, strawberry, avocado, watermelon, etc.; edible nuts such as almond, walnut, cashew, peanuts, peanut butter, pecans, etc.; vegetables such as potato, tomato, mushroom, cucumber, beet, cabbage, radish, carrot, onion, broccoli, spinach, pumpkin, seaweed, chestnut, eggplant, turnip, sweet potato, lettuce, cauliflower, etc.; cereals such as corn or maize, wheat, rice, barley, oats, sorghums, millets, rye, etc.; animal products such as milk, cheese, butter, chicken, egg, egg whites, meat, beef, pork, fish, honey, shrimp, lobster, octopus, crab, etc.; spices such as celery, chilies, turmeric, clove, pepper, cinnamon, cardamom, ginger, garlic, etc.; oils such as mustard, flax seed, soybean, sunflower seed, coconut, olive, beverages such as wine, coffee, tea, alcohol, vodka, beer, etc.

It has become mandatory in many countries to print the nutritional value of the food item on the label. This gives consumers an idea of what they are eating, which is very necessary due to the increasing intake of fast food items such as pizza, burger, chips, etc., in our diet.

ALMOND

Almond and almond oil is used extensively in ancient medical techniques like Ayurveda and Unani medicines. Despite being a seed, it boasts of being counted in the premium health food category consisting whole foods such as other nuts.

Presence of high amounts of nutrients produces energy:

- *Nutrition Facts and Information about an Almond*: Almond is incredibly rich in minerals like Mangnese, Magnesium, Copper, Phosphorus, Iron, Zinc and Potassium. However, Selenium is also present in good amount.
- *Vitamin Content of an Almond*: These small nuts are a powerhouse of Vitamin E, Riboflavin, Thiamin, Niacin and Folate. Good amounts of Vitamin B6 and Pantothenic Acid are also present.
- *Calorie Content of an Almond*: Almonds have a large calorie content, being 575.0 per 100 gm.
- *Health Benefits of an Almond*: The small sized almond comes packed with sizeable amount of health benefits. It lowers the risk of gallstones, weight gain, high blood pressure, cardiovascular disease and diabetes. It reduces blood sugar level, weight and LDL (bad) cholestrol, including almonds in your diet keeps heart and blood healthy.

AVOCADO

Avocado is a fat-rich fruit having a fat content of about 23 per cent. It contains dietary fibres. It is rich in minerals such as copper, magnesium, manganese, and contains some amounts of iron, calcium, iodine, selenium, zinc and phosphorus.

- *Vitamin Content*: Avocado is well known for its high vitamin K and Vitamin A content. It also contains small amounts of Vitamin B, Vitamin C, Vitamin E, Thiamin, Riboflavin, Niacin, Vitamin B6, Biotin, and Folate.
- *Calorific Content of Avocado*: Fruits are normally not rich in calories and are eaten for their ability to provide vitamins, minerals and digestive fibrous content. However, avocado owing to its high fat content provides good quantity of calories. A 100 gm of edible portion of the fruit provides about 215 calories.
- *Health Benefits of Avocado*: The nutritional value of avocado

makes it good for indigestion, hair care, heart health, skin care, psoriasis, and bad breath.

APPLE

An apple a day keeps the doctor away. The health benefits of apple are enormous making it one of the most valuable and savored fruits throughout the world.

- Nutrition Facts and Information about Apple: Apple contains minerals such as magnesium, copper, manganese, copper, calcium, iron, potassium and phosphorus in small quantities. Apple also contains dietary fibre, which help in reducing the bad cholesterol levels.
- *Vitamin Content*: Apple is rich in Vitamin A and Vitamin C. Vitamin. A concentration is higher in the outer skin than the flesh. Like potatoes, Vitamin C concentration is higher just below the skin in apples also. Hence the skin of the apple should not be discarded. Other vitamins present in apple include Vitamin K, Thiamin, Riboflavin, and Vitamin B6.
- *Calorie Content of Apple*: Apple does not have calories as high as avocado or olives, yet, it is an excellent source of energy. The calorie content varies as per the type of apple. Further, apple contains sugars which are easily absorbed by the body. Hence, the weak and ill are often advised to eat apples for gaining weight and fast recovery.
- *Health Benefits of Apple*: The nutritional value of apple makes it useful for digestion, stomach disorders, anaemia, wekness, dental care, dysentry, heart disease, rheumatism, eye disorders, cancer, gout, and skin care.
- *How to Choose an Apple:* When you buy an apple make sure that the apple skin is shiny. Further, the apple should be firm and free of wrinkles. Apricot and Watermelon

APROCPT AMD WATERMELON

APRICOT

Apricots can be related to the Peach family, and usually they are found first at the arrival of summers. This fleshy fruit with less juice is a rich source of Beta-Carotene and Lycopene. Apricots have a velvet like skin, it's kernels resemble and tastes like almonds and are used well as their substitute. Interestingly, not only the fruit but its kernel too has cancer fighting nutrient, in kernels it is Amygladin and the fruit contains Lycopene. An Apricot can be consumed raw, in the fruit salad or even canned, interestingly canned ones are relatively high on Beta-Carotene as compared to raw.

- *Nutrition Facts and Information about an Apricot*: An Apricot is a rich source of potassium, manganese and copper. Iron, magnesium and phosphorus are present in small amounts. Traces of calcium and zinc are also found in it.
- *Vitamin Content of an Apricot*: An Apricot can be said to be loaded with Vitamin A and Vitamin C. It is enriched with Vitamin E, Vitamin K, Niacin and Vitamin B6. Whereas Thiamin, Riboflavin, Folate and Pantothenic Acid are present in small quantities.
- *Calorie Content of an Apricot*: Apricots are rich in many nutrients and fibre but has a calorie count of just 48.0 per 100 gm.
- *Health Benefits of an Apricot*: An Apricot's high content of Vitamin A protects eye sight. Its large Beta-Carotene and Lycopene content provides immunity to heart related disease. The carotenoid Lycopene has been found useful in the prevention of Prostate cancer in men. Presence of good amount of fibre makes an Apricot a must to eat fruit to avoid digestive problems.

WATERMELON

This king sized fruit certainly is loaded with the power of quenching your thirst and meeting your physiological needs for nutrients. Just in case you are only thinking of savoring the fruit content, may we let you know that in China even the rind left is either pickled or stir fried to make it a delicious serving. Its seed which is high in fat and protein is also found useful as a snack or else as an oilseed.

Altogether, it is a real treat to savor in extreme summers:

- *Nutrition Facts and Information about Watermelon*: It is not largely enriched with minerals but has considerable amounts of potassium, manganese, magnesium and copper. While calcium, iron, phosphorus, zinc and selenium are found in minute quantity.
- *Vitamin Content of Watermelon*: A Watermelon largely constitutes Vitamin A and Vitamin C. However, small amounts of Thiamine, Vitamin B6 and Pantothenic Acid are also present. Consists of Riboflavin, Niacin and Folate in small traces.
- *Calorie Content of Watermelon*: It counts 30.0 per 100 gm on the calorie metre.
- *Health Benefits of Watermelon*: This large sized fruit comes packed with large health benefits which ranges from prevention against

cardio- vascular diseases to improving insulin sensitivity. The presence of antioxidants and lycopene scavenge free radicals, maintains a good eye vision, prevents from colon cancer, prostate cancer, breast cancer and endometrial cancer. It is a vital source of energy.

BANANA

- *Nutrition Facts and Information about Banana*: Banana is rich in potassium. It also contains other minerals such as calcium, iron, magnesium and phosphorus in large quantities. It is also rich in fibres making it a useful laxative and good for easing constipation.
- *Vitamin Content of Banana*: Banana is rich in Vitamin C. It also contains other vitamins such Vitamin A, and Vitamin B, especially folate.
- Calorie Content of Banana: Banana contains about 90 to 93 calories per 100 gm. This energy is easily absorbed by the body and hence eating 3-4 bananas daily, especially with milk, is often recommended to gain weight. At the same time, banana is useful for loosing weight. Since it has only 90 calories per 100 gm., banana reduces your calorie intake and thus helps in weight loss. Overweight people, should of course, stop eating banana chips to lose weight.
- *Health Benefits of Banana*: The nutritional value of banana makes it useful for weight gain as well as weight loss, constipation, bowel problems, anaemia, blood pressure, heart problems, ulcers, brain stimulation, depression, nervous disorders, stress, morning sickness, menstruation, etc.

KIWI FRUIT

- *Nutrition Facts and Information about Kiwi*: Kiwi or chinese gooseberries is rich in copper and potassium. Other minerals present in the fruit include calcium, manganese, magnesium, phosphorus, iron, and zinc. Like Apple, it also provides dietary fibre. This fibre makes it good for controlling blood sugar, colon and cardiovascular problems.
- *Vitamin Content of Kiwi*: Kiwi fruit is known for its high Vitamin C content. About 70gm of the fruit will be sufficient for your daily Vitamin C intake. It is also rich in Vitamin K. Kiwi fruits also contains some amount of Vitamin A, Vitamin E, Vitamin B.
- *Calorie Content of Kiwi Fruit*: Most of fruit is made up of water. Hence, 100 gm of Chinese Gooseberries contain about 61 calories only. However, as seen in many fruits, it is easy

for the body to absord these calories.

- *Health Benefits of Kiwi*: The nutritional value of kiwi fruit makes it useful for high blood sugar, asthma, cardiovascular health, heart disorders, diabetes, infant growth, increasing immunity, cancer, colon disorders, cataract, macular degeneration, etc.

WHEAT AND BARLEY

WHEAT

Wheat grains are used to make flour, which is transformed into doughs and then breads, which is a staple food in every country and culture. Eating whole grains are advisable to women for staying slim and healthy. It is rich in protein and provides daily requirement of energy. Works as a good laxative. It has wide culinary uses, from the making of breads, pasta and cakes to fermentation of alcoholic beverages.

- *Nutrition Facts and Information about Wheat*: It contains manganese, phosphorus, magnesium and selenium in very large quantities. Rich in zinc, copper, iron and potassium. However, calcium is also present in small amounts.
- *Vitamin Content of Wheat*: It is rich in Vitamin B6, Niacin, Thiamin, Folate, Riboflavin and Pantothenic Acid. Vitamin E and Vitamin K are also present in small but considerable amounts.
- *Calorie Content of Wheat*: Wheat has a calorific value of 339.0 per 100 gm. Being a grain, it is very appropriate in calories and hence, filling as a food.
- *Health Benefits of Wheat* : Consumption of whole wheat isnecessary for a healthy metabolism, as it prevents Breast Cancer, Gallstones, childhood Asthma and heart risks. Definitely an essential food to intake for women for gastro-intestinal health, also reduces risk of high blood pressure, Diabetes and high cholestrol. To add up to it all, it has phytonutrients which promotes better health through maintaining high blood levels.

BARLEY

It is a staple cereal grain, popular for breakfast meals and savored for its rich flavour which reminds you of nuts. It is loaded with dietary fibre and proteins for an energetic and healthy metabolism.

- *Nutrition Facts and Information about Barley*: Barley is rich in manganese, selenium, phosphorus, copper, magnesium, iron, zinc and potassium. While calcium is found in a small quantity.

- *Vitamin Content of Barley*: Barley is rich in Vitamin B6, Thiamin, Niacin, Riboflavin and Folate. Whereas, Vitamin K and Pantothenic Acid are present in small quantities.
- *Calorie Content of Barley*: Barley has a calorific value of 352.0 per 100 gm.
- *Health Benefits of Barley*: Including Barley in your diet surely helps in prevention from high cholestrol, intestinal dysfunctions, Atherosclerosis, Heart ailments, Diabetes, Gallstones, Childhood Asthma and Cancer diseases. With presence of Phosphorus formation of ATP is enhanced and repair of tissue system is supported.

BEEF

The use of lean and clean beef is advisable to include in diet, it could be as an ingredient in stews or traditional recipes. Beef is a popular meat rich in protein, being a red meat had always made it a bad food when it comes to studies and researches. However, it has been established that a lean beef adds to health benefits related to heart and prevention of cancer. As a matter of fact, no one can deny that beef is an important source of protein.

- *Nutrition Facts and Information about Beef*: Beef is found to be very rich in zinc, selenium, phosphorus, potassium and magnesium. Sodium and copper are found in good quantities. However, minute quantities of calcium and mangnese are also present.
- *Vitamin Content of Beef*: Beef is one of the best source for Vitamin B12, Vitamin B6 Niacin and Riboflavin. However, it is also rich in Thiamin and Pantothenic Acid. Small amounts of Vitamin E, Vitamin K and Folate are present.
- *Calorie Content of Beef*: The calorie count of Beef per 100 gm is 155.0, it is meat which is higher in protein and moderate in fat.
- *Health Benefits of Beef*: Beef is good for bones and teeth. It enhances immunity against infections of ear, etc., and prevents blood vessel walls from damaging. Moderate consumption of lean beef is altogether good for cardiovascular health and to prevent cancer risks.

PORK

Pork makes to the position of most widely consumed meat till today, with being bred almost in all major parts of the world. It is a rich source of proteins and fats. This meat being used to make sausages, ham and bacon is an essential part of people's daily nutrients requirement in many countries.

No doubt, Pork has always been an energy packed food:

- *Nutrition Facts and Information about Pork*: Pork has a high mineral content of phosphorus, selenium, sodium, zinc, potassium and copper. The two minerals which are present in good quantities are iron and magnesium, while calcium and mangnese are found in traces only.
- *Vitamin Content of Pork*: Pork is highly enriched with Vitamin B6, Vitamin B12, Thiamin, Niacin, Riboflavin and Pantothenic Acid. However, Vitamin A and Vitamin E are found in very small amounts.
- *Calorie Content of Pork*: Calorific value of Pork is 458.0 per 100 gm. This is quite high when compared to other animal products like chicken.
- *Health Benefits of Pork*: Consumption of Pork in moderate quantities is helpful in gaining energy. It is good for skin, eyes, nervous system, bones and mental performance. Intake of Pork also ensures better immunity to body due to presence of essential antioxidants.

VODKA AND BEER

VODKA

Vodka is one of the most popular alcoholic beverages. It is made by fermentation of wheat mash, corn mash, potato mash or rye mash.

- *Calorie Content of Vodka*: Vodka is rich in calories. It contains about 228 calories every 100g serving. So if you are trying to lose weight, limit your intake of vodka.
- *Vitamin Content*: Vodka is devoid of vitamins. It contains only traces of Vitamin B.
- *Nutrient Facts and Information of Vodka*: So does vodka contain any minerals? Again, vodka is almost devoid of any minerals. It contains small quantities of phosphorus, potassium and sodium.
- *Health Benefits of Vodka*: It is believed that vodka helps in treating heart problems and certain cancers. There are indicative scientific studies proving this; however, these studies are preliminary and no conclusion can be drawn based on this. Remember—excessive drinking affects your liver and your health is best maintained when you abstain from excessive intake of alcohol.

BEER

Beer is another popular alcoholic beverage:

- *Calorie Content of Beer*: Beer is a good source of calories. It contains about 42 calories every 100gm serving. So if you drink one bottle of beer which contains about 750 ml, your calorie intake will be about 340 calories. Normally people who drink 2-3 bottles of beer a day find that their weight has increased drastically after few days. This is due to the large amount of calories present in beer.
- *Vitamin Content*: Like vodka, beer also contains traces of Vitamin B.
- *Nutrient Facts and Information Beer*: Beer is not rich in any mineral. It contains small amounts of calcium, magnesium, phosphorus and sodium.
- *Health Benefits of Beer*: It is claimed that beer is beneficial in reducing stress, heart diseases, facilitating urination and inducing sleep. Of course all this is applicable when one drinks beer in limited amount.

BEET AND RADISH

BEET

Beet has always been a vital source of energy enriched with nutrients and fibre. It is biennial and available almost throughout the year. Be it the modified root itself or Chard like edible green leaves both are incredibly contributing to a healthy metabolism. While *Beta vulgaris* is widely being relished in the form of salad with spicy and lemon like flavour and pickles, the edible green leaves too are loaded with rich vitamin and mineral content. It's subspecies are sources for highly nutritious garden beet juice, sugar production and animal fodder.

- *Nutrition Facts and Information about Beet*: Beet is a rich source of potassium, iron, magnesium, manganese, phosphorus and copper. Whereas calcium, sodium, zinc and selenium are present in small amounts.
- *Vitamin Content*: Beet consists of Vitamin C, Folate and Betaine in large quantities. Vitamin A, Thiamin, Riboflavin, Niacin, Vitamin B6 and Pantothenic Acid are also present in small amounts. It also constitutes traces of Beta Carotene.
- *Calorie Content of Beet*: Beets are known for being rich in nutrients and low on calorie, having a calorific value of 43.0 per 100 gm. As a result it forms an important part of salads for people under controlled diet.
- *Health Benefits of Beet*: Beet has been found useful in the

treatment of Colon Cancer and birth related defects. It is a natural cleanser which removes toxins from the body and nourishes the bloodstream. Beet is useful in the treatment of liver related dysfunctions like Jaundice, Cirrhosis, etc. Garden Beet juice is a good source of energy and is essential for human body. It is not advisable to feed beet to infants below six months but it is of good use to women under menstruation.

RADISH

Radish is a root vegetable with a rich flavour. It is used in most of the world cuisines but is very popular in Japanese and Chinese cuisine.

- *Nutrition Facts and Information about Radish*: Radish has excellent levels of copper, manganese and potassium. It is also a good source of calcium, magnesium, iron, phosphorous, zinc and sodium.
- *Vitamin Content*: Radishes are a very good source of Vitamin C and Vitamin K. They also contain Riboflavin and Vitamin B6.
- *Calorie Content of Radish*: 100gm of radish contains 16 calories only. Radish is low in saturated fat and very low in cholesterol. They are also very good source of dietary fibre.
- *Health Benefits of Radish*: Radish has anti-bacterial as well as anti-fungal properties. It is beneficial for cough, respiratory problems, digestive disorders, asthma, bronchitis and liver and gallbladder troubles.

CABBAGE AND ICEBERG LETTUCE

CABBAGE

Cabbage is a leafy vegetable, which is eaten raw as salads and used in many other recipes. The high nutrient content and numerous medicinal properties of cabbage make it popular throughout the world.

- *Nutrition Facts and Information about Cabbage*: Cabbage is an excellent source of manganese, calcium and potassium. It is a very good source of iron, phosphorous, magnesium. It is also a very good source of fibre, folate and omega-3 fatty acids. Further, sodium, zinc and copper are found in good amounts in cabbage.
- *Vitamin Content*: Cabbage is an excellent source of Vitamin C. Cabbage is also a good source of Thiamin, Riboflavin, Niacin, Vitamin B6. It contains good amounts of Vitamin K, Folate, Vitamin A and protein.
- *Calorie Content of Cabbage*: 100g of cabbage contains only 25 calories. This food is low in saturated fat, cholesterol and a good source of dietary fibre and folate. It largely contains carbohydrates.
- *Health Benefits of Cabbage*: Cabbage is low in calories and therefore it is good for weight loss. It also has anti-inflammatory properties. It is believed that cabbage juice helps in treating peptic ulcers. Since cabbage is abundant in Vitamin C, it is good for protection from free radicals.

ICEBERG LETTUCE

Iceberg lettuce is a main constituent in salads and is known for its crunchy texture. It has comparatively less nutrients than the other greens.

- *Nutrition Facts and Information about Iceberg Lettuce*: Iceberg lettuce is an excellent source of potassium and manganese and a very good source of iron, calcium, magnesium and phosphorous. It also contains traces of sodium, copper, zinc.
- *Vitamin Content*: Iceberg lettuce is an excellent source of Vitamin A, Vitamin K and Vitamin C. It is also a good source of Thiamin, Vitamin B6, Folate.
- *Calorie Content of Iceberg Lettuce*: Iceberg lettuce contains 14 calories/100 gm. It mainly has water and dietary fibre. This food is low in sodium and very low in saturated fat and cholesterol.
- *Health Benefits of Iceberg Lettuce*: Iceberg lettuce has high water content and is low in calories. Therefore, it is good in weight loss. However, it has relatively low amounts of nutrients. It is considered that, owing to folate content, iceberg lettuce helps in fighting heart diseases and strokes.

TOMATO AND CARROT

TOMATO

- *Nutrition Facts and Information about Tomato*: Tomato is a good source of calcium and iron. It also contains some amounts of phosphorus, sulfur and potassium.
- *Vitamin Content*: Tomato is rich in Vitamin C and contains some Vitamin B and Vitamin A. The vitamin C content increases as the vegetable ripens.
- *Calorific Content of Tomato*: 100 gm of tomato contains only 20 calories. These calories are easy to absorb by the body. The low calorie content of tomato makes it a favourite of obese people. It is often recommended in weight loss programmes as it provides you some of the essential minerals and vitamins, fills your stomach and does not add calories to your body.
- *Health Benefits of Tomato*: The nutritional value of tomato makes it good for weight loss, obesity, eye disorders, night blindness, urinary tract infection, liver disorders, jaundice, indigestion, morning sickness, constipation, diarrhea, intestinal disorders, and diabetes. It also helps in cleansing the body of toxiccompounds.

CARROT

- *Nutrition Facts and Information about Carrot*: Carrot is a good source of minerals such as potassium, and manganese. It also contains some amount of sodium, fluoride, phosphorus, iron, zinc, copper, selenium, and calcium.
- *Vitamin Content*: Carrot is an excellent source of beta carotene. It also contains large amount of Vitamin K. Further, carrot contains traces of Vitamin C, Vitamin E, and Vitamin B.
- *Calorific Content of Carrot*: 100gm of carrot contains about 43 to 48 calories.
- *Health Benefits of Carrot*: The nutritional value of carrot makes it good for eye disorders, cataract, tooth disorders, skin care, nervous disorders, indigestion, constipation, diarrhoea, arthritis, gout, and lung cancer.

CASHEW AND CHESTNUT

CASHEW

Cashew, a kidney shaped seed, is a vital ingredient to include in your diet plan. It works as a health booster and is a good source of monosaturated fats and protein. It has originated from Brazil and is now being cultivated in many other countries.

- *Nutrition Facts and Information about Cashew*: Cahsews are said to be packed with huge amounts of minerals like copper, magnesium, manganese, phosphorus, zinc, iron, selenium and potassium. Calcium is present in good quantity. Further, sodium is found in traces only.
- *Vitamin Content of Cashew*: Huge amounts of Vitamin K, Thiamin, Vitamin B6 and Pantcthenic Acid are present. Further, cashews are also rich in Vitamin E, Folate, Niacin and Riboflavin but consists of Vitamin C in traces only.
- *Calorie Content of Cashew*: Cashew has a calorific value of 553.0 per 100 gm.
- *Health Benefits of Cashew*: Like other nuts Cashew too has an obesity and gallstones fighting property. Presence of high amount of magnesium ensures healthy bones and teeth structure, while copper produces energy and increases capability of antioxidant defences. Effects in a healthy heart and bloodstream. Thus, the risk of heart related disease, diabetes and obesity is greatly reduced. Iron controls red-blood cell function and enzyme activity.

CHESTNUT

Chestnuts which crumble in the mouth to give a sweet flavour, unlike other nuts, are low in fat. Being low in fat, it is often compared to grains. It also has good amount of dietary fibre. It's cultivation is spread across the world and comes in many varieties.

- *Nutrition Facts and Information about Chestnut*: Chestnuts are enriched with large amounts of manganese, potassium, copper, phosphorus, magnesium and iron. Zinc and calcium are also present in small amounts.
- *Vitamin Content of Chestnut*: These nuts are a power house of Vitamin C. Vitamin B6, Thiamin, Folate and Riboflavin are the other nutrients which chestnuts are enriched with. Good amounts of Niacin and Pantothenic Acid are present. Traces of Vitamin A are also found.
- *Calorie Content of Chestnut*: Calorie count of Chestnuts is 213.0 per 100 gm.
- *Health Benefits of Chestnut*: Like all other nuts, chestnuts prevent heart risks, provides energy, are very low in cholestrol and mainly are good to include in diet as other grains. Preventing common cold and enhancing fertility in men are the health benefits which comes with the presence of Vitamin C.

CHERRY AND STRAWBERRY

CHERRY

Cherry is a bright red coloured fruit, which can be eaten fresh. These fruits are found in yellow colour as well. Cherries are eaten raw and are also used for flavouring foods and preparation of wine.

- *Nutrition Facts and Information about Cherry*: Cherry is an excellent source of potassium and manganese. It is a very good source of magnesium and copper. Good amounts of iron and phosphorous are found in cherries. Other minerals present in cheries include calcium and potassium, which are present only in trace amounts.
- *Vitamin Content*: Cherry is an excellent source of Vitamin C, Vitamin K and is a very good source of thiamin, riboflavin, Vitamin B6 and pantothenic acid. It also contains traces of niacin, folate and Vitamin A.
- *Calorie Content*: 100g of cherries contain 63 calories. It is also a good source of dietary fibre. This food is primarily made up of water and carbohydrates ad is low in saturated fat, cholesterol and sodium.
- *Health Benefits of Cherry*: Cherry can reduce the pain of arthritis, goutand headaches. Cherry contains anthocyanin, a red pigment, which acts as an antioxidant. The plant pigment along with Vitamin C strengthens collagen. Cherry juice contains melatonin, which is important for the function of the immune system.

Cherries are used as a sedative in nausea and vomiting. Wild cherry bark is an important cough remedy. Cherry is also beneficial in treating bronchitis, asthma and chronic diarrhoea. It has been found that cherries can reduce the risk of heart attack and the risk of cancer by fifty per cent.

STRAWBERRY

Strawberry is a common fruit which can be consumed fresh, frozen or made into preserves. Strawberries are a popular addition to dairy products and are used as a natural acid/base indicator.

- *Nutrition Facts and Information about Strawberry*: Strawberry is an excellent source of potassium and magnesium. It contains very good amount of phosphorous, sodium, calcium, copper and manganese. Strawberry is a good source of iron.
- *Vitamin Content*: Strawberries are an excellent source of Vitamin C. Infact they have more Vitamin C than citrus fruit. Strawberry is also a good source of folate, thiamin, riboflavin,

niacin, Vitamin B6, omega-3 fatty acids, Vitamin E, Vitamin A and Vitamin K.

- *Calorie Content of Strawberry*: Strawberries contain 32 calories/100 gm, which are mostly carbohydrates. They are a very good source of dietary fibre and iodine. Strawberries also contain an array of beneficial phytonutrients, including flavonoids, anthocyanidins and ellagic acid.
- *Health Benefits of Strawberry*: Strawberries have numberous medicinal properties includings its ability to lower the risk of cancers of the gastrointestinal tract due to presence of Vitamin C. Strawberry is an excellent anti-oxidant. It is also packed with flavonoids; these flavonoids help keep bad cholesterol from damaging artery walls. Strawberries can significantly decrease blood pressure, which may reduce the risk of heart disease. Strawberries are found to enhance memory function and reduce rheumatoid arthritis.

❒

Chapter - 2

Food Safety and Security System

Food security describes a situation in which people do not live in hunger or fear of starvation. World-wide around 852 million men, women and children are chronically hungry due to extreme poverty; while up to 2 billion people lack food security intermittently due to varying degrees of poverty.

A direct relationship exists between food consumption levels and poverty. Families with the financial resources to escape extreme poverty rarely suffer from chronic hunger; while poor families not only suffer the most from chronic hunger, but are also the segment of the population most at risk during food shortages and famines.

Two commonly used definitions of food security come from the UN's Food and Agriculture Organization (FAO) and the United States Department of Agriculture (USDA):

- Food security exists when all people, at all times, have access to sufficient, safe and nutritious food to meet their dietary needs and food preferences for an active and healthy life. (FAO)
- Food security for a household means access by all members at all times to enough food for an active, healthy life. Food security includes at a minimum
    * The ready availability of nutritionally adequate and safe foods,
    * An assured ability to acquire acceptable foods in socially acceptable ways (that is, without resorting to emergency food supplies, scavenging, stealing, or other coping strategies). (USDA)

The stages of food insecurity range from food secure situations to full-scale famine. "Famine and hunger are both rooted in food insecurity.

Food insecurity can be categorized as either chronic or transitory. Chronic food insecurity translates into a high degree of vulnerability to famine and hunger; ensuring food security presupposes elimination of that vulnerability. Chronic hunger is not famine. It is similar to undernourishment and is related to poverty. It exists mainly in poor countries."

FOOD INSECURITY

Food insecurity has been described as "a condition in which people lack basic food intake to provide them with the energy and nutrients for fully productive lives." Hunger Task Force

Food insecurity is defined as not having access to enough food every day of the year. The U.S. federal government collects statistics on this based on surveys. Thus a "food insecure household" is one in which any member experienced one or more days in a given year when they didn't have enough food because of poverty or a lack of resources. This poverty measure takes into account participation in food assistance programmes such as school breakfast, school lunch and Food Stamps.

The USDA report cited below asks the question, "How often were people hungry in households that were food insecure with hunger?" Around 4 percent of people reported going hungry at least once a year, while on any given day the figure is estimated to be between 0.5 percent and 0.8 percent.

Chronic Nutritional Deficiencies

Many countries experience perpetual food shortages and distribution problems. These result in chronic and often widespread hunger amongst significant numbers of people. Human populations respond to chronic hunger and malnutrition by decreasing body size, known in medical terms as stunting or stunted growth. This process starts *in utero* if the mother is malnourished and continues through approximately the third year of life. It leads to higher infant and child mortality, but at rates far lower than during famines. Once stunting has occurred, improved nutritional intake later in life cannot reverse the damage. Stunting itself is viewed as a coping mechanism, designed to bring body size into alignment with the calories available during adulthood in the location where the child is born. Limiting body size as a way of adapting to low levels of energy (calories) adversely affects health in three ways:

- Premature failure of vital organs occurs during adulthood. For example a 50 year old individual might die of heart failure because his/her heart suffered structural defects during early development.

- Stunted individuals suffer a far higher rate of disease and illness than those who have not undergone stunting.
- Severe malnutrition in early childhood often leads to defects in cognitive development.

"The analysis points to the misleading nature of the concept of subsistence as Malthus originally used it and as it is still widely used today. Subsistence in not located at the edge of a nutritional cliff, beyond whichlies demographic disaster. Rather than one level of subsistence, there are numerous levels at which a population and a food supply can be in equilibrium in the sense that they can be indefinitely sustained. However, some levels will have smaller people and higher normal mortality than others."

Dictatorship and Kleptocracy

As the Nobel Prize-winning economist Amartya Sen has observed that "there is no such thing as an apolitical food problem." While drought and other naturally occurring events may trigger famine conditions, it is government action or inaction that determines its severity, and often even whether or not a famine will occur. The 20th century is full of examples of governments undermining the food security of their own nations – sometimes intentionally.

Socialist anti-Western governments do this much more than authoritarian, pro-Western ones. Prime examples are North Korea since 1980, and the Soviet Union in the mid-20th century. Lesser known are Cambodia under Pol Pot, and the Sandinistas in Nicaragua in their attempt to starve the Misquito Indians into submission.

When governments come to power by force or rigged elections, and not by way of fair and open elections, their base of support is often narrow and built upon cronyism and patronage. Under such conditions "The distribution of food within a country is a political issue. Governments in most countries give priority to urban areas, since that is where the most influential and powerful families and enterprises are usually located. The government often neglects subsistence farmers and rural areas in general. The more remote and underdeveloped the area the less likely the government will be to effectively meet its needs. Many agrarian policies, especially the pricing of agricultural commodities, discriminate against rural areas. Governments often keep prices of basic grains at such artificially low levels that subsistence producers can not accumulate enough capital to make investments to improve their production. Thus, they are effectively prevented from getting out of their precarious situation."

Further Communist parties, as well as dictators and warlords have used food as a political weapon, rewarding their supporters while denying food supplies to areas that oppose their rule. Under such conditions food becomes a currency with which to buy support and famine becomes an effective weapon to be used against the opposition.

Governments with strong tendencies towards kleptocracy can undermine food security even when harvests are good. When government monopolizes trade, farmers may find that they are free to grow cash crops for export, but under penalty of law only able to sell their crops to government buyers at prices far below the world market price. The government then is free to sell their crop on the world market at full price, pocketing the difference. This creates an artificial "poverty trap" from which even the most hard working and motivated farmers may not escape.

When the rule of law is absent, or private property is non-existent, farmers have little incentive to improve their productivity. If a farm becomes noticeably more productive than neighbouring farms, it may become the target of individuals well connected to the government. Rather than risk being noticed and possibly losing their land, farmers may be content with the perceived safety of mediocrity.

As pointed out by William Bernstein in his book *The Birth of Plenty*: "Individuals without property are susceptible to starvation, and it is much easier to bend the fearful and hungry to the will of the state. If a farmer's property can be arbitrarily threatened by the state, that power will inevitably be employed to intimidate those with divergent political and religious opinions."

Economic Approaches

There are many economic approaches advocated to improve food security in developing countries. Three typical approaches are listed below. The first is typical of what is advocated by most governments and international agencies. The other two are more common to non-governmental organizations (NGO's).

Westernized View

Conventional thinking in westernized countries is that maximizing the farmers profit is the surest way of maximizing agricultural production; the higher a farmer's profit, the greater the effort that will be forthcoming, and the greater the risk the farmer is willing to take.

This view holds that it is the governments job to place into the hands of farmers the largest number and highest quality tools possible (tools is used here to refer to improved production techniques, improved seeds, secure land tenure, accurate weather forecasts, etc.) However, it is left to the individual farmer to pick and choose which tools to use, and how to use them, as farmers have intimate knowledge of their own land and local conditions.

As with other businesses, a percentage of the profits are normally reinvested into the business in the hopes of increasing production, and hence increase future profits. Normally higher profits translate into higher spending on technologies designed to boost production, such as drip irrigation systems, agriculture education, and greenhouses. An increased profit also increases the farmer's incentive to engage in double-cropping, soil improvement programmes, and expanding usable acreage.

Food Justice

An alternative view takes a collective approach to achieve food security. It notes that globally enough food is produced to feed the entire world population at a level adequate to ensure that everyone can be free of hunger and fear of starvation. That no one should live without enough food because of economic constraints or social inequalities is the basic goal.

This approach is often referred to as food justice and views food security as a basic human right. It advocates fairer distribution of food, particularly grain crops, as a means of ending chronic hunger and malnutrition. The core of the Food Justice movement is the belief that what is lacking is not food, but the political will to fairly distribute food regardless of the recipient's ability to pay.

Poverty and Food Insecurity in Africa

In sub-Saharan Africa, a large and increasing proportion of the population subsist on per capita income of less than one dollar a day. The share of the population falling below the poverty line is as high as 50 per cent. Although all indices of poverty are well manifested in sub-Saharan Africa's Human Development Indices, the heart of the problem is food insecurity. From statistical projections, aggregate cereals demand and supply balances for African countries indicate a likely increase in imports from 9 million metric tons in 1990 to 27 million metric tonnes by 2020. And given the obvious difficulties in mobilizing resources to finance imports and the implications on local food availability, deterioration in the food security will result, unless revolutionary departures are made from current production patterns.

Agriculture is not only the primary source of food in Africa; it is the principal means of livelihood in its predominant rural settlements. The challenges then are, not only to drastically reduce net import demands and make agriculture a major source of export earning, but more critically, to achieve agriculture-led industrialization towards the attainment of structural reforms as are called for by increasing world integration. Although the problems are both policy-induced and structural in nature, our concern is on the structural challenges that tend to constrain the desired social and economic transformation of agriculture and that reinforce poverty and food insecurity.

A look at Measurement Issues

The evidences of poverty and food insecurity have never been so clear and alarming in their proliferation as in the last decade. But more worrisome is the conflict in the manifestations. The World Food summit secured international commitment, in 1990, to reduce the number of undernourished people by half by the year 2015. Five years on, statistics show that an increasing number of people remain food insecure (800 million by 2000). Yet this contracts with the supposed progress being made to reduce by half the world's population living in absolute poverty over the same period, which indicates that the international development community is on track. This implies that different indices are being measured or equally likely that progress in one area is negatively affecting the other. So, is hunger or food insecurity a symptom of poverty and in what ways are they linked?

The above paradox makes a clear distinction between food production and food access. Here is where poverty comes into the equation of food security. A poor nation may increase its food production, national food self- sufficiency and economic growth to lift itself upward in the poverty statistics, but sections of its people may remain food insecure because of other factors that affect their access to the food. Suffice it, then, to say that development indices that focus on increased production of food alone are inadequate to capture the pattern of its distribution between populations and within populations.

Poverty characteristics are important in the construction of poverty indicators. Therefore, the relevance of human development indicators (HDI) rather than money-metric or income measures, GDP measures or other macroeconomic structure have been seen to be more appropriate (Human Development reports). The characteristics of the poor are also contextual and so are the manifestations of poverty in different populations. The need for the voice of the people in poverty assessment and the design of poverty reduction measures therefore remain very valid. The PRSP strategy is aimed at streamlining the objectives of macroeconomic growth with those of human development. It also emphasizes the contextual sing poverty knowledge and reduction strategies.

The gender dimension of poverty is particularly reinforced in agrarian economies where the poor are characterized by landlessness, invariable (inelastic) supply of labour, likely to live in female-headed households, likely to be farm labourers rather than farm owners, remote form development assistance due to time constraints, hunger as well as literacy and health constraints and so on. As a result, the consonance of gender development indicators with other human development measures is a necessary condition in poverty assessment. The relationship of growth with poverty has been shown not to be a foregone conclusion, as nations, which recorded high economic growth especially during structural adjustment, also recorded high levels of poverty incidence and high-income concentration. The distributional aspects of growth are therefore more relevant to the measurement of poverty. This view is reinforced by the fact that there is considerable correlation between the trends in Human Development Indicators, Gender Development Indicators and Human Poverty Indices.

Table: Poverty Indicators for Selected Countries

Indicator	Human Development Index	Gender Development per capita)	Human Poverty	Macroeconomic Growth (GDP	Indicator
$/year					
Norway	0.934	0.932	3.9	36806	
Thailand	0.745	0.766	18.7	2593	
Ghana	0.556	0.552	35.4	399	
Nigeria	0.439	0.421	37.6	256	

The Table above shows dimensions of the linkages of gender development with growth and poverty reduction. It shows synergy, not only between growth and poverty reduction, but also between the human development indices and gender development indices. This implies that growth is a necessary but insufficient condition for poverty reduction. Sub-Saharan Africa has lagged behind both in its macroeconomic structure, human development and gender development indicators, compared with other developing and developed areas. It would then be tempting to say that the problem of poverty in SSA is induced both by slow growth and social inequalities and that pro- growth policy like liberalization are insufficient to achieve balanced and sustainable growth with equity. Liberalization policies, in their standard prescription will need to be looked at through a different kind of lens.

Expectations from Liberalization for African Agriculture

The perspective goal of market liberalization worldwide and especially in Africa, as embodied by different forms of economic (structural) adjustment, is *structural transformation (ST)*. This is hinged on market-led growth strategies rather than protectionist 'soft' government for Africa's predominant agricultural sector.

ST entails the development of manufacturing and service sectors, such that the relative importance of agriculture declines (over time). That is, the percent of labour-force in agriculture and the percent of GNP from the sector decline as labour specialization proceeds. An interrelated set of changes in economic structure, including internal consumption, production mechanism, external trade and capital flows, domestic savings and investment behaviour are necessary mechanisms that must catapult the primary production system into a higher technological realm which is required to sustain industrial development. In short, globalization as epitomized by liberalization policies is expected to be the cure-all for Africa's poverty and food insecurity, if and only if Africa's economic structure can be modified towards more efficient production system, systemic industrialization, modernization of agriculture via increased commercialization, specialization, based on comparative advantage and a gradual shift from agricultural-led to industrial-led macroeconomic development.

In assessing the linkages, Kanji identifies two main approaches, which may yield different results. Mainstream economic approach and Socio-economic approach. The former takes the neoclassical view of liberalization whereby potential effects of SAPs for instance are beneficial:

- Free movement of goods and services
- Increased specialization based on comparative advantage
- Increased allocative efficiency in resource use
- Increased technical efficiency by using more capital and technology rather than inefficient labour
- Enhanced production towards export-led growth
- Appropriate pricing leading to positive supply response
- Increased aggregate production leading to increased food security
- Increased farm income leading to poverty reduction (at least in money-metric terms).

However, these standard response parameters do not consider the way that policies are specified and their differential outcomes, if all cannot respond according to these standards. As a result, the poor and other vulnerable groups may not benefit. Also the perspective of food security is over-generalized.

Food security is not about the food or the commodity but about people and hunger. Nominal production of food does not guarantee affordability to the poor or accessibility to non-producers. In the last two decades, world output of food has doubled but the world's population of the hungry has also doubled. As empirical proof, SSA's dependence on trade, as measured by share of GDP from trade increased from 38 per cent to 43 per cent between 1988 and 2000. At the same time, her share of world trade had declined in real terms. Its dependence on primary goods still remained above 80 per cent from oil and non-oil, mainly agriculture. Price volatility of primary commodities led to declining terms of trade which was 21 per cent below its 1970 level. Over the same period, the percentage of poor people remained the same in 1998 as it was in 1987, in spite of increased trade volume. Social indicators also showed a decline, going by HDI estimates. The conclusion is that growth effects need to consider other related social variables, mainly distribution effect of increased income. Growth in the poor's income need to be decomposed into growth and distribution effect.

The socio-economic approach introduces the realities of capabilities, vulnerabilities and sustainability of livelihoods. Desirable outcomes, therefore, go beyond income gains to welfare gains, reduced vulnerability, improved food security and sustainable use of natural resources, which have strong equity considerations and therefore work up from micro to macro.

Inequality Concerns in the analysis of globalization

Divergence is a feature of current globalization. The inherent equity consideration in the implementation of globalization policies lies in:

1. Use of rules that benefit the powerful countries at the expense of he weaker nations or regions, leading to unequal rate of economic and social development which shows as deepening poverty of developing countries compared to developed ones (Human Development Reports)
2. Its human expression which hinges on the extent to which all groups within a nation can participate in its income–growthprocess. Unequal participation of people and groups in the new trade opportunities created by globalization bring about the paradox of income growth and increasing poverty, of segments of the same population.

In many instances especially in agrarian economies of SSA, equality of participation, equality of response to opportunities is something that cannot be guaranteed. Therefore, while many of the earlier analysis of liberalization effects have been positive on growth, more recent studies have shown that these benefits of globalization are not automatic and are contingent on the management of other evolving phenomena, the two principal concerns being inequalities and market volatility. Thus a people-centred analysis of globalization effects cannot take a purely neoclassic view of economic growth but rather, a human development approach.

Neoclassical economic analysis assesses outcomes of policy in a gender neutral or household or per capita unit of analysis. Distributional effects are considered or emphasized. Resultant inequalities are seen as incidental rather that the cause and effect of mainstream policies. Emphasizes aggregates of growth, efficiency, income and consumption.

Heterodox (feminist) economic analysis goes beyond the unitary analysis to a disaggregated view of society to answer the question: are these outcomes equal for all groups or socio-economic groups. If not, growth and efficiency have been attained at the expense of social justice and equity or at the price of inequity. That is why the theory of inequality is central to the analysis of poverty effects of macro policies such as liberalization.

The Nature and Measurement of Gender Inequality

First let us look at the dimensions of inequality with a view to situating gender inequality. Inequality exists in a development system which concentrates opportunities. It results in distributional imbalances in development outcomes such as economic well being, paucity of it or simply lack of it. Its measurement is usually a measure of concentration, which is estimated as the Gini Coefficient – a measure of the level of evenness of distribution.

Amartya Sen identifies several faces of inequality, with gender inequality being the most profound, being that it crosscuts other forms of inequality. At the micro level therefore, gender inequality has been seen as that which mostly undermines human development. At the macro level, such inequalities transmit their effects either to enhance or to constrain growth. In the latter, where inequality enhances growth, this has been termed the capitalist accumulation effect, while in the former, it has been termed theunderdevelopment effect. Either way, inequality manifests as varying levels of lack or poverty, food insecurity (hunger) being a major manifestation. Gender inequality reinforces the structural dimension of poverty which has also been a concern in the measurement of poverty.

The major types of Gender Inequality that are mostly related to economic production are:

- Employment Inequality reflected often as increased labour feminization without increased gender development or economic empowerment of women;
- Persistent wage gaps between men and women in employment;
- Ownership Inequality reflected often as resource constraints for women in the same production system;
- Household Inequality reflected as unequal power relations and underlies other derivatives such as employment inequality and political inequality.

Causes of Gender Inequality

- Gender role differentiation imposed by the traditional society on time, ability, availability of men and women to respond to changing opportunities;
- Gendered entitlement systems imposing disparities on access of men and women to common property resources, especially productive assets;
- Gendered nature of production which imposes differential outcomes not only on productivity of men and women but also on returns to production due to valuation bias on outputs of production (productive and reproductive work outputs).

How large is gender inequality

Some schools of thought maintain that gender inequality is not as much of a problem as it is made out to be. So how large is gender inequality? Ravi Kanbur's analysis of the size of gender inequality is very explicit. It posits that there is sub-distribution of gender categories since gender crosscuts all other dichotomies. Total size of inequality is therefore the overall distribution of inequality (V) within each sub group.

Eboh recognizes the presence of multiple gender categories, each one exerting a gendered impact on the development process. An estimation of the size and effect of inequality must decompose along these structural lines. First to effectively capture all facets and two to assess differences in the impact on sub-categories – a distinction or decomposition of the within and the between effects. To this extent, intra-gender power structures have been found to be significant in the analysis of gender relations in primary production systems.

Gender Analysis of Liberalization Policies

Inequality becomes a relevant force in globalization because it sets the initial position of men and women at the onset of changing policies of liberalization. This initial position of advantage or disadvantage determines the responsiveness to the opportunities that liberalization present. On the aggregate, the outcome of liberalization in a production system depends on the gender structure of the actors (producers) and their aggregate supply response. In the next section, we carry out a gender analysis of liberalization impacts in cross-country studies.

Going by its own doctrines of survival of the fittest and capitalist accumulation, liberalization itself initially reinforces inequalities although it is also believed to potentially have the ability to close gender gaps and other forms of inequalities over time. Another possible outcome of liberalization is to move an economy or nation from one kind of inequality to another. Thus different forms of inequality would impose adversities or negative impacts on lives of both men and women. Inequalities of different forms that become self-reinforcing culminate in poverty of those affected and underdevelopment in spite of broadening opportunities for growth.

Gender analysis of liberalization policies is a gendered deconstruction of *Stylized Facts* around its doctrines as it affects women and men and as it affects macroeconomic growth indicators. Impact of Gender Inequality on Economic Growth, Poverty and Food Security: Stylized Facts and Empirical Evidences around the developing world

Impact of gender inequality on efficiency and output of agriculture

The broad macroeconomic outcomes of liberalization are as follows: Increased commercialization, increased specialization and concentration expanded market for output export promotion via the availability of farm surplus, industrial linkages are promoted. The effects on macroeconomic variables are enhanced price of commodities, increased farm income, increased flow of private investment, increased savings and increased paid employment.

However, feminist analysis has brought out other unintended likely and documented outcomes, which are the effects of gender inequalities in the agricultural work force:

Increased feminization of the labour force, increased wage inequality, pressure on women's time budget, pressure on household subsistence, negative impact on health and nutrition, negative environmental consequences as women and the poor exploit natural resources, net shortfalls in consumption.

Several Micro studies in agriculture largely support these outcomes. Quinsumbing et al tested the assumption of *pareto efficient* household allocation of production resources in Burkina Faso. They found that farm level output was shortchanged by up to 10 per cent due to allocative inefficiency in household productive resources – a result of differential gender entitlement, even in households where farm plots were evenly distributed between male and female farmers. The assumption of *pareto efficiency* in outcome was debunked. Thus inequality impedes agricultural growth and household food security.

In Cameroun, gender inequality in technological capability and access as shown by unequal power relations in the control of yield-enhancing technology, led to substantial income loss to poor households. Women farmers persisted in growing sorghum in spite of higher returns on rice and household poverty profiles worsened.

In Zambia, women farmers refused to intercrop female crop (beans) with male crop (maize) despite potential savings of 50 per cent on weeding labour and cost. This was related to land.

Macro studies often give contradictory evidence. Kanbur, 2002 argues that findings are mixed and "the jury is out". In spite of some empirical evidences to the effect of positive benefits of gender equality for growth, the groundswell of opinion is not strong enough. He concedes that inequality impedes growth and redistribution releases constraint on growth and production, leading to welfare gains, although more from he economic and social dimension and less on the power dimension. Nonetheless, it is shown that pro-growth policy choices are promoted when endowments and capabilities are more equally distributed between women and men. The evidence against the relative importance of power inequalities needs to be reassessed against the above evidences from Zambia and Cameroun!

Biliamoune on the other hand, supports the hypotheses that increased inequality between countries of north and the south are stronger for African women than they are for African men. While globalization has favoured certain nations at the expense of others, many African countries have lost potential markets, potential foreign capital flows and globalization has forced non- competitive producers out of the market. The results show that globalization has an ambiguous effect on gender inequality in a mixed sample of developing countries, but does have a negative effect on gender inequality in Africa. This implies that gender inequality in Africa is rising as globalization proceeds.

Impact of Liberalization on Employment

The normal stylized argument is that as liberalization progresses, income growth in the productive sector leads to massive entry of women into the labour force. However as income growth progresses, the rate of feminization changes depending on the stage of development. This is the theory of the Feminization U'. Many empirical studies support this theory but the study by Darity and Ertuk clarifies the segmented effect in different countries at different stages of economic growth.

Changes in feminization ratio can apply through two different effects:

Buffer hypothesis: women's labour is secondary due to lower labour value and so as industrialization proceeds, female labour declines

Substitution hypothesis: SAP induced substitution of female labour for male labour as a cost reducing strategy. Feminization enhances economic growth.

In the craft economy (agrarian), at the initial stage of market expansion, there is massive feminization. Feminization rate however falls with rising income due to greater competition with (male) skilled labour. Job losses result for women.

In middle income (semi-industrialized) countries, feminization rate proceeds at the same rate as income growth because net job loss tends to equate net job gains as women's education and skill increases.

In high income countries, feminization rate increases with increasing income (economic growth) because the opportunity cost of women's time is now higher than its subsistence value. You may find the phenomenon of "sit- at-home-husbands".

Recent efforts towards conceptualizing gendered impacts of openness (liberalization) through price, income and employment have verified this U- shaped feminization effect in many newly industrializing nations. Export promotion and trade liberalization have led to massive movement of women into the labour force. Whether this is good for women or good for growth has also been a subject of further analysis. Ertuk and Darity showed that the new global division of labour between the North and the South could thwart economic benefits normally associated with trade liberalization.

In one likely effect, female unpaid labour in the household subsidizes the reproduction of labour. This is a cost on women, which diminishes and passes to the market as higher cost of household welfare and food security as labour force feminization proceeds. On the other hand, wage discrimination against women in the paid employment is a net gain on growth.

Floro examines the same effect in agricultural households in the Philippines and notes substantial substitution of labour between men and women as agricultural export increases, putting pressure on subsistence and welfare. In Nigeria, the substitution effect on household welfare and nutrition was evident during the structural adjustment programme.

Impact of liberalization policies on value of labour

The reproduction of labour is normally subsidized by women via domestic roles of nurturing, welfare provisioning etc. As income growth proceeds and labour force is feminized, cost of reproducing labour becomes positive as industrialization proceeds. In a craft economy, the burden of care falls on the market and because of infrastructural deficiencies and underdeveloped goods and services markets, the value of labour increases as labour quality is compromised leading to inefficiency in production, declining output, declining income, high food prices and food insecurity.

In an industrialized economy, the cost of labour is minimized due to efficient goods and services market. Thus liberalization may leave the value of labour unchanged.

Effect on composition of output

With industrialization, composition of output changes from primary products to industrial goods and export-led industrialization. Female labour has been seen to subsidized production of industrial goods as unionization breaks down (sweatshop effects). Economies change production to industrial goods at the expense of women's sweat.

The phenomenon has been noted in Export Processing Zones (EPZ) and in Commodity Value Chains (Kenya), although they have been shown to provide great opportunities for women to benefit from globalization, with short-term benefits for income and household poverty.

Impact on Investment and Savings

Where the substitution effect is higher, labour force feminization is efficient. Investment increases due to the minimal cost incentive. In a cross country analysis, empirical data not only shows that GDP growth is positively related to gender wage inequality but that part of the impact is transmitted through its positive effect on investment.

During liberalization such as SAP, women's work burden increases due to cut down in governments social spending. The share of household goods that substitutes for market defeminization, leading to desaving. But the higher the household provisioning, the higher the savings. Poverty management and food security occurs at the expense of women.

Higher subsistence leads to higher savings and declining poverty. On the other hand, higher market income leads to increasing opportunity cost of female labour, decreasing subsistence and decreasing savings. Liberalization may affect savings negatively.

Increased Paid work leads to economic empowerment for women

Again, findings are highly mixed and contextual. While in agrarian economies, the economic opportunities are enlarged for women, in other subsistence and newly industrializing economies, there are often less clement effects on women's position in the workforce.

Changes in the conditions of (paid) work due to more informalisation of work, less unionization have led to depressed wages and the sweatshop syndrome. Wage differentials are reinforced. In developed countries, there is evidence of drop in gender wage gaps, given enhanced competition between men and women skilled workers in the work place. In developing countries, wage gaps are exacerbated due to low skill of new female market entrants, high supply of labour and low bargaining power of the unskilled vis a vis the skilled. Work normalization and feminization of work rather is the norm to the advantage (capitalist accumulation) of the market economy.

Occupational segregation also persists due to skill differentiation and because skill upgrading is costly for women. Net job creation effects may be unclear. Net job creation increases for women irrespective of skill category. But net job destruction is also rising in high technology-intensiveenvironment. Volatility of employment and income is therefore on the rise for female labour.

For large industrial firms, the above picture is clearer. Extensive studies in South East Asia and Latin America have been more amenable to the analysis. For agriculture, the informal nature of employment, smaller firms, and high- unpaid work burden makes t more difficult to show the effects from cross- sectional data because of preponderance of unskilled workers. Net job creation may appear to be higher. However income effect is usually negative while wage gap effects are reinforced.

Trend analysis of agricultural data shows the structural effect more clearly as the sector is being transformed in size and technology and income. Income effect becomes lower and wage gap between skilled and unskilled jobs increases. In developed economies, the reverse is usually the case. So in agrarian economies, the stylized feminization 'U' shows up only at the later stages of structural transformation.

Impact on Agricultural Growth via Small

Farmer Commercialization (SFC)

Increased commercialization of agricultural production is seen as a positive response to adjustment policies. The optimal response is expected to 'hasten' the process of structural transformation. Therefore, any constraints to supply-response would naturally show down the rate ofcommercialization. Conversely, optimal trends in the factors that are critical determinants of supply-response should be positively related to the pace of commercialization. In the sense that such factors or the availability of factors of production vary by gender, it is expected that rate of commercialization will vary by gender.

An identification of the critical determinants of supply response and differentials in these parameter estimates for male and female farmers (degree and dimensions of gender inequality in assets ownership, capabilities and accessibility) will lead to different set of outcomes than projected by policies. Priorities for bridging gender gaps are called for in hastening the process of agricultural commercialization and growth.

Some of the determinants of commercialization have been analyzed conceptually and empirically and gender differentials are estimated. The critical determinants are largely related to the macroeconomic growth variables, albeit at the micro level.

Level of investment which may derive from capital accumulation from women in terms of inelastic labour demand is shown to be important. Gender inequality in labour utilization may enhance commercialization for men. On the aggregate, the gross investment is likely to be shortchanged. Credit becomes crucial in an analysis of investment behaviour of commercialfarmers. Therefore, what credit volume is available to male and female farmers is a determinant of commercialization.

Land Asset is another critical factor, and consistent with the 'financial hierarchy hypothesis', bigger financial (asset) base predisposes to higher accessto credit and better supply-response or rate of commercialization, inter alia. Land is the most important asset base in small-scale agriculture. To the extent that access of farmers to land vary significantly by gender this variable is crucial to the analysis of commercialization.

Cropping pattern as a derivative of land size is also important. Land, on its own, may be insufficient, rather the optimal land use within the framework, of commercialization is more important. In this sense are the allocation of land to commercial and non-commercial production and the ratio of traded to non- traded crops on male and female farms become critical.

Inequalities in these initial positions during Small Farmer Commercialization (SFC) have been seen to negate the expected aggregate outcomes from SFC. Food security objectives are still paramount with small farmers. In a study of several African countries, the following patterns were observed:

Box: Impacts of Small farmer Commercialization in Africa

SFC is part of a more comprehensive change in rural livelihoods which include off-farm activities especially wage labour for women. Evidence is also given that it is part of a long-term transition from traditional peasant life to new rural lifestyles (globalization effect).

A major finding in the process of SFC is short-term food shortages at the household level due to spontaneous development of a market economy. Intensification of staple crop production does not translate into food availability, rather, enhanced income from a variety of livelihood options buttress food security in the medium term. Food price hikes are common in a SFC environment.

Diversification, rather than specialization was therefore observed. More plot fragmentation took place rather than land amalgamation. Therefore, the food security objective is stronger in Africa's SFC than themercerization objective.

Impact of Socio-cultural variables

In the sense that the socio-cultural variables exert particular power structures between men and women in rural communities, they are all expected to produce differential gender effects on investment behaviour and level of farm commercialization. Variables like literacy will enhance participation in the market economy via greater access to information and higher technological learning. The age and gender of the farmer are important power variables in a rural community. Even among women, age crosscuts with gender to exert particular influences. An older woman in a farm household has the status of a man among other women while her position among the wives may confer her privileges such as greater access to land and other communal property resources. The nature of employment is also important.

Being primarily engaged in a particular crop production confers social capital, which is found in commodity-based social institutions, like farmers associations or cooperatives. Other (part-time) growers may lack suchinfluence while on the other hand, having another source of income apart from rice farming could be a boost to investment capacity. These are contentious issues and contextual in manifestation and therefore need to be empirically validated.

The foregoing has shown the extent that liberalization policies impact of different people in different sectors of an economy. While liberalization policies will be gender-neutral in their indication, they are hardly gender-neutral in their outcomes. It takes an analysis of such outcomes by gender categories to see the differential impact. It has also been shown that such outcomes of gender inequality do impact on the overall economy, mostly in negative ways. One, disincentives are set up, productivity is shortchanged, discrimination in wages either fuel growth of profit-oriented firms but against unethical operating standards and/or creates disenfranchised population of workers. Inequalities in liberalization effects affect productivity and output especially in agricultural systems, thereby worsening food security. It takes a gender analysis framework to unpack these effects. Gender analysis instruments are an important tool for interrogating reform policies in order to provide a framework to mainstream gender in the workings of policies themselves.

DEFINING FOOD SECURITY

Food security is a flexible concept as reflected in the many attempts at definition in research and policy usage. Even a decade ago, there were about 200 definitions in published writings. Whenever the concept is introduced in the title of a study or its objectives, it is necessary to look closely to establish the explicit or implied definition. The continuing evolution of food security as an operational concept in public policy has reflected the wider recognition of the complexities of the technical and policy issues involved.

The most recent careful redefinition of food security is that negotiated in the process of international consultation leading to the World Food Summit in November 1996. The contrasting definitions of food security adopted in 1974 and 1996, along with those in official FAO and World Bank documents of the mid-1980s, are set out below with each substantive change in definition underlined. A comparison of these definitions highlights the considerable reconstruction of official thinking on food security that has occurred over 25 years. These statements also provide signposts to the policy analyses, which have re-shaped our understanding of food security as a problem of international and national responsibility.

Food security as a concept originated only in the mid-1970s, in the discussions of international food problems at a time of global food crisis. The initial focus of attention was primarily on food supply problems—of assuring the availability and to some degree the price stability of basic foodstuffs at the international and national level. That supply-side, international and institutional set of concerns reflected the changing organization of the global food economy that had precipitated the crisis.

A process of international negotiation followed, leading to the World Food Conference of 1974, and a new set of institutional arrangements covering information, resources for promoting food security and forums for dialogue on policy issues. The issues of famine, hunger and food crisis were also being extensively examined, following the events of the mid - 1970s. The outcome was a redefinition of food security, which recognized that the behaviour of potentially vulnerable and affected people was a critical aspect. A third, perhaps crucially important, factor in modifying views of food security was the evidence that the technical successes of the Green Revolution did not automatically and rapidly lead to dramatic reductions in poverty and levels of malnutrition. These problems were recognized as the result of lack of effective demand.

OFFICIAL CONCEPTS OF FOOD SECURITY

The initial focus, reflecting the global concerns of 1974, was on the volume and stability of food supplies.

Food security was defined in the 1974 World Food Summit as:

- "Availability at all times of adequate world food supplies of basic foodstuffs to sustain a steady expansion of food consumption and to offset fluctuations in production and prices."

In 1983, FAO expanded its concept to include securing access by vulnerable people to available supplies, implying that attention should be balanced between the demand and supply side of the food security equation:

- "Ensuring that all people at all times have both physical and economic access to the basic food that they need."

In 1986, the highly influential World Bank report "Poverty and Hunger" focused on the temporal dynamics of food insecurity. It introduced the widely accepted distinction between chronic food insecurity, associated with problems of continuing or structural poverty and low incomes, and transitory food insecurity, which involved periods of intensified pressure caused by natural disasters, economic collapse or conflict.

This concept of food security is further elaborated in terms of:

- "Access of all people at all times to enough food for an active, healthy life."

By the mid-1990s food security was recognized as a significant concern, spanning a spectrum from the individual to the global level. However, access now involved sufficient food, indicating continuing concern with protein- energy malnutrition.

But the definition was broadened to incorporate food safety and also nutritional balance, reflecting concerns about food composition and minor nutrient requirements for an active and healthy life. Food preferences, socially or culturally determined, now became a consideration.

The potentially high degree of context specificity implies that the concept had both lost its simplicity and was not itself a goal, but an intermediating set of actions that contribute to an active and healthy life. The 1994 UNDP Human Development Report promoted the construct of human security, including a number of component aspects, of which food security was only one. This concept is closely related to the human rights perspective on development that has, in turn, influenced discussions about food security.

The 1996 World Food Summit adopted a still more complex definition:

- "Food security, at the individual, household, national, regional and global levels [is achieved] when all people, at all times, have physical and economic access to sufficient, safe and nutritious food to meet their dietary needs and food preferences for an active and healthy life."

This definition is again refined in the State of Food Insecurity 2001:

- "Food security a situation that exists when all people, at all times, have physical, social and economic access to sufficient, safe and nutritious food that meets their dietary needs and food preferences for an active and healthy life."

This new emphasis on consumption, the demand side and the issues of access by vulnerable people to food, is most closely identified with the seminal study by Amartya Sen. Eschewing the use of the concept of food security, he focuses on the entitlements of individuals and households. The international community has accepted these increasingly broad statements of common goals and implied respo-nsibilities. But its practical response has been to focus on narrower, simpler objectives around which to organize international and national public action. The declared primary objective in international development policy discourse is increasingly the reduction and elimination of poverty.

The 1996 WFS exemplified this direction of policy by making the primary objective of international action on food security halving of the number of hungry or undernourished people by 2015. Essentially, food security can be described as a phenomenon relating to individuals. It is the nutritional status of the individual household member that is the ultimate focus, and the risk of that adequate status not being achieved or becoming undermined. The latter risk describes the vulnerability of individuals in this context. Vulnerability may occur both as a chronic and transitory phenomenon. Food security exists when all people, at all times, have physical, social and economic access to sufficient, safe and nutritious food which meets their dietary needs and food preferences for an active and healthy life.

Household food security is the application of this concept to the family level, with individuals within households as the focus of concern. Food insecurity exists when people do not have adequate physical, social or economic access to food.

HOUSEHOLD MEASUREMENTS: THE FOCUS ON CHRONIC HUNGER AND POVERTY

Sub-nutrition, often assumed in official literature to be synonymous with the more emotive term hunger, is the result of food intake that is continuously insufficient to meet dietary energy requirements. Measurement is typically indirect and based on food balance sheets and national income distribution and consumer expenditure data. Linking hunger and sub-nutrition with inadequate food intake allows the measurement of food insecurity in terms of the availability and apparent consumption of staple foods or energy intake.

This type of measurement corresponds to the earlier narrower definitions of chronic food insecurity. Where international cross-sectional and national time series comparisons are undertaken, as in SOFI 2001, national estimates are based on average per capita availability of staple foods, or apparent consumption.

The estimates may also be weighted by evidence of food expenditure by income categories for countries where consumer expenditure surveys are not available. Because poverty lines, such as those calculated by the World Bank, also reflect assumptions about dietary energy intake, there is inevitably a high degree of correlation in these cases with estimates of poverty and extreme poverty. The international comparison of country estimates of chronic food insecurity therefore reflects cross-sectional patterns and trends in food production, supplemented by what is recorded about trade in basic foodstuffs as incorporated into national food balance sheets.

These comparisons show broad differences in food security between the development categories of low, middle and upper income countries, as well as considerable variance within categories. Attempts to explain these differences within categories, and in changes over time in the incidence of sub-nutrition, have met with limited success. SOFI 2001 notes that groups of variables that reflect shocks and agricultural productivity growth are significant influences in explaining periodic differences in country performance but concludes: "...attempts to seek one simple cause for either good or bad performance are not very useful. The power of just a few variables to explain changes in highly diverse, and indeed unique national situations is limited."

The factors that underpin this form of statistical investigation include the association of a single dependent variable to represent chronic food insecurity, with proxy variables for differences amongst countries and changes in agricultural trade regime. However, these are not suitable for studying trade and food security. The problem of unreliable data on production and unrecorded trade is unavoidable, but may be serious for many of the most food insecure countries in sub-Saharan Africa. The current crisis in Southern Africa highlights this issue. Malawi appears to have been one of the twelve best-performing countries since the early 1990s in improving food security. However, there is currently much debate about the reliability of food production data, particularly for roots and tubers in this country.

Trends for countries in which these are important staples, especially in subsistence, and comparisons between these and other countries are a source of ambiguity. An important intra-country gap exists in current analyses of food insecurity, which focus on national level or the individual level, as reflected either in averages derived as ratios of national aggregates or a national survey estimate. That gap is most apparent for larger countries such as Brazil, India, Nigeria or the Russian Federation. Substantial intra-country regional or zonal differences in the structure and dynamics of food security are also likely—for example, as a result of more rapid agricultural development in the Punjab and Haryana States in India or temporarily because of drought in Northern Nigeria. The trends in food security, as in poverty, may not be fully evident at a national level.

Therefore, an investigation of a process such as trade liberalization that involves cross-country comparisons should be sensitive to possibly important variability within larger economies. This implies the need for regional analyses to complement country level investigations. The case study of Guatemala shows the intra-country dimension missing from national food security assessments. The definition of sub-nutrition includes poor absorption and/or poor biological use of nutrients consumed. The most convenient assumption for an agricultural economic analysis would be to ignore these factors. However, and again the current crisis in Southern Africa serves as a reminder, there may be significant differences between countries in these factors and the way they are changing.

The deteriorating health situation in Southern Africa may be eroding nutritional status, not only with the recrudescence of malaria and tuberculosis, but most evidently because of the rapid spread of HIV/AIDS, with an incidence of 25 per cent and more amongst the economically active adult population. People may become more vulnerable, and so the economy more fragile and sensitive to ever-smaller shocks. This is also a reason for reassessing the importance of transitory, acute food insecurity.

FOOD SOVEREIGNTY

A third approach is known as food sovereignty; though it overlaps with food justice on several points, the two are not identical. It views the business practices of multinational corporations as a form of neocolonialism. It contends that multinational corporations have the financial resources available to buy up the agricultural resources of impoverished nations, particularly in the tropics. They also have the political clout to convert these resources to the exclusive production of cash crops for sale to industrialized nations outside of the tropics, and in the process to squeeze the poor off of the more productive lands. Under this view subsistence farmers are left to cultivate only lands that are so marginal in terms of productivity as to be of no interest to the multinational corporations.

It advocates banning the production of most cash crops in developing nations, thereby leaving the local farmers to concentrate on subsistence crops. In addition it opposes allowing low-cost subsidized food from industrialized nations into developing countries, what is referred to as "import dumping".

World Food Summit

The World Food Summit was held in Rome in 1996, with the aim of renewing global commitment to the fight against hunger. The Food and Agriculture Organization of the United Nations (FAO) called the summit in response to widespread under-nutrition and growing concern about the capacity of agriculture to meet future food needs. The conference produced two key documents, the Rome Declaration on World Food Security and the World Food Summit Plan of Action.

The Rome Declaration calls for the members of the United Nations to work to halve the number of chronically undernourished people on the Earth by the year 2015. The Plan of Action sets a number of targets for government and non-governmental organizations for achieving food security, at the individual, household, national, regional and global levels.

Achieving Food Security

"The number of people without enough food to eat on a regular basis remains stubbornly high, at over 800 million, and is not falling significantly.

Over 60 per cent of the world's undernourished people live in Asia, and a quarter in Africa. The proportion of people who are hungry, however, is greater in Africa (33 per cent) than Asia (16 per cent). The latest FAO figures indicate that there are 22 countries, 16 of which are in Africa, in which the undernourishment prevalence rate is over 35 per cent." – Food and Agriculture Organization (FAO)

From The State of Food Insecurity in the World 2003

'In general the countries that succeeded in reducing hunger were characterised by more rapid economic growth and specifically more rapid growth in their agricultural sectors. They also exhibited slower population growth, lower levels of HIV and higher ranking in the Human Development Index'.

USAID [3] proposes several key steps to increasing agricultural productivity which is in turn key to increasing rural income and reducing food insecurity. They include:

- Boosting agricultural science and technology. Current agricultural yields are insufficient to feed the growing populations. Eventually, the rising agricultural productivity drives economic growth.
- Securing property rights and access to finance.
- Enhancing human capital through education and improved health.
- Conflict prevention and resolution mechanisms and democracy and governance based on principles of accountability and transparency in public institutions and the rule of law are basic to reducing vulnerable members of society.

The First Millennium Development Goal is to Eradicate extreme hunger and poverty, and agricultural productivity is likely to play a key role if it is to be reached on time.

"Of the eight Millennium Development Goals, eradicating extreme hunger and poverty depends on agriculture the most.

The Agriculture-hunger-poverty Nexus

Eradicating hunger and poverty requires an understanding of the ways in which these two injustices interconnect. Hunger, and the malnourishment that accompanies it, prevents poor people from escaping poverty because it diminishes their ability to learn, work, and care for themselves and their family members. Food insecurity exists when people are undernourished as a result of the physical unavailability of food, their lack of social or economic access to adequate food, and/or inadequate food utilization. Food-insecure people are those individuals whose food intake falls below their minimum calorie (energy) requirements, as well as those who exhibit physical symptoms caused by energy and nutrient deficiencies resulting from an inadequate or unbalanced diet or from the body's inability to use food effectively because of infection or disease.

An alternative view would define the concept of food insecurity as referring only to the consequence of inadequate consumption of nutritious food, considering the physiological utilization of food by the body as being within the domain of nutrition and health. Malnourishment also leads to poor health hence individuals fail to provide for their families. If left unaddressed, hunger sets in motion an array of outcomes that perpetuate malnutrition, reduce the ability of adults to work and to give birth to healthy children, and erode children's ability to learn and lead productive, healthy, and happy lives. This truncation of human development undermines a country's potential for economic development – for generations to come.

There are strong, direct relationships between agricultural productivity, hunger, and poverty. Three-quarters of the world's poor live in rural areas and make their living from agriculture. Hunger and child malnutrition are greater in these areas than in urban areas. Moreover, the higher the proportion of the rural population that obtains its income solely from subsistence farming (without the benefit of pro-poor technologies and access to markets), the higher the incidence of malnutrition. Therefore, improvements in agricultural productivity aimed at small-scale farmers will benefit the rural poor first.

Increased agricultural productivity enables farmers to grow more food, which translates into better diets and, under market conditions that offer a level playing field, into higher farm incomes. With more money, farmers are more likely to diversify production and grow higher-value crops, benefiting not only themselves but the economy as a whole."

Biotechnology for Smallholders

The area sown to genetically enhanced crops in developing countries is rapidly catching-up with the area sown in industrial nations. According to the International Service for the Acquisition of Agri-biotech Applications (ISAAA), genetically enhanced (biotech, GM) crops were grown by approximately 8.5 million farmers in 21 countries in 2005, up from 8.25 million farmers in 17 countries in 2004. The largest increase in biotech crop area in any country in 2005 was in Brazil, provisionally estimated at 44,000 km^2 (94,000 km^2 in 2005 compared with 50,000 km^2 in 2004. India had by far the largest year-on-year proportional increase, with almost a threefold increase from 5,000 km^2 in 2004 to 13,000 km^2 in 2005.

Current high regulatory costs imposed on varieties created by the more modern methods are a significant hurdle for development of genetically enhanced crops well suited to developing country farmers by modern genetic methods. Once a new variety is developed, however, seed provides a good vehicle for distribution of improvements in a package that is familiar to the farmer.

Currently there are some institutes and research groups that have projects in which biotechnology is shared with contact people in less-biotechnological methods that do not involve high research and registration costs, such as conservation and multiplication of germplasm andphytosanitation.

FOOD SYSTEM

The Indian food supply is abundant and affordable and it is acknowledged by many to pose an acceptable level of risk. The food system has evolved from one that provided consumers with minimally processed basic commodities for home meal preparation to today's availability of highly processed products that are ready-to-eat or require minimal preparation. Food preservation processes have changed dramatically from traditional salting, curing, drying, and heating. Today's products are the result of many technological developments such as pasteurization, irradiation, and genetic engineering. Likewise, food distribution systems have changed greatly. The broad introduction of refrigerated railcars and trucks, freezers, and air transport created a national and now global food system. These changes allow out-of-season availability, convenience, variety, and improved sensory attributes.

The size and complexity of the Indian food system raise many safety issues, for example:

- The emergence of new foodborne pathogens such as *Escherichia coli* 0157:H7 and the re-emergence of previously identified pathogens such *as Salmonella* have resulted in new microbiological hazards.
- Advances in science and technology that allow the development of genetically modified foods and the construction of modified macronutrients require new ways of evaluating the safety of substances added to the food supply, and this need will increase.
- Heightened consumer interest in raw or minimally processed fruits and vegetables, partly in response to dietary recommendations, has created a year-round demand for fresh produce, which can be met out-of-season only through increased imports. This increased produce volume requires additional attention to possible contamination of domestic as well as imported fruits and vegetables.
- Americans eat fewer home-prepared meals than ever before, in response to changes in the US workforce and to developments in food processing and food service that offer

greater convenience and variety in available foods. The potential for contamination increases as food is handled by more people.

- As technology has advanced, a smaller number of food facilities provide food to larger numbers of Indian consumers, increasing the extent of harm that can arise from a single incident.
- The remarkable success of modern medicine in extending the lifespan and increasing the quality of life for many people has placed new demands on the food system and on those responsible for guarding its safety. Increasing numbers of people have immune systems that are compromised because of age, illness, or medical treatment. These people are highly susceptible to illness and death from microbial pathogens, and might be more sensitive to new food ingredients and recently identified natural components of the diet.

Increasing consumption of fortified foods and dietary supplements, including herbals, has raised new questions about the safety of "natural" substances not normally in the diet, or normally part of the diet but at much lower concentrations, and about the health effects of consuming high concentrations of nutrients ordinarily considered safe.

Thus, the developments that have provided the American consumer with a wide array of food products have also introduced risks. Government has attempted to address such developments by adding structures and processes without always considering their effects on other aspects of the system. As a result, inefficiencies and apparent conflicts within the system have arisen. Some have been corrected (for example, pesticides have been exempted from the Delaney clause's ban oncarcinogens), but others remain. For example, inspectors from multiple agencies oversee parallel and nearly identical processes in the same food processing facility.

The current food safety system has evolved piecemeal over almost a century in response to changes in the food supply and to changes in the biophysical and social environments in which the system operates. The present system is not the product of planning, and it is often not equipped to anticipate changes. But the situation is not just haphazard; changes in risks have made the system outmoded. The role and organization of government entities have remained largely unchanged, and the food safety system has fallen behind today's needs.

Scope of The Food Safety Problem

Over the years, as the agriculture and marketing systems have evolved to provide food to a growing and increasingly sophisticated population, complex processes built on advances in science and technology have been developed to evaluate and manage the risks associated with the food supply. In spite of well-established systems that control many food risks, serious hazards to public health remain. Although estimates vary greatly, there is agreement that foodborne illness is a serious problem. In the United States, an estimated 81 million cases of foodborne illness may occur each year, resulting in as many as 9,000 deaths. The estimated annual medical costs and productivity losses due to seven major foodborne pathogens range from $6.6 billion to $37.1 billion. The system because the wholesomeness and safety of a food are influenced by all the people and processes that handle or transform it from production to consumption. Federal, state, and local governments play major roles in managing risks to protect the public from hazards in the food supply. Regulatory agencies are empowered to prescribe rules, standards, and processes to control risks; to develop and maintain research programmes to apply contemporary science and technology to safety decisions; to monitor risks in the food supply; and to provide information and education to all components of the food system. In authorizing and funding efforts to ensure the safety of the food supply, the government must balance the interests of diverse groups and allocate finite resources among competing needs.

Faulty handling of a product at any point in the system can transform a safe product into one that can cause serious harm. Producers, shippers, importers, processors, wholesalers, retailers, handlers, and consumers all influence the health risks associated with food products. Consumers play a particularly important role in the control of microbiological risks, both in their food handling practices and in their demand for an effective, efficient food safety system.

Food safety issues also involve the interplay of domestic and international legal, political, scientific, social, and economic forces. Intense debates about desired levels of protection and about the appropriateness of different control measures can arise as parties discuss the scientific bases for risk decisions, public expectations, and relative costs and benefits of intervention in different ways and in different components of the food system.

Science must play a vital role in food safety decisions through risk assessment, that is, the identification of hazards and the determination of the likelihood and severity of risk under given conditions of exposure. Hazards are biological, chemical, or physical substances that can cause adverse consequences. Hazards associated with food include microbiological pathogens, naturally occurring toxins, allergens, intentional and unintentional additives, modified food components, agricultural chemicals, environmental contaminants, animal drug residues, and excessive consumption of some dietary supplements. In addition, certain methods of food preparation in the home can contribute to increasing some of these hazards. However, a hazard does not pose a risk in the absence of exposure. The susceptibility of the consumer and the magnitude of exposure determine whether those hazards cause immunological changes, genetic and developmental changes, cancer, or death.

Hazard identification is the basis for estimating risk. A food safety risk is the probability of harm to health resulting from a food-related hazard at a particular exposure to a specified person or group. It is important to recognize that safety is an intellectual concept, not an inherent biological property of a substance; safety has been defined as the judgment of an acceptable level of risk. Thus, "safe food" involves a subjective evaluation of social issues and values, as well as a scientific assessment of risk.

Food Safety Regulation

Regulation of food safety was largely the responsibility of state and local officials until the first decade of the twentieth century. The emergence of a national market for food, combined with shocking stories of practices in the food industry, spurred the federal government to reassess its responsibility to ensure food safety.

Although those seminal laws provide the basic legal and institutional framework for the federal regulation of food safety that we observe today, they are very different in their implementation and responsibilities. Their core was similar: each prohibited the shipment in interstate commerce of food that met any of several definitions of "adulteration." Those definitions, or proscriptions, targeted products that were spoiled, contaminated with filth, derived from diseased animals, or contained unsafe substances. In short, both laws sought to prevent the sale of food that could offend consumers or cause them to become ill.

The original Meat Inspection Act and Pure Food and Drugs Act focused on different sectors of the food market and, from the beginning, supported different approaches to ensuring compliance. The Meat Inspection Act, which has been administered by the US Department of Agriculture (USDA) since its inception, requires continuous on-site factory inspections by government inspectors using sight, smell, and touch to detect problems. The USDA also administers the 1957 Poultry Products Inspection Act, which requires continuous inspection of poultry and poultry products and the 1970 Egg Product Inspection Act, which requires continuous inspection of the processing of liquid, frozen, and dried egg products. Animal carcasses and processed products cannot be shipped from the processing plant until they have been inspected and deemed to be unadulterated by the USDA inspector.

The 1906 Pure Food and Drugs Act was administered by the USDA Bureau of Chemistry, which was renamed the Food and Drug Administration (FDA) in 1930. In 1940, FDA was transferred to the Federal Security Agency, and in 1953 it became a separate entity in the Department of Health, Education, and Welfare, later retitled the Department of Health and Human Services. FDA, with a more varied and ever-expanding industry to regulate, has used a sampling strategy in which far fewer inspectors pay periodic visits to settings where food is produced, processed, or stored to verify compliance with its requirements or to uncover and punish violations. In 1958, when Congress enacted the Food Additives Amendment to the Food, Drug, and Cosmetic Act of 1938, the FDA was given premarket review and approval authority over chemical additives to foods.

The meat and poultry inspection system still requires sight, smell, and touch inspections, which are ineffective in addressing the current issues of food safety. Expert opinion that USDA inspection procedures do not adequately address the microbiological problems associated with meat and poultry led to the adoption of a new approach to inspection using the Hazard Analysis Critical Control Point (HACCP) system. In contrast to the reactive characteristics of traditional food safety strategies, the HACCP system focuses on preventing hazards that could cause foodborne illness by applying science- based controls at each step of the process from raw material to finished product.

Following the recommendation of a National Academy of Sciences committee, FDA adopted the HACCP approach for seafood inspection in December 1995, and USDA began the implementation of HACCP for meat and poultry inspection in January 1997 with completion of the implementation by January 2000.

Agencies other than USDA and FDA-such as the National Marine Fisheries Service (NMFS) in the Department of Commerce, the Environmental Protection Agency (EPA), the Centres for Disease Control and Prevention (CDC), and the National Institutes of Health (NIH)-also have roles in food safety. NMFS conducts a voluntary seafood inspection and grading programme and does research on seafood safety. The EPA Office of Prevention, Pesticides, and Toxic Substances is responsible for risk assessment, product approvals, tolerance setting, and research on pesticide residues in or on human food and animal feed. State health departments in conjunction with CDC are responsible for the surveillance and investigation of illnesses related to foods, and NIH conducts research related to foodborne disease. Many state and local agencies are also involved in food safety regulation and inspection.

With so many agencies involved in food safety, decisions and priorities often focus on specific issues rather than strategies, and they are not always well-integrated. The system that has evolved in the federal government for regulating food safety is complex, fragmented, and cumbersome.

The Committee And Its Charge

Congress directed USDA's Agricultural Research Service to contract with the National Academy of Sciences to conduct a study on the scientific and organizational needs of an effective food safety system. The Academy appointed an ad hoc Food Safety Oversight Commission composed of selected members of the Institute of Medicine's Food and Nutrition Board, the National Research Council's (NRC) Board on Agriculture, and the NRC Commission on Life Science's Board on Environmental Studies and Toxicology; in turn, the ad hoc commission convened the Committee to Ensure Safe Food from Production to Consumption.

The committee was charged with determining the scientific basis of an effective food safety system; assessing the effectiveness of the current US system to ensure safe food; identifying scientific and organizational needs and gaps in the current system at the federal level; and providing recommendations to move toward the scientific foundation and organizational structure of a more effective food safety system for present and future generations. If organizational changes were recommended, a subsequent study on implementing the recommendations was to follow, if requested. Given the constraints on time and funding, the committee focused on the role of the federal government in ensuring safe food.

The committee is aware that safe food is and always will be a moving target with respect to both changing hazards and changing degrees of acceptance of risk. This report is not and cannot be a comprehensive, all-inclusive discussion of these issues and adoption of its recommendations will not end the effort to make food safer. It is not possible to foresee how risk acceptance will change or how the problems will change in decades to come, but federal food safety efforts must be designed effectively to deal with what is known and what is not known.

THE FOOD SYSTEM LEAVES THE FARM

Refashioning the genetic structure of crops and animals, important as it is, represents only one face of the technological revolution which has marked the appearance of the modern food system. Just as nature has been redesigned from within, through animal genetics and plant biotechnology, it has been transformed from without, by leading, in turn, to changes in the physical environment, or countryside. These changes in the 'face of the land', themselves stimulated by technological change and accompanying shifts in the labour process have contributed to new social conflicts and political demands around what has come to be seen as the Green agenda. The development of the food system implies a major change in the 'natural' environment, as well as in the genetic composition of the species. The scope of this change can hardly be overestimated.

The environmental effects of modern agriculture point to contradictions within the entire model on which the modern food system is based. Modern agriculture developed out of the partial separation of 'farming' activities from the natural resource base on which these activities were traditionally dependent. This led to technological innovation, and accompanying policy incentives, which have presented problems for the planned evolution of the food system.

In some sectors, such as the production of chemical fertilizers, plant breeding and pesticides, innovation developed 'autonomously', according to a scientific and industrial logic only loosely related to the cycle of agricultural production. The reintroduction of new industrial components into agriculture, and the food system more generally, posed problems in two ways: some processes were taken out of 'farm' production (appropriation) and others were substituted, especially in food processing activities (substitution).

These transformative technological changes were associated with major shifts in the labour process, not only on the farm but in the household and in the food industry. However, an area of equal concern has emerged during the last decade or so, which promises to pose even more serious problems for the evolution of the food system: the environment. Recent decades have witnessed a series of policy interventions designed to reduce, or reverse, the unforeseen or negative effects of the food system on the environment, largely in the industrialized countries. No area of concern demonstrates the difficulty of managing the contradictions of the food system as clearly as the environment.

Conflicts over the rural environment, and over food quality, have come to represent the clearest indication yet of the problems which the modern food system poses for sustainable development, and for the model of economic growth based on intensive accumulation which, as we have seen, spawned the modern food system itself.

This chapter examines the impact of the modern food system on the environment, in both the developed and developing countries, and the social responses which these environmental changes have evoked in recent years. The analysis begins by considering the changes within the food system which have undermined long-term sustainability, changes which were associated with the transference of economic activities between the farm and other components of the wider system. The major agricultural policy instruments which have been brought to bear on the rural environment in the industrialized countries are examined, notably the effects of price-support policies and economic incentives in the introduction of more capital intensive, 'high'- technology agriculture.

The effects on the environment of these policy mechanisms, including the loss of genetic resources, the pollution of water and soils, the threats to sustainable utilization posed by land degradation and the effects of agricultural change on amenity and recreation in rural areas. These environmental effects of the modern food system are considered as first-, second- and third-order problems, each of which requires major adjustments, at the international as well as the national level. Finally, the chapter examines the role of management interventions and environmental movements in seeking to modify or reverse these processes. A conceptual framework is outlined, which explores different forms of 'resistance' to the development of the modern food system, and concentrates attention on the epistemological and political aspects of these responses.

The description of farming in Hooten Pagnell contains most of the elements of what was still, in the 1930s, looked upon as a 'natural' farming system, heavily dependent on the cyclical and seasonal quality of rural life. Animals were left to graze in the fields, or fed on fodder crops produced on the farm, bought inputs such as fertilizers and pesticides played a negligible part in the farm accounts, a sizeable part of the food for home consumption was still provided by the farm, marketing was still in its infancy, and the 'farm family' (largely the women) processed and prepared food in the home. Each of these elements, as we have seen, has been removed (partially or fully) from the farm economy and relocated, usually in an industrial form, elsewhere in the food system.

In contrast to this picture, modern agriculture, as we have seen, is dependent on very high levels of protein and energy transfer, linking the production process on the farm with sectors in which value is added to farm production. These linkages, both upstream and downstream, have broken into the cycle of renewal, failing to return to the resource base what has been removed from it, a principle which marks sustainable agricultural systems. Thus, in modern farming, animal waste disposal has become a 'problem' rather than an essential part of a natural recycling process.

In the same way, advanced systems of crop and animal husbandry, using every protective device from pesticides to antibiotics, are made more necessary by the conditions under which animals are kept, and the genetic make-up of delicately engineered plant varieties. Given the commitment to high yields, consistent quality, and the major investments in research and development which underpin these technologies, once they are established there is apparently no cost-effective alternative to capital-intensive, energy-wasteful production regimes.

Nevertheless, in the process of establishing these regimes the 'knot' which tied agriculture to the environment has been un-done, and the costs of modern agriculture are counted elsewhere. In the United States for example, it has been estimated that the cost of soil erosion off the farm was US$6.1 billion in the mid-1980s. Similarly, in the United Kingdom, £200 million in capital costs and an annual expenditure of £10 million will be required, over a twenty-year period, to bring all drinking water up to the European Community's standard for nitrate concentrations.

In the developing countries the so-called 'externalities' are often higher still. Repetto *et al* (have argued that although gross domestic product (GDP) in Indonesia grew at an annual rate of 7.1 per cent between 1970 and 1984, if this was corrected to take account of the depletion of timber, petroleum and top soil, the rate of economic growth falls to only 4 per cent, and for four of the fourteen years was actually negative. Similarly, by calculating the effects of soil erosion on agricultural growth over ten years, Bishop and Allen have shown that in Mali soil erosion accounts for up to 16 per cent of agricultural GDP. Costs of this sort are not included in the national accounts, and hence calculations about the benefits of agricultural growth rarely reflect the real losses sustained over long periods.

There are several important respects in which attention has shifted to the problems the modern food system presents to the environment. First, the increased dependence on differently located components of the agricultural production and food processing system has served to transfer environmental costs from one part of the system to another. For example, as we have argued elsewhere, the use of soya meal and manioc for intensive cattle production in Europe, has transferred some of the costs of maintaining feedstock systems to other countries, such as Brazil and Thailand, which can ill afford it. Second, increasingly intensive production has led to problems of waste disposal, pollution and disease control, all of them problems which have accompanied intensification.

Table: Intermediate Consumption in French Agriculture (Billion Francs)

	1970	1975	1981
Animal feed	6.8	14.9	33.0
Fertilizers	4.2	9.0	19.1
Fuel and repairs	3.2	6.8	15.4
Crop protection	1.2	2.9	9.6
Building maintenance	0.8	1.4	3.2
Veterinary costs	0.9	1.9	4.5
Other goods	2.5	4.8	9.5
Other services	1.4	2.4	5.0

Total intermediate consumption as proportion of output 30.0 percent 36.0 percent 46.0 percent

These problems frequently assume major importance in two directions: for the farm they represent increased costs which need to be incorporated in the farm accounts, and the market viability of the enterprise; and for the local environment they represent major threats to the existing ecological systems, species diversity and habitats. With increasing demands for financial security, but tighter economic margins, expenditure on what are termed 'intermediate goods' now represents nearly half the value of agricultural output of some industrialized countries such as France.

European Parliament Working Document A 2-207/85 Report on behalf of the Committee on the Environment, Public Health and Consumer Protection.

This table, which expresses the costs of intensification both in current money terms, and as a percentage of total production costs, clearly points to the increasing financial burden of maintaining intensification, which is borne by the farmer in the first instance, but indirectly by the consumer and taxpayer and, at another remove, by agricultural competitors in less protected markets. The environmental costs of this pattern of financial and resource management on the farm are paid in a number of ways, not all of which are easily 'accountable' in monetary terms.

The third aspect of the removal of 'natural' processes from the farm, and the relocation of these processes in other sectors of the food system, has been to transform, in some cases fundamentally, the pattern of land use in rural areas. The modern food system has brought unprecedented interference with traditional land uses and the rural landscape, especially through activities like drainage, land levelling and deforestation.

There has also been a reduction in soil quality, arising from the poor management of soil resources. Current problems, as we shall see, include precipitation of acid rain on land, the discharge of toxic wastes and the uncontrolled spread of sewage on land. As a result of these and other factors, the usable agricultural area within the European Community declined by almost 8 per cent between 1962 and 1984, from almost 100 million hectares to under 92 million hectares.

The combination of several different processes, whose cumulative effect is to undermine the quantity of under-graded land available for both agricultural and non-agricultural uses (including conservation) has led to a rural resource crisis in Europe of serious dimensions. As the Food and Agricultural Organization (FAO) of the United Nations has put it, in rather august language:

A complex web of economic policies provides, at considerable cost to the environment, many of the incentives and institutional mechanisms needed to support the high level and intensity of agricultural production. This situation is compounded by over-production of some commodities in the agricultural sector and rapidly rising economic costs from policies intended to encourage production and raise income. It is to this 'complex web of economic policies' that we need to turn next.

Policy Instruments and Mechanisms

In a document by the European Parliament itself, we are reminded of the lack of attention to long-term sustainability in the development of the European Community's agricultural policy. Emphasizing the five fundamental objectives of the Common Agricultural Policy (CAP) of the European Community (article 39 of the Treaty of Rome)—to increase agricultural productivity, improve farm living standards, stabilize markets and ensure a secure supply of foodstuffs at a reasonable price—the document continues by stating that 'the pursuit of these objectives clearly betokens a productivist and materialist ideology which takes no account of environmental concerns'.

Community preference follows logically from the establishment of a single agricultural market, but it is also clear that establishing this market is expensive in terms of export subsidies 'and that it does not necessarily contribute to the rational location of different types of production'. Similarly, within the European Agricultural Guidance and Guarantee Fund (EAGGF) of the European Community, 'guidance' to farmers (which might assist with the painful process of restructuring for farm households) only amounts to one twentieth of the total expenditure: the hulk of expenditure under this fund takes the fonn of subsidies to agricultural producers.

The scale of agricultural subsidies1 as we shall see1 makes any serious attempt at environmental protection in European agriculture extremely difficult, since fanners vvho are normally subsidized for doing what is harmful to the environment also expect to be subsidized for not doing what is environmentally harmful. The cost of the CAP is 1 as Simpson remarks 'legendary'

Only part of the tota1 cost of the CAP is attributa hlP to the purchase, storage and export subsidies for farm production: a 'mere' El8 billion per annum, equivalent to £5.91a week for a family of four in the Community. In addition, the same family has to pay almost t\'\rice this amount weekly tn,,vards the cost of fixing FC prices above prevailing world market levels. The total cost is £42 billion per annun1. These figures provide an indication of 'a policy which sacrifices long-term interests to immediate concerns1 and one scarcely needs reminding that most environmental issues arise from a concern for the long term future/.

It is worth paying attention to the policy framework for agriculture within the European Community, because in intention, although not always in its choice of 1nechanisms, it mirrors the approach of other industrialized countries1 such as the United States and Japan. The policy framework for European agriculture, as vve have seen1 ·was established vvith a vie\1\r to protecting rural incomes through production subsidies, and ensuring food sufficiency V\rithln member counb"ies. One consequence of these policies is that the benefits and costs of agricultural policy are shared "/ery unequally betvveen producers and consumers. For example, if we compare France ..vvith the United Kingdom, we can appreciate that because of the larger size of the French agricultural sector, the absolute value of protection is higher than in the United Kingdom.

Hovvever, if ·we t:tke individual farmers the reverse is true: British farmers do rather better under the CAP because they work, on average, larger farms. In France in 1980 the average farm size was 25.4 hectares compared with 68.7hectares in the United Kingdom. As Cheshire makes dear, 'large farmers, because they produce more, effectively receive more support than poorer, smaller fanners'. The aggregate effect of these distributional factors is highly unequal: three-quarters of EC support to fanners goes to the richest quarter of farmers.

The level of expenditure under the CAP far outstripped most other budgetary items within the control of the Community. Taxpayers and consumers effectively supported 40 per cent of the value of farmers' produce during the years 1983-7, vvhen agricultural spending in real tenns increased by 4 per cent a year. In the United Kingdon1, in 1984, n1ore V\ras spent on farmers and the food industry (£6.9 billion) than was spent on unemployment benefit and supplementary benefit combined (£5 billion).

Senior also points to the fact that only a dozen people work for the European Commission on consumer affairs, while 800 work in DG.VI, the directorate responsible for agriculture. And within the European Community it is DG.VI that makes agricultural policy, in consultation with the agricultural producers' group COPA, the Council of Agricultural Ministers and the Agricultural Committee of the European Parliament.

The effect of close collaboration between farming interests, and the virtual exclusion of the consumers' interest from food policy discussions, is that policy not only favours large farmers over smaller ones, it also favours wealthier families over poorer ones. In 1988 in the United Kingdom the poorest 25 per cent of households spent 29 per cent of their disposable income on food. The richest 25 per cent of households spent 14 per cent on food. The relatively

'rich' West Germans spent 14 per cent on food, while the relatively 'poor' Greeks spent 36 per cent.

Simpson observes that 'if poor people were paying to help other poor people and keep them on the land that may be some consolation. But they are not'. Very little influence is wielded within European Community circles by the consumer interest, and environmental considerations still do not enter into the design of agricultural policy, as one might expect. As we have seen, this lack of political influence is in marked contrast with the position of the agricultural lobby. In explaining the ideological dominance of this lobby, we must take account of the level of farm support in the past. The level of farm support has been fundamental to the shift in agricultural practices, most of which, as we shall see, are prejudicial to the environment. It is not difficult to demonstrate that the mechanisms, and the level, of farm support in the European Community is highly inegalitarian in its effects. Can it be demonstrated that these policy mechanisms are ultimately responsible for the environmental problems that afflict the countries of Western Europe?

The cumulative effects of high levels of farm support on the rural environment may be complex and subtle, but they are also increasingly well documented. The agricultural technology/policy model encouraged the rapid adoption of new technology in the United States and Western Europe. The high level of farm support, expressed through high farm prices, has encouraged more investment in research and development, and the acquisition of more capital equipment by farmers. Price support has also stimulated intensification through its effect on land values.

Throughout the period between the mid-1950s and the late 1970s agricultural land values increased in the United Kingdom, in fact they tripled in real terms. After 1979, when the rate of increase of CAP price began to fall, and particularly after 1984 when milk quotas were introduced, land prices began to decline, for the first time in decades. The intensification of agriculture was given a considerable stimulus by the capitalization of land as an asset, and the need to maximize returns on this asset.

It is also clear, from evidence such as that of Traill that high support prices for farmers induce more capital investment, and the substitution of capital equipment, where possible, for labour. In West Germany, in 1989, there were

8.5 milking machines for every 100 cows; 2.8 combine harvesters and 12.4 tractors for every 100 hectares of land. This level of mechanization was higher than in the United Kingdom because the farm structure was different: under a regime of high support prices, and accompanying subsidized credit and guaranteed markets, there is every inducement for even the smallest farmers to mechanize production.

Second, although the legal and financial inducements to farm amalgamation are few within the European Community, the economic gains from larger units, from 'shedding' labour and acquiring ever more capital equipment, are considerable. The pressures on the production margins of small farmers, even those with milking machines and tractors, are further accentuated by the concentration of farm ownership. One effect of agricultural support and the technological treadmill is, therefore, greater specialization. It is in the automatic consequence of inducing investment, and losing employment, in farming.

PUBLIC INVESTMENT CRITICAL TO FOOD SECURITY

Agriculture must figure prominently in poverty alleviation strategies of developing countries.

Accelerated public investments are needed to facilitate agricultural and rural growth through:

- Yield-increasing crop varieties, including those that are drought and salt tolerant and pest resistant, and improved livestock
- Yield-increasing and environmentally friendly productiontechnology
- Reliable, timely, and reasonably priced access to appropriate inputs such as tools, fertilizer, and, when needed, pesticides, as well as the credit often needed to purchase them
- Strong extension services and technical assistance to communicate timely informationand developmentsin technology and sustainable resource management to farmers and to relay

farmer concerns to researchers
- Improved rural infrastructure and effective markets
- Particular attention to the needs of women farmers, who grow much of the locally produced food in many developing countries
- Primary education and health care, clean water, safe sanitation, and good nutrition for all.

These investments need to be supported by good governance and an enabling policy environment, including trade, macroeconomic, and sectoral policies that do not discriminate against agriculture, and policies that provide appropriate incentives for the sustainable management of natural resources, such as secure property rights for small farmers. Development efforts must engage poor farmers and other low-income people as active participants, not passive recipients; unless the affected people have a sense of ownership, development schemes have little likelihood of success. Developing countries must reverse present declining levels of public investment in agriculture.

On average, they devote 7.5 per cent of government spending to agriculture. For their part, donor countries must redress the precipitous decline in aid to agriculture and rural development, which plunged by nearly 50 per cent in real terms between 1986 and 1996. Overall development aid has also fallen in recent years. Ironically, our research has found that aid to developing country agriculture not only is effective in promoting sustainable development and poverty alleviation, but it leads to increased export opportunities for industrial countries as well, including, paradoxically, increased agricultural exports. Donors must also rethink their rather inflexible emphasis of the past two decades on less government and a smaller public sector, which has contributed to public disinvestment in agriculture in the developing countries.

AGRICULTURAL RESEARCH IS ESSENTIAL

Public investment in agricultural research is of particular importance for achieving food security in developing countries. The private sector is unlikely to undertake much of the research needed by small farmers because it cannot expect sufficient returns to cover costs. IFPRI research has shown that the annual rates of return to agricultural research and development are, on average, 73 per cent. Benefits to society from agricultural research can be extremely large but will not be obtained without public investments. We have also found that even minor increases in aid to agricultural research for developing countries can significantly accelerate food supplies, while relatively small cuts could have serious negative effects. Despite this evidence, low-income developing countries grossly underinvest in agricultural research: less than 0.5 per cent of the value of their agricultural production, compared to 2 per cent in higher- income countries. Sub-Saharan Africa, which desperately needs productivity increases in agriculture, has only 42 agricultural researchers per million economically active persons in agriculture, compared with 2,458 in industrial countries. Efforts to improve longer-term productivity on small-scale farms, with an emphasis on staple food crops, must be accelerated.

Research and policies are also needed to help farmers, communities, and governments better cope with risks resulting from such factors as poor market integration, poorly functioning markets, and climatic fluctuations. More research must be directed to the development of appropriate technology for sustainable intensification of agriculture in resource- poor areas, where a high percentage of poor people live, and where environmental risks are severe.

The needed research must join all appropriate scientific tools together, with better use of the insights of traditional indigenous knowledge. Research and technology alone will not drive agricultural growth. The full and beneficial effects of agricultural research and technological change will materialize only if government policies are conducive to and supportive of poverty alleviation and sustainable management of natural resources.

THE CHALLENGES TO FOOD SECURITY

In developing countries, 800 million people are undernourished, of which a significant proportion live on less than US$1 per day, despite a more than 50% decline in world food prices over the past 20 years. Global food production has soared, making a variety of foods available to all consumers. Although the decline in food prices in developed countries has benefited the poor who spend a considerable share of their income on food, this trend has not had much impact on the majority in the developing world, with sub-Saharan Africa painting the gloomiest picture.

Due to the substantial price reduction in this commodity sector, cereals have become the staple foods in the diet of poor people. While yield increases in the major cereal crops has meant more calorific intake of food, micronutrient malnutrition remains a serious problem. Regional analyses depict sub-Saharan Africa as the only region where both the number and proportion of malnourished children have consistently risen in the past three decades. However, malnutrition in South Asia is also very high.

The world population is projected to reach 8 billion by 2025, and it is estimated that most of this growth will occur in developing countries. Feeding and housing an additional 2 billion people will cause considerable pressure on land, water, energy and other natural resources. Looking at projections to 2020, the worldwide per capita availability of food is expected to increase by approximately 7%, *i.e.* 2900 calories per person per day. Nonetheless, an average availability of 2300 calories is projected for individuals in sub-Saharan Africa, a figure that is just above the recommended minimum calorie intake for an active and productive life. In terms of agricultural output, preliminary world estimates for 2001 suggested that growth was as low as 0.6%. Annual rates also demonstrate a trend of decreased productivity, particularly in developing-country regions. Output growth in Asia has systematically declined over the past five years the rates experienced in sub-Saharan Africa are lower than average. Agricultural productivity is important for food security in that it has an impact on food supplies, prices, and the incomes and purchasing power of farmers. Improving food security at the national level requires an increase in the availability of food through increased agricultural production, or by increasing imports.

To augment domestic production and maintain an adequate supply of food, food-insecure countries often rely on imports and food aid. Export earnings are frequently low and do not suffice to provide foreign exchange to finance imports. Thus, in the long term, importing food is unsustainable. Historically, increased food production in the developing countries can be attributed to the cultivation of more land rather than to the deployment of improved farming practices or to the application of new technologies. By its very nature, agriculture threatens other ecosystems, a situation that can be exacerbated by over-cultivation, overgrazing, deforestation and bad irrigation practices. However, increased demands for food in Asia, Europe and North Africa have to be met by increasing yields because most land in these areas is already used for agriculture.

The potential to expand agricultural land exists in Latin America and sub-Saharan Africa only, where much of the remaining land is marginal for agricultural expansion. The implication, therefore, is that the increase in food production needed to feed the world's growing population can only be met by increasing the amount of food produced per hectare. Recognizing the extent of environmental degradation caused mainly by human activities, the multilateral agreements that arose from the UNCED meeting of 1992 were intended to address the compromised food-security situation on a global scale. One such agreement is the United Nations Convention to Combat Desertification. This agreement promotes the implementation of practices intended to reverse desertification for sustainable land use and food security. As the more affluent developed countries tend to produce more food, some argue that redistribution of these surpluses could feed the escalating populations of developing countries. Redistribution, however, requires policy changes that may be impossible to implement on a global scale. Therefore, a substantial proportion of the food demands of developing countries will have to be met by the agricultural systems in these countries. Enabling a consistent and sustainable supply of food will require an overhaul in the production processes and the supporting infrastructure. Finding solutions to declining crop yields requires an effort that will improve the assets on which agriculture relies; namely, soils, water and biodiversity.

Transforming the agricultural systems of rural farmers by introducing technologies that integrate agro-ecological processes in food production, while minimizing adverse effects to the environment, is key to sustainable agriculture. In addition, increases in crop yield must be met with the use of locally available low-cost technologies and minimum inputs without causing damage to the environment.

ATTAINING FOOD SECURITY

Within the context of the definition, three distinct components appear central to attaining food security: availability, accessibility and adequacy. Within each component, questions are raised which may need to be addressed to improve the food security situation at a national, regional or international level.

The questions raised here are intended to demonstrate the complexity of the issue and are by no means exhaustive:

- *Availability*: is there enough food available through domestic production or imports to meet the immediate needs? Is production environmentally sustainable to meet long-term demands? Are the distribution systems effective in reaching low-income and rural communities?
- *Accessibility*: do the vulnerable in society have the purchasing power to attain food security? Can they afford the minimum basic diet of 2100 calories per day required for an active and productive life?
- Adequacy: does the food supply provide for the differing nutritional needs, *i.e.* a balanced diet, offering the necessary variety of foods at all times? Is the food properly processed, stored and prepared?

Global food productivity is undergoing a process of rapid transformation as a result of technological progress in the fields of communication, information, transport and modern biotechnology. A general observation is that technologies tend to be developed in response to market pressures, and not to the needs of the poor who have no purchasing power. As agriculture is the main economic activity of rural communities, optimizing the levels of production will generate employment and income, and thus uplift the wealth and well-being of the community.

Improving agricultural production in developing countries is fundamental to reducing poverty and increasing food security. Investment to raise agricultural productivity can be achieved through the introduction of superior technologies such as better-quality seeds, crop rotation systems etc. It is argued, however, that the adoption of earlier agricultural technologies has led to the emergence of more virulent strains of pests, pathogens and weeds, soil deterioration and a loss of biodiversity.

The Green Revolution, in particular, focused on wheat and rice—not much attention was paid to staple crops such as sorghum, cassava or millet. Also, the seeds and fertilizers required to grow the higher-yielding varieties were expensive and therefore not accessible to all. Reaffirming support for the principles agreed upon at the UNCED, the United Nations Millennium Development Goals have set a road map for protecting the environment. Embraced in these time-bound goals is a new development ethic that demands sustainability in a framework where progress is measured in terms of actions reconciling the economic and ecological factors of food production for the benefit of present and future generations?

Extending this understanding to agriculture, sustainable agriculture is defined as:

- Environmentally sound, preserving resources and maintaining production potential;
- Profitable for farmers and workable on a long-term basis;
- Providing food quality and sufficiency for all people;
- Socially acceptable; and
- Socially equitable, between different countries and within each country.

A secure food system is one in which the ecological resources on which food production depends allow for their continued use, with minimum damage for present and future generations.

In other words, food security and sustainable agriculture are interlinked and both are central to the concept of sustainable development. The FAO Anti- hunger Programme reported that increasing investment in agriculture and rural development can reduce hunger. To reduce the number of hungry people by half by 2015, it estimated that funding of US$24 billion would be required for agricultural research, emergency food assistance, and improving rural infrastructure.

By contrast, at the current rate of progress, the number of food-insecure would fall by only 24%. For people to be food-secure, they must have access to the resources needed to buy or produce their own food.

Breaking the poverty cycle of rural communities, whose livelihoods depend on agriculture, will require investment in different technologies to address the different constraints experienced in different world regions. The production problems experienced by farmers vary between countries and communities, and technological solutions need to be relevant to those circumstances, *i.e.* one solution will not be suitable everywhere.

The potential of some of these technologies has been demonstrated in various world regions— for instance, agro-ecological improvement programmes involving:

- Better harvesting and conservation of water, even in rain-fed environments;
- A reduction of soil erosion by adopting zero tillage combined with the use of green manure and herbicides as in Argentina and Brazil; and
- Pest and weed control without pesticide or herbicide use, *e.g.* Bangladesh and Kenya, has been well tested and established.

Indeed, such programmes are now widely accepted as being at the core of sustainable agriculture. The communities that participated in these projects were able to transform food production through the use of resource-management strategies that focused on improving the soil by growing leguminous crops and applying agro-forestry, zero tillage and green manure.

These and other projects have proved that the sustainability of any farming practice and the conditions under which production can be maintained at reasonable levels cannot be predicted with absolute certainty. Some regions may be better able to transfer high-yielding technologies with varying degrees of success.

The uptake of new production systems has proved successful where the programmes have included the participation of entire communities and have not been introduced to isolated groups of farmers. Producing nutritionally enhanced properties in staple crops eaten by the poor could reduce the burden of disease in many developing countries. Scientists at the International Crops Research Institute for the Semi-Arid Tropics have developed a pearl millet variety enhanced with beta-carotene. The trait naturally occurs in two Burkina Faso millet lines from which it was transferred by conventional breeding methods. Genetic modification of japonica rice with a ferritin gene has not given superior results compared to rice with an 80% increase in iron density produced by conventional plant breeding at the International Rice Research Institute. Research and technology alone will not drive agricultural growth. Inadequate infrastructure and poorly functioning markets tend to exacerbate the problem of food insecurity. The cost of marketing farm produce can be prohibitive for small-scale farmers, as their isolation prevents the link between agricultural and non-agricultural activities among adjacent villages and between rural and urban areas.

Building roads in rural areas is vital to facilitating growth, trade and exchange of farm and non-farm products in rural communities, even those that can adequately feed themselves. For instance, government investment in irrigation projects, storage and transport facilities, roads connecting villages to larger markets in the rural areas of China and India, has made an impressive impact on employment and productivity and ultimately provided opportunities for poverty alleviation in the affected areas. UNDP, basic thresholds in roads, power, ports and communications must be reached in order to sustain growth.

❐

Chapter - 3

Skills of Food Production

FOOD PRODUCTION

In 1900 most food was still processed locally, either in the home or in small establishments, like bakeries, supplying a limited market. Food- processing factories were already well established for certain products, but their contribution was, in relative terms, much smaller than it was to be by midcentury.

To some extent this can be associated with social factors: the middle-class housewife, at least in Europe, prided herself on her household management and disdained ready-prepared food. With domestic help still easily available she could afford this prejudice; moreover, while the prejudice existed, the food manufacturers had no great incentive to improve quality. With the poorer working-class housewife the situation was different: quantity was at least as important as quality, and she was quite happy to see some of her domestic chores translated to the factory.

In the USA, with its predilection for labour-saving techniques of all kinds, there was a different attitude, at least in the rapidly growing urban communities. Processed food was welcome also in the areas of pioneering activity where ordinary sources of supply did not exist and the acquisition and storage of fresh food presented considerable problems.

We must recall, too, that new food-producing areas were developing far from the main areas of consumption and — so far as perishables like meat, fish, and fruit were concerned — their products could not be marketed at all unless processed in some way on the spot. Even in the case of non-perishable materials, such as wheat, the products of the new areas often could not be satisfactorily handled without the development of new technologies. The hard wheats of North America, for example, did not lend themselves to the traditional stone-milling methods of Europe.

MODERN FOOD TECHNOLOGY

At the beginning of this century certain aspects of modern food technology were already well developed but others, which had become commonplace by 1950, had scarcely developed at all. We may, therefore, conveniently begin our study by outlining the situation in 1900.

By that time the canning industry had been firmly established for meat, fish, fruit, and vegetables. Although great improvements were to be made both in the technique itself and in the quality of the product, canned food was widely used for both its convenience and its cheapness. The fact that it would keep almost indefinitely was a most important point in its favour — as much for the housewife anxious to hold a reserve against unexpected demand as for the military victualler meeting the requirements of an army in the field.

Refrigeration, too, was firmly established as an important means of preservation, and large cargoes of frozen meat were coming into Europe from the new sources of supply in Australia, New Zealand, and North and South America. The quality left something to be desired, however, partly because of imperfections in the freezing process, which affected the taste, and partly because of the inferior quality of much of the product, reared under conditions very different from those on European farms. Nevertheless it was acceptable and, because of its cheapness, it found a ready market. As opposed to canned products, however, which would keep more or less indefinitely, refrigerated products had a relatively short life because the cost of fuel made it uneconomic to freeze for long periods.

The magnitude of the trade is indicated by the fact that in 1900 New Zealand exported four million carcasses of mutton and lamb and the Argentine more than two million. There was also a rapidly growing trade in frozen beef:

20 000 tons from the Argentine in 1900. The freezing of fish was less successful, however, and in the fish trade refrigeration was generally on a short-term basis sufficient to cover transit from the increasingly distant fishing grounds to the ports. Fruit, vegetables, and eggs did not at that time lend themselves to preservation in this way.

The processing of dairy products, too, was being gradually moved from the farm to the factory. By 1850 cheese factories were established in both the USA and Australia, but in Britain and elsewhere in Europe they met fierce opposition from farmers and dairymaids alike: the one feared for his position as the traditional cheese producer and the latter for her employment.

Nevertheless, the first English cheese factory — at Longford, Derby — was in operation in 1870, under the guidance of American advisers, and within five years there were ten such factories, processing the milk of 8000 cows. Production of factory-made cheese increased steadily, but the larger farmers, able to buy modern equipment and assimilate new techniques, contrived to hold their own.

In butter-making the move to the factory was fostered by the invention of the centrifugal cream-separator by the Swedish engineer de Laval in 1877, which made possible great savings in labour and space. While the traditional dairy-farming countries continued to be major suppliers, the new producers, notably Australia and New Zealand, made rapidly growing contributions.

All producers found a rival, however, in margarine. Invented in the 1860s by the French chemist H. Mège-Mouriés, its large-scale manufacture had been firmly established, especially in Holland, by 1900. An important discovery here, made in 1899, was that certain oils, too soft for margarine manufacture, could be hardened by hydrogenation in the Sabatier-Senderens reaction. This process began to be worked on an industrial scale about 1910.

Milk is another important perishable food whose handling changed rapidly. With the extension of the railways and the growth of the urban areas, the towns increasingly drew their supplies from the countryside in bulk. The milk travelled in tinned-steel churns and was delivered from smaller churns at the doorstep. Some surplus milk was condensed or dried. Pasteurization was introduced about the turn of the century, originally with the commercial objective of prolonging the life of the milk and later it was used more widely for the sake of health in general and for the prevention of tuberculosis in particular.

In the first half of this century the trends indicated above continued, with emphasis on preservation and factory processing. Development was facilitated by a better understanding of the scientific principles involved. In addition, some quite new processes came into general use, especially after the Second World War.

The most important of these were freeze-drying, which allowed easy reconstitution of many products, and deep-freezing, which went hand in hand with the availability of domestic cold-storage lockers. Before studying these innovations, however, we may conveniently consider progress in established food technology.

DAIRYPRODUCTS

Throughout the first half of this century milk and products derived from it remained of major importance. At mid-century world milk production was around 180 million tons annually, and from this were made some three million tons of butter and two million tons of cheese. Most countries remained more or less self-supporting in respect of these commodities: few imported more than 10 per cent of their over-all needs. The position of the United Kingdom was quite different, however: in 1939 she imported 80 per cent of her butter and 50 per cent of her cheese. The main exporters were New Zealand, by far the largest, followed by Australia, Denmark, and Holland. While technological developments, notably mechanization of existing methods and centralization of manufacture, ensured that quantities were sufficient, this was not always the case so far as quality was concerned. Factory-made butter was the least affected, in that the process of its manufacture is relatively simple. With cheese, however, the decline was very evident, and mainly the result of commercial factors. The full flavour of a cheese is realized only as the result of a long ripening process governed by a complex system of enzymes. If this process is curtailed, the product, though unimpaired from the nutritional point of view, may be relatively tasteless and of poor texture; such curtailment did occur in the cheese factories and stores, though it would be idle to suggest that all farmhouse cheese was perfect.

Much of the decline was promoted by changing demand. Bread and cheese was the traditional meal of the industrial worker in the factory and the demand was for quantity rather than quality. To satisfy this, quickripening moist cheeses were produced on the basis of rapid turnover and larger profits. Less cheese was stored in lofts, to ripen, but more in cold-stores where microbiological action was suspended. Worse, means were discovered of making cheese from pasteurized milk.

At first the process denatured milk proteins and prevented coagulation with rennet, but this was overcome by using a somewhat lower pasteurization temperature. The result was 'processed' cheese, first manufactured in Switzerland at the beginning of the century and later made elsewhere in Europe and in North America. From the purely practical point of view it has much to commend it: although its moisture content is higher than that of real cheese, thus making it poorer value for money, it keeps indefinitely and there is no wasteful rind. Its disadvantage is its taste and texture.

We have already noted the advent of margarine as a rival to butter. The original product was in effect little more than an emulsion of purified beef tallow with milk, from which the fatty fraction was then precipitated by addition of ice and worked to a buttery consistency. It was not very palatable but it was cheap and nutritious. In the twentieth century vegetable fats and oils were introduced and the skim milk used was subjected to lactic fermentation.

Great improvements were made in the emulsification process, and incorporation of vitamins A and D (compulsory in Britain during the Second World War) was common. By 1950 the palatability of margarine and its nutritional value had been greatly enhanced. By careful control of the manufacturing process, products could even be made suitable for different climatic conditions. World production in 1938 amounted to more than one million tons, roughly one-third that of butter.

Milk contains approximately 87 per cent water; it is not surprising therefore that there has long been an interest in drying (or condensing) it, not only as a means of indefinite preservation but also to reduce its bulk. Most early processes depended on direct heating: the milk was allowed to run over a hot roller and the dry residue was then scraped off. Unfortunately this causes considerable change in flavour and the lost water is not easily reabsorbed when desired. Nevertheless, it provides a product useful for various purposes in the food industry.

During the Second World War spraydrying processes were developed in which a spray of skimmed milk was allowed to fall through a rising current of hot air; by the time the droplets reached the bottom of the plant they have turned to powder. Again, however, there was difficulty in reconstituting the product. In 1946 this was overcome by an agglomeration process developed in the USA by the Instant Milk Company. Spray-drying was also used to dry eggs.

There were some important changes in the process of pasteurization. From the 1920s this was done in bulk rather than in bottles and consisted in holding the milk for half an hour at about 65°C; it was then rapidly cooled. During the Second World War, however, this method began to be replaced by the so- called HTST (High Temperature Short Time) process in which the working temperature was about 72°C but the operating time only a quarter of a minute. It was followed by the UHT (Ultra High Temperature) process in which the milk is superheated to about 150°C for only a few seconds. The short heating periods of these last two processes demanded the development of elaborate heat exchangers.

MEAT AND FISH

For meat and fish, and for fruit, vegetables, and condensed milk, canning continued to be the most important means of preservation. The basic principle remained unchanged but there were significant developments in practice, organization, and, of course, in scale; in 1950 the USA, which had become the world's greatest producer of canned foods, used some 10 000 million cans.

At the same time developments in bacteriology — a science which had not even been born when Nicolas Appert introduced his preservation process in 1810 on a purely empirical basis — made it possible to conduct the process more efficiently and, above all, more safely. An essential requirement was proper understanding of the heat-transfer process: it was essential that the whole of the food mass was held for long enough at the required temperature.

The essence of canning is to destroy by heat all the micro-organisms that cause food to go bad and then to seal the container completely so that there can be no subsequent contamination until it is opened. Contamination, should it occur, is usually harmless but certain organisms can produce severe, and sometimes fatal, food poisoning. This was not uncommon in the early days of canning but is now very rare.

In Appert's original process the food to be preserved was put into loosely stoppered glass bottles which were then immersed in boiling water for what experience indicated was 'long enough'. The stoppers were then driven home and luted round the edge. This procedure presented two hazards: some organisms can survive the temperature of boiling water and there might be leakage round the stopper.

The first hazard was overcome by replacing the water by a solution of calcium chloride, which boils at a much higher temperature (246°F), and later, in the 1870s, by using autoclaves in which the boiling-point of water is raised by application of pressure; this was a technique widely adopted for sterilizing surgical instruments. By the end of the century large reliable autoclaves were in general use. They remained in normal practice until the 1960s, when the process of flame sterilization began to be used. In this, the cans are spun rapidly (two revolutions per minute) while a gas flame is applied to their surface. Under these conditions heat transfer is so rapid that there is no local overheating.

The risk of contamination after sterilization was largely overcome by using cans made of tinplate instead of glass containers. The end discs were soldered on and a small hole was left in the upper disc to be closed by soldering when heat treatment was complete. It was a slow and laborious process: even a good artisan could make no more than about 600 cans a day.

The development of can-making machinery was, therefore, essential to the expansion of the industry: by mid-century such machines were capable of making 600 cans in two minutes. The major development here was the advent of the sanitary or open-top can about 1905. This was made from seamed tubing double-seamed at top and bottom; the need for soldering was eliminated.

For most of the period in question, tinplate was the standard material for making cans, the thickness of the tin, which is expensive, being progressively reduced: in 1950 a thickness of 0.0001 inch was normal. Such thin films were easily damaged and any imperfection could be a site of corrosion; to avoid this it became customary to lacquer the tinplate. After the Second World War the cheapness of aluminium led to its use in making cans, especially for vegetables and drinks; for the latter, the pull-ring opener was introduced. At the same time, steel coated with an exceedingly thin film of chromium/ chromium oxide began to replace tinplate; this, too, was lacquered.

The storage and transport of refrigerated food was well established by the end of the nineteenth century, but it was generally believed that if food was cooled below -2°C it would suffer irreversible and deleterious changes. In 1929, however, Clarence Birdseye showed that quick freezing to lower temperatures is satisfactory for many products, mainly because the ice crystals formed are much smaller. This opened the way to the enormous frozen-food industry which, as a complement, demanded the general adoption of domestic deep-freeze lockers in addition to refrigerators.

A very important innovation in this area was accelerated freeze-drying, originally developed in Sweden in the 1930s for drying biological materials of pharmaceutical importance. It is based on the fact that at low pressures ice will sublime —that is to say, it passes directly into the vapour phase without melting. The dehydrated residue is left in a powder form which readily reabsorbs water to reconstitute the material in something very like its natural form.

Freeze-drying has been used for many vegetables; for meat and fish; and for coffee. During the Second World War it was used for the purification of penicillin, but the first commercial plant for food preservation seems to have been opened in Russia in 1954. It is an expensive process in terms of energy consumption but against this it can be argued that the product can be stored indefinitely vdthout further delnand for energy, such as is necessary for refrigerated goods.

MILLING AND BAKING

We have already mentioned the new pattern of wheat production and the problems arising from the introduction of new types of wheal having physical properties different from those to which millers were accustomed. A compensation, hovvever_ was that increasing use of the combine harvester by 1938 50 per cent of American wheat \Vas harvested in this x.vay - gave cleaner grain.

At the same time, the increasing mechanization of doughmaking for bread- and of the making of cakes and biscuits too - demanded production of a uniform product. Ne\v milling processes had to take account, in particular, of two characteristics of the grain: it'i hardness and its shape1 especially that of its longitudinal crease.

The steel rollers that replaced the traditional mill stones served a double purpose. First, a set of fluted rollers crushed the grain and effected some separation of bran from flour. Then the grain was put through a series of pairs of reduction rolls1 one rotating at a slightly different rate from its companion in order to introduce a shearing movement, before being sie.../ed. The most important changes in this process as the century ad·vanced ·V\rere a great reduction in the size of the rollers, relative to throughput, and the introduction of air-flotation techniques, rather than sieving, for separating flour grains of different degrees of fineness.

The proportion of the wheat that could be converted into flour varied, and S01 other things being equat there vvas a tendency to favour new varieties offering a high extraction rate. Other things were not ah,vays equal, however; thus many of the more productive strains pruved to contain excessive amounts of amylase, an enzyme that breaks starch doV\ rn into sugar.

Much bread is still made by the traditional method of selling the dough aside for two or three hours to let it ferment or rise. Shortly after the Second vVorld War, however, American bakeries adopted a dough development process based on mechanical manipulation, which cut this preliminary stage to a few minutes, and saved much space and labour. This development made it possible to bake continuously, instead of in batches, in tunnel ovens.

Production was also speeded by the use of improvers. Flour, like wine, improves with keeping, as a result of spontaneous chemical changes. In the nineteenth century, when flour was imported from abroad, the maturing process took place during the voyage but when Britain and other European importers bought grain from North America and did their own milling this no longer happened. To overcome this difficulty, certain chemical improvers were developed which accelerated the ageing process; they also had the advantage of producing a more uniform type of flour and one that led to a more easily workable dough.

FOOD ADDITIVES

In the nineteenth century food adulteration was widely practised, for a variety of reasons. Sometimes the motive was simply greed, as when an expensive commodity was 'extended' by mixing in a cheap one. Sometimes the aim was to improve the appearance or keeping qualities of the food, as when vegetables were kept green by adding copper salts to the water in which they were boiled. In some cases the adulterants were harmless and no more than a cheat, but some were dangerous and might even be fatal.

By 1900 most western countries had introduced restrictive legislation to deal with the problem. In Britain legislation dates effectively from the amended Adulteration of Food and Drugs Act of 1875; in the USA the Food and Drugs Act was introduced in 1906.

The legislation was designed not to forbid food additives altogether but to restrict their number to those regarded as safe and to lay down the concentrations at which they might be used. In the first half of the twentieth century some additives were forbidden, on the ground that they had shown previously unsuspected toxic properties, and others were added as research and experience showed them to be both safe and useful. After the Second World War there was particular emphasis on the elimination of potentially carcinogenic substances.

There were, however, few internationally agreed standards, and this inevitably had some effect on the growing international trade in processed foods: a product quite acceptable in one country might be forbidden in another. The USA tended to be more nervous than Europe, sometimes justifiably.

Among widely used additives were sulphur dioxide (and other closely related chemicals), benzoic and propionic acids, certain antibiotics, and esters of gallic acid. One of their most important roles was as an antioxidant, preventing fats and oils from becoming rancid. Such rancid materials are not only unpalatable but many also cause more or less serious digestive disorders. The ageing of flour by means of additives has already been mentioned.

In the early years of this century, but more particularly in the 1920s, it was realized that the nutritional value of foods could not be expressed simply in terms of their content of protein, fat, and carbohydrate. They also contained accessory food factors, known as vitamins, which — even though present only in minute quantities — were essential for health. In a good mixed diet containing fresh food the body normally obtains sufficient vitamins, but heavy reliance on processed foods can lead to deficiency and ill health.

A classic example was Christiaan Eijkman's discovery in 1890 that beriberi, a serious disease widely prevalent in the East, was due to lack of vitamin B; in rice-eating countries intake of this is normally quite adequate because it is contained in the husk of the rice grain. When polished rice is eaten, however, this source of the vitamin is lost and more or less serious deficiency symptoms will appear.

Many vitamins are heat-sensitive substances and may be destroyed in cooking or in preservation processes such as canning. As this hazard became generally recognized, many manufacturers began to add vitamins, especially vitamins B and C (the anti-scurvy factor), to make good the loss. We have already noted the addition of vitamins A and D to margarine to make it comparable in this respect with butter.

ORGANIZATION

In conclusion, we must mention two major organizational changes in the food industry. Apart from the steady trend towards centralized production, there developed an increasingly close association between the food processor and the producer. Many farmers, for example, would grow crops such as peas or rhubarb under contract to a particular processor. Similarly meat and fish factors would have long-term supply contracts. Such arrangements were beneficial to all concerned, including the customer, for the contracts normally embodied strict clauses about the quality of the product. Very often the precise variety of crop to be grown, and the stage at which it was to be harvested, was laid down.

The second organizational change also directly concerned the customer. In the 1930s European food shops still followed traditional lines; such commodities as butter, tea, bacon, meat, and fish were weighed out from bulk to the customer's requirements by assistants in the open shop.

But in the USA signs of change had appeared as early as 1912, when the first selfservice store opened in Memphis; by 1929 there were at least 3000 such shops. In Europe, the self-service shop made rapid headway after the Second World War. In these shops food offered for sale is exposed to constant handling by customers, and for reasons of hygiene virtually all items must, therefore, be wrapped. This development had profound consequences for the packaging industry.

BIOTECHNOLOGY AND FOOD PRODUCTION

Scientific innovation and its derivative benefits have had profound implications to humanity within the last century. The exciting discipline of biotechnology has drawn the interests of traditional biologists, biochemists, microbiologists, medical and agricultural scientists into applying mathematical and engineering models to understanding biology. Furthermore, several scientists in the exact sciences of mathematics, physics, and chemistry have begun to use system approaches to unravel the mystery and complexity of biology. And from the side, diagnostic, biopharmaceutical, biochemical and agriculcultural industries are rapidly drawing from and applying the research results of biotechnology.

Biotechnology is experiencing a revolution like none before in the life sciences and is affecting every facet of our lives, from crop improvement to commerce, and drugs to sustainable development. This technology has the potential to address problems not solved by conventional research.

At the same time, biotechnology may speed up research process and increase research precision. GM crops have been developed and rapidly disseminated since the early 1990s. At present, there is very little commercial utilization of results from modern biotechnology research in developing countries. As a result, the potential contributions of biotechnology to poverty alleviation, enhanced food security and nutrition in developing countries have received little attention, beyond blanket statements of support or opposition.

THE GENE REVOLUTION

Mendel's laws of genetics were rediscovered in 1900. Mendel had published his work on inheritance patterns in pea in 1865, but it took 35 years for others to grasp their significance. Since 1900, there has been steady progress in our understanding of the genetic makeup of all living organisms ranging from microbes to man. A major step in human control over genetic traits was taken in the 1920s when Muller and Stadler discovered that radiation can induce mutations in animals and plants.

In the 1930s and 1940s, several new methods of chromosome and gene manipulation were discovered, such as the use of colchicine to achieve a doubling in chromosome number, commercial exploitation of hybrid vigour in maize and other crops, use of chemicals such as nitrogen mustard and ethyl methane sulphonate to induce mutations and techniques like tissue culture and embryo rescue to get viable hybrids from distantly related species. The double helix structure of DNA, the chemical substance of heredity, was discovered in 1953 by James Watson and Francis Crick. This triggered explosive progress in every field of genetics. Just as it took 35 years for biologists to understand the significance of Mendel's work, it may take a couple of decades more to understand fully the benefits and risks associated with genetically improved foods. It would be prudent to apply scientific and precautionary principles in areas of human health and environmental safety. The 1990s have seen dramatic advances in our understanding of how biological organisms function at the molecular level, as well as in our ability to analyse, understand, and manipulate DNA molecules, the biological material from which the genes in all organisms are made. The entire process has been accelerated by the Human Genome Project, which has poured substantial resources into the development of new technologies to work with human genes.

The same technologies are directly applicable to all other organisms, including plants. Thus, the new scientific discipline of genomics has arisen, which has contributed to powerful new approaches in agriculture and medicine, and has helped to promote the biotechnology industry. The quality of food and food plants can be modified and optimized to meet the nutritional and health needs of atrisk and compromised populations prevalent in most of the developing countries. High rates of malnutrition, infectious disease as well as diet-related diseases such as diabetes and hypertension are prevalent in many developing countries.

These are as a result of compromised immune function, inadequate sources of nutritious and quality foods and limited access to healthy and suitable foods. Bioceptability and adoption of biotechnology products in certain developing countries, achievements such as the development of high- vitamin A rice have greatly increased the acceptability of biotechnology for human food applications among hitherto skeptical consumers. Furthermore, it provides insights into the potential for application of biotechnology in developing improved quality and functional foods for human nutrition and health, rather than simply for use in agricultural technology for improved yields and pest resistance.

The production of increased levels of beta-carotene in plants is especially important, as its precursor, lycopene has been shown to have physiological chemo-preventive effects with regard to various cancers. Furthermore, lycopene, commonly found in various carotenoid containing plants such as tomatoes and carrots, is an essential ingredient in maintaining eye health and vision. Modifications that have been targeted and developed by various biotechnology companies include improvement in the oil content and composition of oil seeds such as legumes. Improvement in soybean oil quality includes stabilization of the unsaturated fatty acids by increasing levels of the antioxidant, vitamin E. These successes indicate a relevant and important role for biotechnology in improving food quality and developing functional foods, particularly those targeted for needy populations in developing countries, such as children and pre-natal women.

GENETICALLY MODIFIED CROPS

Modern agricultural biotechnology is still in an early phase, and the focus is overwhelmingly on production in industrial country farms and for industrial country markets. In 1998, 85% of the land planted with genetically improved crops was in just five developed countries with the United States alone accounting for about 75% of the area. Argentina, China, Mexico, and South Africa cultivated the remaining 15%, and the countries other than China include a substantial number of large-scale, capital-intensive farms that produce primarily for industrial country markets.

Among the crops produced in these four developing countries are insectresistant cotton and maize, herbicide-resistant soybean, and tomatoes with a long shelf life. Globally, herbicideresistant soybean, insect-resistant maize, and genetically improved cotton account for 85 per cent of all plantings.

The unprecedented rapid adoption of transgenic crops during the initial five-year period when genetically modified crops were first adopted, reflects the significant multiple benefits realised by large and small farmers in industrial and developing countries that have grown transgenic crops commercially. Between 1996 and 2000, a total of fifteen countries - 10 industrial and 5 developing - contributed to more than a twenty five fold increase in the global area of transgenic crops from 1.7 million hectares in 1996 to 44.2 million hectares in 2000.

The accumulated area of transgenic crops planted in the five-year period 1996 - 2000 total 125 million hectares, equivalent to more than 300 million acres. Adoption rates for transgenic crops are unprecedented and are the highest for any new technology by agricultural industry standards. High adoption rates reflect growing satisfaction with products that offer significant benefits ranging from more convenient and flexible crop management, higher productivity and/or net returns per hectare, health benefits and a safer environment through decreased use of conventional pesticides, which collectively contribute not only to improved weed and insect pest control but also benefits of lower input and production costs; genetically modified crops offer significant economic advantages to farmers compared with corresponding conventional crops. The severity of weed and insect pests varies from year to year and hence this will have a direct impact on pest control costs and the consequent economic advantage.

Despite the on-going debate on GM crops, particularly in countries of the European Union, millions of large and small farmers in both industrial and developing countries continue to increase their plantings of GM crops because of the significant multiple benefits they offer. This high adoption rate is a strong vote of confidence in GM crops, reflecting grower's satisfaction. Many recent studies have confirmed that farmers planting herbicide-tolerant and insect-resistant Bt crops are more efficient in managing their weed and insect pests.

An estimated 3.5 million farmers grew transgenic crops to health and economic advantages. In coming years, the number of farmers planting GM crops is expected to grow substantially and the global area of GM crops is expected to continue to grow. Global population would exceed 6 billion by 2050, when approximately 90% of the global population will reside in Asia, Africa and Latin America.

Today, 815 million people in the developing countries suffer from malnutrition and 1.3 billion are afflicted by poverty. Transgenic crops, often referred to as GM crops, represent promising technologies that can make a vital contribution to global food, feed and fibre security. During the six-year period 1996 - 2001, the global area of transgenic crops increased by more than 30-fold, from 1.7 million hectares in 1996 to 52.6 million hectares in 2001.

This high rate of adoption reflects the growing acceptance of transgenic crops by farmers using GM technology in both industrial and developing countries. During the six-year period 1996 - 2001, the number of countries growing transgenic crops more than doubled, increasing from 6 in 1996 to 9 in 1998, to 12 countries in 1999 and 13 in 2000 and 2001. The experience of the first six years, 1996 to 2001, during which a cumulative total of over 175 million hectares of transgenic crops were planted globally in 16 countries, 10 industrialized and 6 developing, has vindicated the vision of the pioneers of crop biotechnology who have seen their early promises of transgenic crops fulfilled - GM crops have met the expectations of large and small farmers planting transgenic crops in both industrial and developing countries. The unprecedented rapid adoption of transgenic crops during the first six-year period, 1996 - 2001, reflects the significant multiple benefits realised by large and small farmers. There is a growing body of evidence that clearly demonstrates the improved weed and insect pest control attainable with transgenic herbicide-tolerant and insect resistant Bt crops that also benefit from lower input and production costs. Despite the ongoing debate on GM crops, particularly in countries of the European Union, millions of large and small farmers in both industrial and developing countries continue to increase their plantings of GM crops because of the significant multiple benefits they offer.

More specifically, the use of transgenic crops results in:

- More sustainable and resource-efficient crop management practices that require less energy and fuel and conserves natural resources.
- More effective control of insect pests and weeds.
- A reduction in the overall amount of pesticides used in crop production, which impacts positively on biodiversity, protects predators and non-target organisms and contributes to a safer environment.
- Less dependency on conventional pesticides that can be a health hazard to producers and consumers; the potential health benefits associated with fewer pesticide poisonings from Bt cotton in China is an important finding, with significant implications for other developing

- Countries where small farmers may be at similar risk from heavy and over-use of conventional pesticides.
- Bt maize, which has reduced levels of the fumonisin mycotoxin provides safer and healthier food and feed products.
- Greater operational flexibility in timing of herbicide and insecticide applications.
- Conservation of soil moisture, structure, nutrients and control of soil erosion through no or low-tillage practices as well as improved quality of ground and surface water with less pesticide residues.

There is now considerable evidence that transgenic crops are deliveringsignificant economic benefits. The global economic advantage to farmers deploying herbicide tolerant soybean, HT canola and Bt corn was estimated to be of the order of $ 700 million in 1999, equally shared between developing and industrial countries. In addition to these direct economic advantages that farmers derive from transgenic crops, there are also significant additional indirect benefits to others in society. For crops such as herbicide-tolerant soybean, these indirect benefits to consumers globally can be of the same order of magnitude as the direct economic advantages to farmers.

Thus, the global direct and indirect economic advantage of GM crop in 1999 was of the order of $ 1 billion or more. 2001 is the initial year of the second quinquennium during which GM crops is being comercialized. In 2001, coincidental with increased political, policy and institutional support for GM crops due to their acknowledged contribution to global food security, the global area of transgenic crops benefited from renewed growth which resulted in a 19% increase in global GM crop area in 2001 - almost twice the growth rate in 2000. The number of farmers that benefited from GM crops increased from 3.5 million farmers in 2000 to an estimated 5.5 million in 2001. More than three-quarters of the GM farmers that benefited from GM crops in 2001 were resource-poor farmers planting Bt cotton, mainly in eight provinces in China and also in the Makathini Flats in KwaZulu Natal province in South Africa.

The well documented experience of China with Bt cotton presents a remarkable case study where 5 million small resourcepoor farmers in 2001 are already benefiting from significant agronomic, environmental, health and economic advantages - this is a unique example of how biotechnology can impact on poverty alleviation, as advocated in the 2001 UNDP Human Development Report. The China experience with Bt cotton lends itself for introduction and replication to carefully selected developing countries in Asia, Latin America and Africa where resource-poor farmers can learn, share and benefit from the rich experience of

China – the majority of the hectare of global cotton is grown in developing countries. Following a successful launch of Bt cotton in 2001, Indonesia is also expected to expand its Bt cotton in 2002, and India, the largest cotton growing country in the world, has approved commercial cultivation of Bt cotton in 2002. There is cautious optimism that global area and the number of farmers planting GM crops will continue to grow in 2002 in the six principal countries already growing GM crops - USA, Argentina, Canada, China, South Africa and Australia.

The other seven countries growing transgenic crops in 2001 are expected to report modest growth in GM crop area in 2002. The commercialization of herbicide-tolerant soybean in Brazil will be dependent on resolving the outstanding regulatory issues between the Ministries of Agriculture, Environment and Justice. The commercialization of GM crops in India and Brazil would represent a watershed for GM crops in developing countries in that the three most populous countries in Asia - China, India and Indonesia with 2.5 billion people, as well as the three major economies of Latin America, Argentina, Brazil and Mexico, plus South Africa would then all be commercializing and benefiting from transgenic crops. As new and novel products with input and output traits will become available for commercialization in the near future, it is critical that these products be deployed in an integrated strategy in which both conventional and biotechnology applications are applied to attain the challenging goal of global food security. Adoption of such a strategy will allow society to continue to benefit from the vital contributions that both conventional and modern plant breeding offer.

Technology is only one of several elements that can contribute to an integrated global food security strategy where population control and improved food distribution systems are also essential elements. Biotechnology can play its appropriate and essential role in achieving food security in the developing world. The experience of China, Argentina and South Africa, that are already deriving significant benefits from GM crops, can be shared with other developing countries in the three continents of the South which face similar challenges.

ADAPTING BIOTECHNOLOGY FOR INCREASED CROP PRODUCTION

What is needed in developing countries is an understanding that goes beyond conventional, orthodox wisdom to work more strategically in developing and implementing effective, international, national and regional policies. Funding for agricultural research has declined 50% on a worldwide basis. Funding for research in general is at a dismal low in developing countries.

The intrusion of intellectual property rights into the arena of crop improvement, while beneficial to the economies of the developed world is making the lives of many researchers even more difficult. Private industry has dominated research in biotechnology. Consolidation of the industry has proceeded rapidly since 1996, with more than 25 major acquisitions and alliances worth US$15 billion. Little private-sector agricultural biotechnology research so far has focused on developing country food crops other than maize. Production of genetically modified crops is not a complex technology and is clearly within the capabilities of national research institutes in many developing countries. Genetic modification of crops using recombinant DNA technology is also within reach of the institutes of the Consultative Group on International Agricultural Research, including Centro Internacional de Mejoramiento de Maiz y Trigo in Mexico, International Rice Research Institute in The Philippines, and the International Institute for Tropical Agriculture in Nigeria.

Furthermore, these institutes have already assumed responsibility for biotechnological research and a number of crop improvement projects are under way. These institutes see biotechnology as a tool and not as an end in itself. Crop improvement through biotechnology need not be equated with transgenic plants.

For example, marker-assisted breeding is a powerful biotechnology that can find widespread application with the crops of the poor. Detailed linkage maps of these crops will be tremendously useful. As these CGIAR institutes focus on their needs, they will want and need to reach out to public institutions in developed countries. Alliances such as the Cassava Biotechnology Network that bring together researchers from many countries are an effective way to create synergy towards a common goal.

The private sector leads in every aspect of the agricultural biotechnology revolution and activities in the public sector will have to marshal the strength of the private sector through public-private partnerships. Such partnerships must be based upon mutual trust and common goals. The private sector can work with the CGIAR institutes and with national research institutions of developing countries to transfer technologies, train scientists, provide hands-on experience in intellectual property management, and facilitate the nocost or low-cost licensing of inventions. Since the cost of these inventions is being charged to the consumers in developed countries, such approaches amount to a transfer of wealth by large corporations from the developed world to the developing world.

The application of biotechnology to the problems of the poor will not be straightforward and the models we have from developed countries will probably not be applicable. Agricultural research for the crops and problems of the poor has to proceed from the bottom up, not from the top down. Crops have to be created that fit not only in the agro-ecology of the poorest regions often characterized by marginal and heterogeneous environments, but the crops must also fit into the social and economic systems. Agricultural research has to start with studying farming practices, asking the farmers - men and women - what they want, allowing the farmers to make choices between often conflicting objectives such as higher yield versus yield stability, and examining the possibility of marketing the excess production. Researchers have to begin by soliciting the help of the farmers to describe farming practices and analyse these practices to pinpoint problem areas and opportunities. Together, the researchers and farmers have to generate a range of choices that the farmers could implement. The major objective of this approach is not the transfer of technology, but empowerment of the farmer to improve production.

MILK AND OTHER DAIRY PRODUCTS

The dairy products vary greatly. Some cows give richer milk than others. Butter may be almost pure fat, or it may contain much water and salt. The cheeses are rich or poor in protein and fats according to method of making. Cottage cheese may be well drained or quite watery. Therefore, this table gives only approximate contents.

	Water	Protein	Fat	Carbohy-drates	Ash	Calories Per lb.
Whole	87.00	3.3	4.0	5.0	0.7	325 milk
Cream	74.00	2.5	18.5	14.5	0.5	910
Buttermilk	91.00	3.0	0.5	4.8	0.7	165
Butter	...	..	82.4	..	..	3475
Cheese	33.70	26.0	34.2	2.3	3.8	1965 whole milk
skimmed milk	45.70	31.5	16.4	2.2	4.2	1320

Milk is not a beverage. It is a food. A quart of milk contains as much food and fuel value as eight eggs or twelve ounces of lean beef. That is, a cupful is equal to two eggs or three ounces of lean beef. This shows that milk should not be taken to quench thirst, but to supply nourishment. Milk is one of our most satisfactory and economical albuminous foods, even at the present high prices. In many foods from 5 to 10 per cent of the protein goes to waste. In milk the waste does not ordinarily amount to more than about 1 per cent.

This fluid generally leaves the stomach within one or one and one-half hours after being ingested. In spite of its merits as a food some writers on dietetics advocate that adults stop using it, giving it only to the young. Milk is an excellent food when properly used. When abused it tends to cause discomfort, disease and death, and so does every other food known to man. Milk is given in fevers and in other diseases, when the digestive and assimilative processes are suspended. This is a serious mistake and has caused untold numbers of deaths. When the digestion has gone on a strike all feeding is destructive.

Milk and meat broths, which are generally given, are about the worst foods that could be selected under the circumstances, for they decay very easily, and are excellent food for the numerous bacteria that thrive in the digestive tract during disease. These foods must decay when they are not digested, for the internal temperature of the body during fevers is over one hundred degrees Fahrenheit. When bacteria are present in excess they give off considerable poison, which makes the patient worse. If circumstances are such that it is necessary to feed during acute disease, which is always injurious to the patient, let the food be the least harmful obtainable, such as fruit juices.

Even they do harm. In our country cow's milk is used almost exclusively. In other lands the milk of the mare, the ass, the sheep, the goat and of other animals is used. The objection voiced against cow's milk is that it is an unnatural food for man, only fit for the calf, which is equipped with several stomachs and is therefore able to digest the curds which are larger and tougher than the curds formed from human milk. It is said that the curds of cow's milk are so indigestible that the human stomach cannot prepare them for entry into the blood. This is probably true, but it is also true of other protein-bearing foods. The digestion and assimilation of proteins are begun in the stomach and completed in the intestines, and the protein in milk is one of the most completely utilized of all proteins.

To call a food unnatural means nothing, for we can call nearly all foods unnatural and defend our position. A natural food is presumably a nutritious and digestible aliment that is produced in the locality where it is consumed, one that can be utilized without preparation or preservation. So we may say that a resident of New York should not use figs, dates, bananas and other products of tropical and semi-tropical climates, for they are not natural in the latitude of New York. We can take the position that it is unnatural for people to eat grains, which need much grinding, for the birds are the only living beings supplied with mills.

We can further say that it is unnatural to eat all cooked and baked foods. But such talk is not helpful. The more a person uses his brain the less power he has left for digestion and therefore it is necessary to prepare some of the foods so that they will be easy to digest. Man is such an adaptable creature that we are not sure what he subsisted on before he became civilized and are therefore unable to say what his natural food is. We know that in the tropics fruits play an important part in nourishing savages, while in the frozen north fat flesh is the chief food. Perhaps there is no natural food for man. Some of those who advocate the disuse of milk have a substitute or imitation to take its place, nut milk made from finely ground nuts and water. Like all other imitations, it is inferior to the original. It is more difficult to digest than real milk and the flavour is quite different. The objection that milk is indigestible is not borne out by the experience of those who give it under proper conditions. It is true that milk disagrees with a few, but so do such excellent foods as eggs, strawberries and Concord grapes, and many other aliments which are not difficult to digest. This is a matter of individual peculiarity. Some can take boiled milk, but are unable to take it fresh, and *vice versa*. Outside of the few exceptions, milk digests in a reasonable time and quite completely. It is easier to digest than the legumes which are rich in protein.

It is also easier to digest than nuts, which contain much protein. The milk sugar causes no trouble and cream is one of the easiest forms of fat to digest, if taken in moderation. The protein in milk will cause no inconvenience if the milk is eaten slowly, in proper combinations and not to excess. The rennet in the stomach curdles the casein. The hydrochloric acid and the pepsin in the gastric juice then begin to break down and dissolve the clots, and the process of digestion is completed in the small intestines.

Those who overeat of milk in combination with other foods will derive benefit from omitting the milk. They will also be benefitted if they continue using milk and omit either the starch or the meat. When foods disagree, in nearly every instance it is due to the fact that too much has been eaten and too many varieties partaken of at a meal. Some may single out the milk or the meat as the offenders.

Others may point to the starches, and still others to the vegetables with their large amount of indigestible residue. They are all right and all wrong, for all the foods help to cause the trouble. However, such reasoning does not solve the problem. If the meals cause discomfort and disease, reduce the amount eaten, take fewer varieties at a meal and simplify the cooking. Those who eat simple meals and are moderate are not troubled with indigestion. Those who eat such mushy foods as oatmeal and cream of wheat usually take milk or cream and sugar with them. This should not be done, for such dressing stimulates the appetite and leads to undermastication. Neither children nor

adults chew these soft starchy foods enough. The result is that the breakfast ferments in the alimentary tract. After a few months or years of such breakfasts, some kind of disease is sure to develop.

Mushy starches dressed with rich milk and sugar are responsible for a large per cent of the so-called diseases of children, which are primarily digestive disturbances. Colds, catarrhs and adenoids are, of course, due to improper eating extending over a long period of time.

Nothing should be eaten with mushy starches except a little butter and salt. After enough starch has been taken, a glass of milk may be eaten. If parents would only realise that they are jeopardizing the health and lives of their dear ones when they feed them habitually on these soft messes, which ferment easily, there would be a remarkable decrease in the diseases of childhood and in the disgraceful infant and childhood mortality, for several hundred thousand children perish annually in this country.

Milk is often referred to as a perfect food, and it is the perfect food for infants. The young thrive best on the healthy milk given by a female of their own species. Every baby should be fed at the breast. The milk contains the elements needed by the body. The ash is composed of the various salts necessary for health, containing potassium, chlorine, calcium, magnesium, iron, silicon and other elements. For the nourishment of the body we need water, protein, fat, carbohydrates and salts, so it will be seen that milk is really a complete food. However, as the body grows the nutritive requirements change and milk is therefore not a balanced food for adults.

It may be interesting to note that there is no starch in milk and that infants fed at the breast exclusively obtain no starchy food. Many babies get no starch for nine, ten or even twelve months, and this is well, for they do not need it. They grow and flourish best without it. Milk is an emulsion. It is made up of numerous tiny globules floating in serum. The size of the globules varies, but the average is said to be about 1/10,000 of an inch in diameter. These globules are fatty bodies. There are other small bodies, containing protein and fat, which have independent molecular movement. The milk is a living fluid. When it is tampered with it immediately deteriorates. Without doubt, nature intended that the milk should go directly from the mammary gland into the mouth of the consumer, but this is not practicable when we take it away from the calf. However, if we are to use sweet milk it is best to consume it as nearly like it is in its natural state as possible.

It is quite common to drink milk rapidly. This should not be done. Take a sip or a spoonful at a time and move it about in the mouth until it is mixed with saliva. It is not necessary to give it as much mouth preparation as is given to starchy food. If it is drunk rapidly like water large curds from in the stomach. If it is insalivated it coagulates in smaller curds and is more easily digested, for the digestive juices can tear down small soft curds more easily than the large tough ones. Milk should not form a part of any meal when other food rich in protein is eaten. Our protein needs are small, and it is easy to get too much. Whole wheat bread and milk contain all the nourishment needed. On such a diet we can thrive indefinitely. This is information, not a recommendation. The bread should be eaten either before or after partaking of the milk. Do not break the bread into the milk. If this is done, mastication will be slighted. Bread needs much mastication and insalivation. When liquid is taken with the bread, the saliva does not flow so freely as when it is eaten dry.

Fruit and milk make a good combination, but no starchy foods are to be taken in this meal. Take a glass of milk, either sweet or sour, and what fruit is desired, insalivating both the fruit and the milk thoroughly. If you have read that the combination of fruit and milk has proved fatal, rest assured that those who made such reports only looked at the surface, for other foods and other influences were having their effects on the system.

Many people die of food-poisoning and apoplexy. These bad results are due to wrong eating covering a long period and it is folly to blame the last meal. It would be queer if fruit and milk were not occasionally a part of the last meal. In winter, figs, dates or raisins with milk make an excellent lunch or breakfast. These fruits take the place of bread, for though they are not starchy, they contain an abundance of fruit sugar, which is more easily digested than the starch. Starch must be converted into sugar before the system can use it. On hot days milk and acid fruit make a satisfying meal. Many believe that milk and acid fruit should not be taken in the same meal, because the acid curdles the milk.

As we have already seen, the milk must be curdled before it can be digested. If this step in digestion is performed by the acid in the fruit no more harm is done than when it is performed by the lactic acid bacteria. Fruit juices and milk do not combine to form deadly poisons. If fruit and milk are eaten in moderation and no other food is taken at that meal the results are good. However, if fruit, milk, bread, meat, cake and pickles make up the meal, the results may be bad. Such eating is very common. But do not blame the fruit and the milk when the whole meal is wrong.

Likewise, if a hearty meal has been eaten and before this has had time to digest a lunch is made of fruit and milk, trouble may ensue. All the foods may be good, but a time must come when the body will object to being overfed. In summertime much less food is needed than during the cold months. Nevertheless, barring the Christmas holidays and Thanksgiving, people overeat more in summer than at any other time of the year. Picnics often degenerate into stuffing matches. We should expect many cases of serious illness to follow them, and such is the case.

Sometimes the milk is so carelessly handled that it becomes poisonous and at other times the fruit is tainted, but generally bad combinations and overeating are the factors that cause trouble when the fruit and milk combination is blamed. Buttermilk and clabbered milk are more easily digested by many than is the fresh milk. In Europe sour milk is a more common food than in this country. Here many do not know how excellent it is.

Two glasses of milk, or less, make a good warm-weather lunch. Those who have a tendency to be bilious should use cream very sparingly. Bilious people always overeat, otherwise their livers would not be in rebellion. The fat, in the form of cream, arouses decided protest on the part of overburdened livers.

A theory has found its way into dietetic literature, sometimes disguised as a truth, to the effect that boiled or hot milk is absorbed directly into the bloodstream without being digested. This is contrary to everything we know about digestion and assimilation, and although it is a fine enough theory it does not work out in practice. We have seen bad results when nothing but a small amount of the hot milk was fed to patients with weak digestive power. Perhaps others have had better results. When the system demands a rest from food, nothing but water should be given. Boiled or natural milk is then as bad as any other food, and worse than most, for in the absence of digestive power it soon becomes a foul mass, swarming with billions of bacteria. The system is compelled to absorb some of the poisons given off by the micro-organisms and the results are disastrous.

Every food we take must be modified by our bodies before entering the circulation, and milk is no exception. When milk is allowed to stand for a while the sugar ferments, through the action of the lactic acid bacteria. The sugar is turned into lactic acid, which combines with the casein and when this process has continued for a certain length of time the result is clabbered milk or sour milk. The length of time varies with the temperature and the care given the milk. If milk remains sweet for a long time during warm weather, discharge the milkman and patronize one whose product sours more quickly, for milk that remains sweet has been subjected to treatment.

All kinds of preservative treatment cause deterioration. If extraordinary care is taken with the milk and it is kept at a temperature of about forty-two degrees Fahrenheit, it may remain sweet five or six weeks, provided it is not exposed to the air, but such care is at present not practicable in commercial dairies. The milk contains unorganized ferments which spoil it in time without exposure to bacterial influences. These ferments cause digestion or decay of the milk.

Fresh butter is a palatable form of fat, which digests easily. Like all other milk products, it must be kept clean and cold, or it will soon spoil. Butter absorbs other flavours quickly and should therefore not be placed near odourous substances. It is best unsalted and in Europe it is very commonly served thus. When people learn to demand unsalted butter they will get good butter, for no one can palm off oleomargarine or other imitations under the guise of fresh unsalted butter.

Unsalted butter must be fresh or it will be refused by the nose and the palate. Salt and other preservatives often conceal age and corruption of foods. Butter combines well with starches and vegetables, in fact, it can be used in moderation with any other food, when the body needs fat. Butter should not be used to cook starches or proteins in. Greasy cooking should be banished from our kitchens.

Milk is a complex food, highly organized, and therefore is easily injured or spoiled. The general rule is that the more complex a food is, the more easily it spoils. It is rather difficult at present to get wholesome milk enough to supply the people of our large cities. When it is boiled, the milk keeps longer, but boiled milk is spoiled milk. The fine flavour is lost, the casein, which is the principal protein of milk, is toughened, the milk, which is normally a living liquid, is killed, the chemical balance is lost, the organic salts being rendered partly inorganic. Milk that is unfit to eat without being boiled is not fit to eat afterwards, for the poisonous end products of bacterial life remain.

The milk is soured by the bacteria it contains. The lactic acid bacteria are harmless. When there is a lack of care and cleanliness, other bacteria get into the milk, and these are also harmless to people in good health, and most of them are not injurious to sick people. The bacteria do not cause disease, but when disease has been established, they offer their kindly offices as scavengers. Bacteria thrive in sick people, especially when they are fed when digestive power is lacking.

Boiling retards the souring of milk, but when fat and protein are boiled together the protein becomes hard to digest. Milk is rich in both fat and protein. Excessive heat turns the milk brown, the milk sugar being carameled. Babies do not thrive on boiled milk. They may look fat, but instead of having the desirable firmness of normal children, they are puffy. Children fed on denatured milk fall victims to diseases very easily, especially to diseases which are due to lack of organic salts, such as rickets and malnutrition.

Pasteurization of milk is very popular. This is objectionable for the same reasons that boiling is condemned, though not to the same extent. Pasteurization is heating the milk to about 140 to 150 degrees Fahrenheit. This kills many of the bacteria, but many escape and when the milk is cooled off they begin to multiply and flourish again. It is estimated that pasteurized milk contains one-fourth as many bacteria as natural milk. So nothing is gained, and the milk is partly devitalized.

The advocates of pasteurization give statistics showing that milk so treated has been instrumental in decreasing infant mortality. But please bear in mind that previously a great deal of milk unfit for consumption was fed to the babies. Those who pasteurize milk generally are careful enough to see that they get a good product in the first place. If we can't get good milk we can do without it, for it is not a necessary food, but we can get good milk if we make the effort. If the milk is filthy, boiling or pasteurizing does not remove the dirt. Gauthier says of pasteurization: "Sometimes it is heated up to 70 degrees with pressure of carbonic acid. But even in this case pasteurization does not destroy all germs, particularly those of tuberculosis, peptonizing bacteria of cowdung, and the dust of houses and streets, etc."

Even boiling does not kill the spores of bacteria unless it is continued until the milk is rendered entirely unfit for food. To kill these spores it is necessary to boil the milk several times. The spores are small round or oval bodies which form within the bacterial envelope when these micro-organisms are subjected to unfavourable conditions.

The spores resist heat and cold that would kill almost any other form of life. When conditions are favourable they develop into bacteria again. After heating, the cream does not rise so quickly nor does it separate so completely as it does in natural milk. This is due to the toughening of the casein in the milk. Heating partly disorganizes the delicately balanced salts contained in the milk.

The result is that they can not be utilized so easily and completely by the body, for the human organism demands its food in an organic state, that is, in the condition built up by vegetation or by animals.

We may consume iron filings and remain anemic, in fact, the effect the iron medication has is to ruin the teeth, digestive organs and other parts of the body as a consequence. But if we partake of such foods as apples, cabbage, lettuce and spinach, the necessary salt is taken into the blood. Heating milk also makes it constipating. True, normal people can take boiled milk without becoming constipated, but how many normal people are there? We are sorely enough afflicted in this way now. Let us have a supply of natural milk or go without it.

It is not my desire to convey the impression that it does any harm to scald or boil milk occasionally, but if done daily it does harm, especially to the young. Scalded milk has its proper place in dietetics. Occasionally we find a person who has persistent chronic diarrhaea. If he is in condition to eat anything, this annoying affliction is usually overcome in a reasonable time if the patient will take boiled or scalded milk in moderation three times a day, and nothing else except water. How are we to obtain good milk? We can do it by using common sense, care and cleanliness.

It is well to remember that there are bacteria in all ordinary milk, and that if the milk is from healthy cows and is kept clean and cold these bacteria are harmless. Most of them are the lactic acid bacteria, which change the milk sugar into acid. When the milk has attained a certain degree of acidity, the lactic acid bacteria are unable to thrive and the souring process is slowed up and finally stopped. Most of the other bacteria in milk perish when lactic acid is formed.

This is why stale sweet milk is often harmful, when the same kind of milk allowed to sour can be taken with impunity. If the milk is kept in a cold place the bacteria multiply slowly. If it is kept in a warm place they increase in numbers at a rate that is marvelous, and consequently the milk sours much sooner. Even if the milk is kept cold, bacterial growth will soon take place, but it will perhaps not be lactic acid bacteria. It may be a form that causes the milk to become ropy and slimy or one that gives it a bad odour.

Bacteria are like other forms of vegetation, such as grass, weeds, flowers and trees, in that some flourish best under one condition and others under dissimilar conditions, and they struggle one against the other for subsistence and existence. Like flowers there are thousands of different forms of bacteria and they vary according to their food and environment. Peculiar odours in milk generally come from certain kinds of food given to the cows, such as turnips; from bacterial action; or from flavours absorbed from other foods or from odours in the air. Milk should not be exposed to odourous substances, for it becomes tainted very quickly.

Sometimes yeast finds its way into milk and causes decomposition of the sugar with the formation of carbon dioxide and alcohol. A count of the bacteria in milk often serves a good purpose, for it shows whether it is good and has had proper care. The consumers have a right to demand milk low in bacteria, for if no preservatives have been used, that means clean milk. If we could live in our pristine state of beatific bliss, if such it was, we would not have to use milk after childhood is past, but our present condition demands the use of easily digested foods and to many milk is almost a necessity.

The milk in the udder of a healthy cow is almost surely free from bacteria, but the moment it is exposed to the air these little beings start to drop into the fluid. The bacterial standards given by various city health departments vary. Those who are mathematically inclined may find the following figures interesting: In some great cities they allow 500,000 bacteria to the cubic centimetre of milk.

A cubic centimetre contains about twenty-five drops. In other words, they allow 20,000 bacteria per drop. This may seem very lively milk, but these bacteria are so small that about 25,000 of them laid end to end measure only about an inch, and it would take 17,000,000,000,000 of them to weigh an ounce, according to estimates. These are the tiny vegetables we hear and read so much about, that we are warned against and fear so much.

Truly the pygmies are having their innings and making cowards of men. The bacteria multiply by the simple process of growing longer and splitting into two, fission, as it is called, and the process is so rapid that within an hour or two after being formed a bacterium may be raising a family of its own.

Some of the milk brought to the cities contains as many as 15,000,000 bacteria per cubic centimeter, that is, about 600,000 per drop. This milk is either very filthy or it has been poorly cared for and should not be given to babies and young children. The filthiest milk may contain several billion bacteria to the cubic centimetre. By using care milk containing but 100, or even fewer, bacteria per drop can be produced.

From the standpoint of cleanliness this is excellent milk. Of course, the dairyman who takes pride enough in his work to produce such milk will sell nothing but what is first-class, and if he has business acumen he can always get more than the market price for his product.

The talk about germs has been overdone, but no one can deny that the study of bacteriology has made people more careful about foods. The filthy dairies that were the rule a few years ago are slowly being replaced by dairies that are comfortable, well lighted and clean. Do not allow the germs to scare you, for if ordinary precautions are taken no more of them will be present than are necessary, and they are necessary.

They thrive best in filth, and they are dangerous only to those who live so that they have no resistance. Wholesome milk can be produced only by healthy animals. Bovine health can be secured by the same means as human health. The cows must be properly fed and housed. They must have both ventilation and light. They must not be unduly worried. If a nursing of an angry mother's milk is at times poisonous enough to kill a baby, you may be sure that the milk from an abused, irritated and angry cow is also injurious.

If the animals are kept comfortable and happy they will do the best producing, both in quality and quantity. It may sound far-fetched to some to advocate keeping animals happy in order to get them to produce much and give quality products, but it is good science and good sense. Happy cows give more and better milk than the mistreated ones. The singing hens are the best layers. Cows should have fresh green food all the year, and this can be obtained in winter time by using silage.

It is a mistake to give cows too much of concentrated foods, such as oil meals and grains. Cattle cannot long remain well on exclusive rations of too heating and stimulating foods. When fed improperly they soon fall prey to various diseases, such as rheumatism and tuberculosis. It is the same with other domestic animals. The horse when overfed on grain develops stiff joints. The hogs that are compelled to live exclusively on concentrated, heating rations are liable to die of cholera. Young turkeys that have nothing but corn and wheat to eat die in great numbers from the disease known as blackhead. It is the same law running all through nature, applying to the high and to the low, that improper nourishment brings disease and death. When cattle roam wild, the green grasses are their principal source of food. Man should be careful not to deviate too much, for forced feeding is as harmful to animals as it is to man.

The following excellent recommendations for the care of milk are given by Dr. Charles E. North of the New York City Milk Commission:

- "No coolers, aerators, straining cloths or strainers should be used.
- "The hot milk should be taken to the creamery as soon as possible.
- "The night's milk should be placed in spring or iced water higher than the milk on the inside of the can. It should not be stirred, and the top of the can should be open a little way to permit ventilation.
- "The milking pails and cans will be sterilized and dried at the creamery, and should be carefully protected until they are used.
- "Brush the udder and wipe with a clean cloth; wash with clean water and dry with a clean towel.
- "Whitewash the cow stable at least twice yearly.
- "Feed no dusty feed until after milking.
- "Remove all manure from cow stable twice daily.
- "Keep barnyard clean and have manure pile at least 100 feet from the stable.
- "Have all stable floors of cement, properly drained.
- "Have abundant windows in cowstables to permit sunlight to reach the floor.
- "Arrange a proper system of ventilation.
- "Do not use milk from any cows suspected of gargot or of any udder inflammation. Such milk contains enormous numbers of bacteria.
- "Brush and groom cows from head to foot as horses are groomed.

- "Use no dusty bedding; wood shavings or sawdust give least dust.
- "Use an abundance of ice in water tank for cooling milk."

Perhaps some will take issue with the doctor on the first paragraph of his recommendation. If straining cloths are used they should be well rinsed in tepid water, washed and then boiled. However, if his recommendations are carried out in letter and spirit no straining is necessary.

Herr Klingelhofer near Dusseldorf, Germany, runs a model dairy. The cows, stables, milkers, containers, in fact, all things connected with the dairy are scrupulously clean. The milkers do not even touch the milk stools, carrying them strapped to their backs. The milk is strained through sterilized cotton and cooled. The cows are six and seven years old and are milked for ten or twelve months and they are not bred during this time. The first part of the milk drawn from each teat is not used, for that part is not clean, containing dirt and bacteria. This milk is practically free from bacteria, for without adding preservatives it will remain sweet, for as long as thirteen days.

If ordinary milk fails to sour in two or three days it shows that it has been treated. According to the Country Gentleman, it will cost from one cent and a quarter to one cent and three-quarters extra per quart to produce clean milk. Healthy adults can take milk teeming with bacteria without harm, but for babies it is best to have very few or none in the milk. At Dusseldorf the babies used to die as they do here when fed unclean milk.

Herr Klingelhofer says that when fed on his product "sterben keine". This is submitted to those who advocate pasteurizing the milk. Denatured milk makes sickly babies. Clean natural milk makes healthy babies. The extra cost of less than two cents a quart is not prohibitive. Most fathers, no matter how poor, waste more than that daily on tobacco and alcoholics.

The extra cost would be more than saved in lessened doctor bills, to say nothing of funeral expenses. The recompense that comes from the satisfaction of having thriving, sturdy, healthy children can not be figured in dollars and cents. Dr. Robert Mond, of London, after investigating for years, has come to the cease that sterilized milk predisposes to tuberculosis, instead of preventing it. He believes that milk so treated is so inferior that he would not personally use it. That sterilized milk predisposes to tuberculosis, as well as to other diseases which can attack the body only when it is run down, is natural.

Any food that has been rendered inferior can not build the robust health that comes to those who live on natural food. Adults who use sterilized milk should counteract its bad effects by partaking liberally of fresh fruits and vegetables. If the milk is clean, put into clean containers by careful milkers and is then kept cold until delivered, it will reach the consumers in good condition. Do not let the fact that when you consume a glass of milk you are also engulfing some millions of bacteria bother you, for bacteria are necessary to our existence. If all the bacteria on earth should perish, it would also mean the end of the human race.

Today the progressive farmer is coming to the fore. He is a man who is justly proud of his work, so it will probably not be long before all city people who desire clean milk can get it. The milk cure consists in feeding sick people on nothing but milk for varying periods. Generally the patient is told to either take great quantities three or four times a day, or to take smaller quantities perhaps every half hour. The milk cure has no special virtue, except that it is a monotonous diet.

The body soon rebels if forced to subsist on an excessive amount of but one kind of food. The individual loses his desire for food and even becomes nauseated. If the advocates of the milk cure would prescribe milk in moderation, instead of in excess, they would have better success. The benefit derived from the milk cure comes from the simplicity, not from the milk. A grape cure, an orange cure or a bread and milk cure would be as beneficial. The milk cure is ancient. It was employed twenty-five centuries ago.

"CLABBERED MILK"

Clabbered milk or sour milk needs no special preparation. Put the milk into an earthen or china dish. Do not use metal dishes, for the lactic acid acts upon various metals. Cover the dish so as to keep particles of matter in the air away, but the covering is not to be airtight. Put the dish in a warm place, but not in the sun.

Milk that sours in the sun or in an air-tight bottle is generally of poor flavour. Clabbered milk is a good food. It does not form big, tough curds in the stomach, it is easy to digest, and the lactic acid helps to keep the alimentary tract sweet. The various forms of milk may be used in similar combinations.

BUTTERMILK"

The real buttermilk is what remains of the cream after the fat has been removed by churning. It is slightly acid and has a characteristic taste, to most people very agreeable. The flavour is different from that of artificially made buttermilk. In composition it is almost like whole milk, except that it contains very little fat. Many people make buttermilk by beating the clabbered milk thoroughly, until it becomes light. The buttermilk made from sweet milk and the various brands of bacterial ferments obtainable at the drug stores is all right.

These ferments have as their basis the lactic acid bacteria, and if the manufacturers wish to call their germs by other names, such as

Bacillus Bulgaricus, no harm is done. It is unnecessary to add any of these ferments, for the milk clabbers about as quickly without them. Buttermilk is an excellent food.

The casein can be seen in fine flakes in the real buttermilk. Adults usually digest buttermilk and clabbered milk more easily than the sweet milk. The lactic acid seems to be quite beneficial. Metchnikoff thought for a while that he had discovered how to ward off decay and old age by means of the lactic acid bacteria in milk. Milk can be clabbered quickly by adding lemon juice to sweet milk.

JUNKET

Add rennet to milk and let it stand until it thickens. The milk is not to be disturbed while coagulation takes place, for agitation will cause a separation of the whey. The rennet can be bought at the drug stores. "Whey" contains milk sugar, some salts, and a little albumin. It is easily digested, but not very nourishing. It is what is left of the milk after the fat and almost all of the protein are removed.

COTTAGE CHEESE

This is sometimes called Dutch cheese or white cheese. It is a delicious and nutritious dairy product that is easy to digest. Put the clabbered milk in a muslin bag, hang the bag up and allow the milk to lose its whey through drainage. In summer this bag must be kept in a cool place. After draining, beat the curds.

Then add enough clabbered milk to make the curds soft when well beaten. A small amount of cream may also be added. Cottage cheese made in this way is superior in flavour and digestibility to that which has been scalded. No seasoning is needed. A little salt is allowable, but sugar and pepper should not be used. Fruit and cottage cheese make a satisfying as well as nutritious meal. Delicious cottage cheese is also made by using the whole clabbered milk.

Hang it up to drain in a bag until it has lost a part of its whey. Then beat it until the curds are rather small, but not fine. No milk or cream is to be added to this, for it contains all the fat that is in the whole milk. Do not drain this cheese so long that it becomes dry.

"OTHER CHEESES"

The various cheeses on the market are made principally from ripened curds, with which more or less fat has been mixed. The ripening is a form of decay, and it is no exaggeration to say that some of the very ripe cheeses on the market are rotten. The flavours are due to ferments, moulds and bacteria, which split up the proteins and the fats.

The mild cheeses are generally good and may be eaten with fruits or vegetables or with bread. Two or three ounces are sufficient for the protein part of the meal, taking the place of flesh. Use less if less is desired. When cheese becomes very odourous and ripe, no one with normal nose and palate will eat it. People who partake of excessive amounts of meats or alcoholic beverages are often fond of these foul cheeses. One perversion leads to another.

Cheese of good quality, eaten in moderation, is a nutritious food, easily digested. Gauthier says of cheese: "Indeed, this casein, which has the composition of muscular tissue, scarcely produces during digestion either residue or toxins." Because good cheese is concentrated and of agreeable flavour, it is necessary to guard against overeating. An excess of rich cheese soon causes trouble with the liver or constipation or both.

Cheese should not be eaten in the same meal with fish, meat, eggs, nuts or legumes, for such combining makes the protein intake too great. There is nothing incompatible about such combinations, but it is safest not to make them. The course dinners, ending up with a savory cheese, crackers and coffee, are abominations. They are health-destroyers. They lead to overeating. As nearly everybody overeats, and because overeating is the greatest single factor in producing disease and premature death, it is advisable not to eat cheese and other foods rich in protein in the same meal. The greater the variety of food, the more surely the diner will overeat. The term,"full cream cheese" is misleading, for cheeses are not made of whole cream. The cream does not contain enough protein for the manufacture of cheese. Some cheeses are made of skimmed milk. Others are made of milk which contains part, or even all, of the cream. Some have cream added. The cheeses containing but a moderate amount of fat are the best.

The popular Roquefort cheese is made of a mixture of goat's milk and sheep's milk. The savor is due to bacterial action and fat saponification, which result in ammonia, glycerine, alcohol, fatty acids and other chemicals in very small quantities. The peculiar colourings which run in streaks through some cheeses that are well ripened are due to molds, bacteria and yeasts.

Gentlemen who would discharge the cook if a moldy piece of bread appeared on the table, eat decaying, moldy cheese with relish. The best cheese of all is cottage cheese. People of normal taste will soon weary of the frequent consumption of strong cheese, but they can take cottage cheese every other day with relish. Occasionally put a few caraway seeds in it if this flavour is agreeable.

Cottage cheese may be eaten plain or with bread, or with fruit or vegetables. It may be used as dressing both on fruit and vegetable salads. Cheese should play no part in the alimentation of the sick, with the exception of cottage cheese, which may be given to almost anyone who is in condition to eat anything. The other cheeses are too concentrated for sick people. In acute disease nothing is to be fed.

"SKIMMED MILK"

It is about the same in composition as buttermilk. It is inferior in flavour, but a good food. It is used a great deal in cooking. Milk should not be used very much in cooking. When cooked it does not digest very readily and it has a tendency to make other foods indigestible."Sour cream" or clabbered cream is best when it is taken from clabbered milk. It may be used as dressing on fruits and salads. Sweet cream will clabber, but it is not as delicious as when it clabbers on the milk."Clotted cream" is made by putting the milk aside in pans in a cool place until the cream rises. Then, without disturbing the cream, scald the milk. Put the pan aside until the contents are cold and remove the cream, which has a rich, agreeable flavour.

This may be used as a dressing. Whipped cream and ice cream are so familiar that they hardly need comment. Cream is such a rich food that it must be eaten in moderation. Otherwise it will cause discomfort and disease. Ice cream is made of milk and cream, in varying proportions, flavoured to taste and frozen. It is not necessary to add eggs and cornstarch. If eaten slowly it is a good food, but taken in too large quantities and too rapidly it may cause digestive troubles. It is not best to chill the stomach.

Those with weak digestion should be very careful not to do so. Buttermilk is sometimes flavoured and frozen. This ice is easy to digest. Some doctors recommend this dish to their convalescents. It is an agreeable change, and can be eaten by many who are unable to take care of the rich ice cream.

SALT AND FOOD TECHNOLOGY

The number of applications fulfilled by salt in foods are as varied as the number of different foods there are. These range from a taste enhancer to a taste suppressant; as a mediator of water activity and a regulator of texture, mouthfeel, juiciness and friability. Blanching in salt water retains colour and crispness in vegetables destined for freezing and salt initiates granule formation producing the unparalleled taste and texture of Parmesano Reggiano cheese.

Salt is not only our oldest known food preservative, but it fulfils a critical anti-microbial function in the most modern hurdle technologies employed in the production of high quality minimally processed chilled foods that have become so popular in recent years.

Despite the myriad established uses of salt in food preparation at home and in the food industry, the overarching attraction of salt for people is sensorial. Simply put—salt makes food taste good. Salt doesn't just deliver salty flavour, it delivers flavour in many ways.

Salt is the oldest, most common and most important single flavouring substance. From a food appeal point of view, salt cannot be considered to be merely desirable, but by far the most satisfying of flavour components for all starchy and protein-based foods. This propensity for humans and animals to prefer a salty taste may originate from our marine evolution or may simply be a mechanism to ensure we receive an adequate amount of this essential nutrient in our diet.

When faced with foods that don't meet their taste expectations, most people will simply take up a salt shaker as add enough to satisfy their needs. Thus, in a country such as Italy, where bread baking traditions result in regional products that vary from high to almost no salt, consumers at home and diners in restaurants will readily make up any taste deficit by voluntarily adding salt at the table prior to consumption.

The same can be said for the consumer response to all other food products—those that demonstrate a deficiency in taste will be corrected by the consumer on a voluntary basis. Throughout history, even during periods when it was a very costly commodity, salt was considered to be an economic necessity of life.

One of the most important uses of salt in taste is to moderate bitterness in certain foods. For example, some of or most nutritious cruciferous vegetables, such as broccoli, spinach, Brussels sprouts, cabbage, kale, mustard greens, radicchio will not be acceptable to consumers unless a certain amount of salt is added.

This is particularly true for children as the most recent results of tests from Ohio State University reveals. Restricting the amount of salt that consumers can add to these foods risks their access to the nutritional benefits they hold. Of course, bitter natural foods such as olives would not be an edible food commodity unless they were fully debittered with salt.

When added in small amounts, salt intensifies the sweetness of many foods such as caramel, taffy, fudge, fruits, mild vegetables and various sauces. For example, lightly salting a slice of watermelon makes it taste sweeter. Salt also make food taste more palatable by suppressing other unpleasant flavours. In these instances the goal of the consumer or manufacturer is not to make a food taste salty, but rather to enhance the overall taste profile and acceptability of the food. Salt has a profound effect on the texture of an incredible array of food products. Because of its functional impact on the gelation properties of proteins, salt is used to respond to consumer preferences for texture, mouthfeel and ease of swallowing for all national and imported cheeses and cheese products, processed meat and fish products.

Items such as bologna, frankfurters, restructured beefsteaks, chicken pieces , dry-cured ham, surimi from all fish sources, battered calamari rings, minced fish balls, etc., etc., serve as some examples. Salt has a critical impact on the texture, colour and cooking loss of a range of fresh, processed and dehydrated vegetables, such as runner beans, carrots, cucumbers, broccoli and cauliflower.

Of course, not only food processors love salt. The use of salt by consumers to improve the texture of foods is very common. Preparing for the holidays, a cursory search on Google using the terms 'brining turkey' yields more than

300,000 citations! As an example, a quote from the San Francisco Chronicle reads, "The Chronicle Food section cooked 28 turkeys to find the best method of producing a plump, juicy bird. Our favourite—by far—was the turkey that we brined before roasting."

The level of salt used in bread manufacture significantly affects the physical nature of the final product. Most standard bread is made from doughs containing somewhere around 1.5-2% salt by weight of flour. Salt has a significant physical effect on the properties of wheat gluten, resulting in a less sticky, more manageable dough.

Salt also affects the rate of fermentation, and its addition is timed after the dough has been partly fermented. The role of salt in controlling fermentation is not only due to the increase in osmotic pressure, but also to the actions of sodium and chloride ions on the semi-permeable membranes of yeast cells. Inadequate levels of salt will result in excessive yeast fermentation, resulting in gassy, soured doughs that are difficult to process and result in loaves with an open grain and poor texture. Many types of flat bread have become widely available in recent years. These include single-layered, leavened dough products such as naan, pizza crust, ciabatta and focaccia, batters such as crepes and pancakes as well as double layered products such as pita bread, and unleavened products like chapattis, paratha and tortillas.

Salt is an essential ingredient in most formulations, many of which are sourdough or yeast-leavened products. Salt, temperature, aeration and flour quality are all used to control bread quality. Salt affects the physical nature and properties of biscuit doughs, especially hard doughs, in a similar way to bread. In doughs with significant gluten development, such as crackers and semi-sweet types, salt toughens the gluten and gives a less sticky dough.

It may also slow down the rate of yeast fermentation. Typical levels of addition are generally less than 2%, based on flour, resulting in about 1.5% in the final product. Salt has a variety of technological functions in meat products. While many of the major effects relate to preservation, especially in cured and salted products, it also has other, direct effects on the nature and quality of the product.

Salt is used in the manufacture of both hard and soft cheeses. The salting of some of the most famous Italian, Swiss and Dutch cheeses is carried out after they are formed into rounds. The rounds are then immersed in saturated salt brine, for up to 20 days. For many traditional manufacturers, the saturated brine baths are a source of pride, some having been in continuous operation for more than 100 years (showing perfectly cubic sodium chloride crystals from 5-6 inches on a side, sitting in crystal clear brine).

Salt is the oldest food preservative known to humankind—it has been used for thousands of years. The main mechanism of salt preservation is through the reduction of water activity.

Microorganisms require water to survive and grow and salt preferentially ties up a portion of the water, leaving the microorganisms without sufficient free water. In inhibiting microbial growth, salt interacts with both the acidity (pH) of the medium and its temperature, as well as other factors present.

Processed Foods and Salt

Salting is one of the oldest food preservation methods. Salt (sodium chloride) helps prevent spoiling by drawing water out of the food, depriving bacteria of the moisture they need to thrive. Salt is also an antibacterial agent, killing some of the bacteria that cause spoiling. At one time, salting was one of the only methods available to help preserve food. But today food processors have many other methods. These include pasteurization, refrigeration/ freezing, dehydration/freeze-drying, irradiation and using chemical preservatives.

Note: Some chemical preservatives, such as sodium benzoate, sodium propionate, sodium citrate and sodium phosphate, contain small amounts of salt.

Each of these newer processes has resulted in the need for less—if any salt—as an ingredient. So why do food manufacturers continue to add salt to processed foods? Here are some reasons:

- Salt makes food more flavourful.
- Salted foods such as soups seem thicker and less watery.
- Salt increases sweetness in products such as soft drinks, cookies and cakes.
- Salt helps cover up any metallic or chemical aftertaste in products such as soft drinks.
- Salt decreases dryness in foods such as crackers and pretzels.

Most Americans consume more than double the recommended daily amount of sodium per day—in part because of a heavy diet of processed foods.

To decrease the amount of salt in your diet:

- Eat fewer processed foods such as potato chips, frozen dinners, and cured meats such as bacon and lunchmeats.
- Choose low-sodium or reduced-sodium processed foods.
- Don't add salt to your food. Instead, use herbs and spices to flavour foods.
- Eat more fresh, unprocessed foods such as fresh fruits, vegetables, lean meats, poultry, fish and unprocessed grains.

How Do Salt and Sugar Prevent Microbial Spoilage?

Protection of foods from microbial spoilage using salt (usually sodium chloride) or sugar (usually sucrose) has ancient roots and is often referred to as salting, salt curing, corning or sugar curing. (Pieces of rock salt used for curing are sometimes called corns, hence the name "corned beef".) Curing may utilize solid forms of salt and sugar or solutions in which salt or sugar is mixed with water.

For instance, brine is the term for salt solutions used in curing or pickling preservation processes. Examples of foods preserved with salt or sugar include the afore-mentioned corned beef as well as bacon, salt pork, sugar-cured ham, fruit preserves, jams and jellies, among others.

There are numerous descriptions and permutations of curing which may include additional preservation techniques such as smoking or ingredients such as spices. However, all curing processes fundamentally depend on the use of salt and/or sugar as the primary preservation agent(s).

Incidentally, these processes not only prevent spoilage of foods, but more importantly serve to inhibit or prevent growth of food-borne pathogens such as *Salmonella* or *Clostridium botulinum* when properly applied.

There are several ways in which salt and sugar inhibit microbial growth. The most notable is simple osmosis, or dehydration. Salt or sugar, whether in solid or aqueous form, attempts to reach equilibrium with the salt or sugar content of the food product with which it is in contact. This has the effect of drawing available water from within the food to the outside and inserting salt or sugar molecules into the food interior. The result is a reduction of the so-in the food that is necessary for microbial survival and growth. The a_w of most fresh foods is 0.99 whereas the a_w necessary to inhibit growth of most bacteria is roughly 0.91. Yeasts and molds, on the other hand, usually require even lower a_w to prevent growth.

Salt and sugar's other antimicrobial mechanisms include interference with a microbe's enzyme activity and weakening the molecular structure of its DNA. Sugar may also provide an indirect form of preservation by serving to accelerate accumulation of antimicrobial compounds from the growth of certain other organisms.

Examples include the conversion of sugar to ethanol in wine by fermentative yeasts or the conversion of sugar to organic acids in sauerkraut by lactic acid bacteria. Microorganisms differ widely in their ability to resist salt- or sugar-induced reductions of aw. Most disease-causing bacteria do not grow below 0.94 aw (roughly 10 per cent sodium chloride concentration), whereas most moulds that spoil foods grow at an aw as low as 0.80, corresponding to highly concentrated salt or sugar solutions.

Yet other microorganisms grow quite well under even more highly osmotic, low a_w conditions. For example, halophiles are an entire class of "salt-loving" bacteria that actually require a significant level of salt to grow and are capable of spoiling salt-cured foods. These include members of the genera *Halobacillus* and *Halococcus*.

Food products that are concentrated sugar solutions, such as concentrated fruit juices, can be spoiled by sugar-loving yeasts such as species of *Zygosaccharomyces*. Nevertheless, use of salt and sugar curing to prevent microbial growth is an ancient technique that remains important today for the preservation of foods.

DEVELOPMENTS IN FOOD TECHNOLOGY

Several companies in the food industry have played a role in the development of food technology. These developments have contributed greatly to the food supply. Some of these developments are:

- *Instantized Milk Powder*: D.D. Peebles (U.S. patent 2,835,586) developed the first instant milk powder, which has become the basis for a variety of new products that are rehydratable in cold water or milk. This process increases the surface area of the powdered product by partially rehydrating spray-dried milk powder.
- *Freeze Drying*: The first application of freeze drying was most likely in the pharmaceutical industry; however, a successful

large-scale industrial application of the process was the development of continuous freeze drying of coffee.

- *High-Temperature Short Time Processing*: These processes for the most part are characterized by rapid heating and cooling, holding for a short time at a relatively high temperature and filling aseptically into sterile containers.
- *Decaffeination of Coffee and Tea*: Decaffeinated coffee and tea was first developed on a commercial basis in Europe around 1900. The process is described in U.S. patent 897,763. Green coffee beans are treated with steam or water to around 20 per cent moisture. The added water and heat separate the caffeine from the bean to its surface. Solvents are then used to remove the caffeine from the beans. In the 1980s, new non-organic solvent techniques have been developed for the decaffeination of coffee and tea. Carbon dioxide under supercritical conditions is one of these new techniques. U.S. patent 4,820,537 was issued to General Foods Corp. for a CO2 decaffeination process.

Powdered milk

Powdered milk is a powder made from dried milk solids. Powdered milk has a far longer shelf life than liquid milk and does not need to be refrigerated due to its low moisture content.

History

Powdered milk was first made in the 20th century and is used extensively today. It is found abundantly in many countries because of reduced transport and storage costs (as it does not require refrigeration). Like other dry foods it is considered non-perishable and is favoured by survivalists, hikers and other people in need of non-perishable easy to prepare foodstuffs.

Processing

Powdered milk is typically made by spray drying non-fat skim milk. Pasteurized milk is first concentrated in an evaporator to about 50 per cent milk solids. The resulting concentrated milk is sprayed into a heated chamber where the water almost instantly evaporates, leaving behind fine particles of powdered milk solids. Alternatively, the milk can be dried by drum drying. Milk is applied as a thin film to the surface of a heated drum, and the dried milk solids are then scraped off with a knife. Powdered milk made by drum drying tends to have a cooked flavour, due to caramelization caused by greater exposure to heat.

Yet another process is the use of freeze drying, freeze drying has the advantage of preserving many nutrients in milk compared to drum drying.

Uses

Powdered milk is often used in baking, in recipes where adding liquid milk would render the product too thin to be used. It is also a common sight in UN food aid supplies, fallout shelter, warehouses and wherever fresh milk is not a viable option.

Trivia

"Powdered Milk Man" is a supervillain, mostly described in a song from The Aquabats.

Freeze drying

In a typical phase diagram, the boundary between gas and liquid runs from the triple point to the critical point. Freeze drying (blue arrow) brings the system around the triple point, avoiding the direct liquid-gas transition seen in ordinary drying (green arrow).

Freeze drying (also known as lyophilization) is a dehydration process typically used to preserve a perishable material or make the material more convenient for transport. Freeze drying works by freezing the material and then reducing the surrounding pressure to allow the frozen water in the material to sublimate directly from the solid phase to gas in a manner similar to that which causes unused ice cubes to shrink in a frost-free freezer. The greatly reduced water content that results inhibits the action of microorganisms and enzymes that would normally spoil or degrade the substance.

The application of high vacuum in freeze drying causes ice to sublimates much more quickly, making it useful as a deliberate drying process. A cold condenser chamber and/or condenser plates provide a surface(s) for the vapour to re-solidify on. These surfaces must be colder than the temperature of the surface of the material being dried, or the vapour will not migrate to the collector. Temperatures for this ice collection are typically below -50 °C.

If a freeze-dried substance is sealed to prevent the reabsorption of moisture, the substance may be stored at room temperature without refrigeration, and be protected against spoilage for many years. Freeze drying tends to damage the tissue being dehydrated less than other dehydration methods, which involve higher temperatures. Freeze drying doesn't usually cause shrinkage or toughening of the material being dried, and flavours/smells also remain virtually unchanged.

Liquid solutions that are freeze-dried can be rehydrated (reconstituted) much more quickly and easily because it leaves microscopic pores in the resulting powder. The pores are created by the ice crystals that sublimate, leaving gaps or pores in its place. This is especially important when it comes to pharmaceutical uses. Lyophilization also increases the shelf life of drugs for many years.

The process has been popularized in the form of freeze dried ice cream and as an example of astronaut food. It is also popular and convenient for hikers because the reduced weight allows them to carry more food and reconstitute it with available water. Freeze drying is used in the manufacture of instant coffee as well as some pharmaceuticals.

In high altitude environments, the low temperatures and pressures can sometimes produce natural mummies by a process of freeze-drying.

In chemical synthesis, products are often lyophilized to make them more manageable or more easy to dissolve in water for subsequent use.

Ultra-high-temperature processing

Ultra-high temperature processing (or UHT) is the partial sterilization of food by heating it for a short time, around 1-2 seconds, at a temperature exceeding 135°C (275°F), which is the temperature required to kill spores in milk. The high temperature also reduces the processing time, thereby reducing the spoiling of nutrients. The most common UHT product is milk, but the process is also used for fruit juices, cream, yoghurt, wine, soups, and stews. UHT milk has seen large success in Europe, 7 out of 10 Europeans drink it regularly. Its largest manufacturer, Parmalat, had $6 billion of sales in 1999. In the North American market, consumers have been uneasy about buying warm milk, and have been much more reluctant in buying it. To combat this, Parmalat is developing UHT milk in old-fashioned containers. Many milk products in North American foods are made using UHT milk anyway, such as McDonalds McFlurries.

UHT milk has a typical shelf life of six to nine months, until opened. However, once contaminated, UHT milk spoils much more rapidly than pasteurized milk because all the lactobacillus in milk has been killed by the high temperature heat treatment. Many people believe that UHT products are inferior in quality to less-aggressively-pasteurized alternatives, but this is disputed by the manufacturers. It can be contrasted with HTST pasteurization (high temperature/short time), in which the milk is heated to 72°C (161.6°F) for at least 15 seconds.

Decaffeination

Decaffeination is the act of removing caffeine from coffee beans and tea leaves. All decaffeination processes are performed on unroasted (green) coffee beans, but the methods vary somewhat. They generally start by steaming the beans. The beans are then rinsed in some solvent that contains as much of the chemical composition of coffee as possible without also containing the caffeine in a soluble form. The process is repeated anywhere from 8 to 12 times until it meets either the international standard of having removed 97 per cent of the caffeine in the beans or the EU standard of having less than 0.10 per cent caffeine by mass in the coffee at the end of the process. Coffee contains over 400 chemicals important to the taste and aroma of the final drink; this effectively means that no chemical reaction will remove only caffeine while leaving the other chemicals at their original concentrations. While they are occasionally referred to informally as "decaffeinated," soft drinks without caffeine are prepared by simply leaving caffeine out in the first place.

Coffea arabica normally contains about half the caffeine of coffea robusta, and a coffea arabica bean containing a tenth as much caffeine as a normal bean has been found by some Brazilian scientists. This may change how low caffeine coffee is produced in the future. But for now, one of several methods is employed.

Roselius process

The first commercially successful decaffeination process was invented by Ludwig Roselius and Karl Wimmer in 1905. It involved steaming coffee beans with a brine (salt water) solution and then using benzene as a solvent to remove the caffeine. Coffee decaffeinated this way was sold as *Cafe sanka* in France and later as *Sanka* brand coffee in the US. Today benzene is considered so unsafe that in the 1990's the US military reformulated Napalm to reduce the benzene level.

Direct method

In the direct method the coffee beans are first steamed for 30 minutes and then repeatedly rinsed with either methylene chloride or ethyl acetate for about 10 hours. The solvent is then drained away and the beans steamed for an additional 10 hours to remove any residual solvent. Methylene chloride is considered a superior solvent because the extraction can be performed at a lower temperature and because it extracts fewer components other than the caffeine. Ethyl acetate can be obtained from various fruits and vegetables, which allows the beans processed with it to be labelled as "Natural Decafs".

Water method

In the water method (also called indirect method) beans are first soaked in hot water for several hours. Then the water is removed and either methyl chloride or ethyl acetate is used to remove the caffeine from the solution. The solution is then heated to evaporate the methyl chloride or ethyl acetate. Finally beans are soaked again in water after the caffeine is removed. The first few batches are tossed out and the water reused so that the water actually has a similar composition to the beans' liquids, except for the lack of caffeine.

CO_2/O_2 process

With the CO_2 process, pre-steamed beans are soaked in a liquid bath of carbon dioxide at 73 to 300 atmospheres. After a thorough soaking, the pressure is reduced allowing the CO_2 to evaporate, or the pressurized CO_2 is run through either water or charcoal filters to remove the caffeine. The carbon dioxide is then used on another batch of beans. This same process can also be done with oxygen (O_2). These liquids work better than water because they are kept in supercritical state near the transition from liquid to gas so that they have the high diffusion of gas and the high density of a liquid.

Filtered water method

This is the same as the Water Method, except a charcoal filter is used instead of methyl chloride or ethyl acetate to remove the caffeine from the water. The charcoal is generally bathed in some carbohydrate, such as sucrose. This prevents the charcoal from absorbing many of the similar molecules in the water.

Triglyceride process

Green coffee beans are soaked in a hot water/coffee solution to draw the caffeine to the surface of the beans. Next, the beans are transferred to another container and immersed in coffee oils that were obtained from spent coffee grounds.

After several hours of high temperatures, the triglycerides in the oils remove the caffeine - but not the flavour elements - from the beans. The beans are separated from the oils and dried. The caffeine is removed from the oils, which are reused to decaffeinate another batch of beans. This is a direct contact method of decaffeination.

❐

Chapter - 4

Food Preservation and Pasteurization

Have you ever eaten methi paranthas in the month of June? If yes, where did the methi come from? Not from the vegetable market, because it is not available in the month of June! On a certain day, if the dishes are not to your liking, you prefer to eat food with pickle or mango chutney. Have you ever wondered how preparations such as pickles, potato chips, tomato sauce, etc., are present in your house throughout the year? Why do they not get spoilt? There are definite months in a year when pickles, papads, chips, squashes, etc., are prepared and stored for the year. In this lesson let us learn about these foods which can be stored for long periods without getting spoilt.

WHAT IS FOOD PRESERVATION ?

The dictionary meaning of the word "preserve" is to keep safe, retain quality, prevent decomposition or fermentation. When we apply this meaning to food preservation it can be defined as: A process by which certain foods like fruits and vegetables are prevented from getting spoilt for a long period of time. The colour, taste and nutritive value of the food is also preserved. Let us understand this definition in a little more detail. The definition says *preventing foods from getting spoilt.* When you keep fruits, vegetables or left over dal in the refrigerator or in a cool place, will this be called food preservation? No, because you can store fruits and vegetables or left over dal in this state for a few days only. The definition of food preservation states that the preserved food should *retain their colour and taste.*

This means that the colour and taste of food which is present at the time of preservation should not change. Let us take the example of preserving grapes as raisins. Raisins are prepared by sun drying grapes. During the drying process the grapes change colour from green to brown, and taste, sweeter. However, once they are dried and stored, they do not change colour or taste. Like colour and taste, a well preserved food should *not change texture.* When your mother makes mango murraba at home, have you observed the texture of the mango pieces? It is firm . In a well made murraba, this firmness of mango pieces should not change after sometime.

Why Do We Need to Preserve Foods

Now that you have understood the definition of food preservation, did you think about why we should preserve foods? Can you think of a few reasons for preserving foods? Let us find an answer to this question by taking an example of one food item. Let us take the example of a fruit, say mango. There are many ways by which mangoes can be preserved. These are: juice, murraba, squash, aam papad, pulp, chutney, pickle, raw mango powder.

You may be able to add a few more to the above list. Mango is a summer fruit and grows in large quantities during the months of April to August. Different varieties of mango are grown in different parts of our country.

Usually all the quantity grown in a region cannot be consumed by the people staying there as there is always an excess. What does the farmer do with this excess quantity? He makes arrangements to transport the excess quantity to regions where either mango is not grown or where that particular variety of mango is not available. If he does not do this, the excess produce will rot and go waste.

The farmer will then lose money. There is still some quantity which is left after the fresh fruit is consumed by the people. It is this quantity which has to be preserved for consumption during the months when mango is not available. Preservation of foods is done during the months when food is available in large quantity and therefore at low cost.

- One of the important reasons for preserving foods is to take care of the excess produce. There are many other reasons for preserving foods. Let us learn about these.
- The second reason for preserving foods is that they add variety to our meals. Have you ever got tired of eating the same vegetables which are in season? Is it not nice to eat peas when they are either very expensive in the market or are not available ? Eating cauliflower in pulav or cauliflower vegetable

during the summer months adds to the interest in meals. In the same way, eating some chatni, papad or pickle along with the meals adds to the variety. Preserving foods when they are in season makes this possible.

- Reaches areas where the food item is not grown. In some areas of Rajasthan which are desert areas and in Himalayan regions that are covered with snow most of the time, very few foods can be grown. Availability of some preserved foods can add to the variety and nutritive value of meals. For example inclusion of dehydrated peas, green leafy vegetables, canned fruits etc., in the meals is a good idea in such areas.
- Makes transportation and storage of foods easier. Preservation of foods usually reduces bulk. This makes their transportation and storage easier since it requires less space. For example, if you dry green leafy vegetables such as mint, methi, corriander, etc, their weight and volume reduces, thus making their storage easy.

Why Does Food Get Spoilt

The definition of food preservation states that preserva-tion is keeping food in such a state that they do not get spoilt for a long period. Before we look at the reasons of food spoilage, let us understand, when is a food spoilt. When you keep bread outside the refrigerator for few days, a spongy growth is seen on it, which may be white, green on black in colour.

The bread thus gets spoilt due to growth of mould and becomes unfit for consumption. Likewise, if cooked dal or vegetables is left outside for sometime, it develops a bad smell and bubbles due to fermentation.

The dal and vegetables are thus spoilt and cannot be eaten. Can you now say when is a food spoilt? Food is said to be spoilt if there is rotting, i.e., bad smell, fermentation, i.e., bubbles/gas in the food or mould i.e., spongy growth on the foodstuff.

Formation of soft spots or soft brown spots on fruits and vegetables is also food spoilage. Why do foods get spoilt? If you know the reasons of food spoilage, you can remove these conditions while preserving food items. Foods get spoilt mainly due to the presence of micro-organisms, enzymes (present in foods), insects, worms, and rats.

Presence of Micro-organisms

Micro means small. Micro-organisms are very small organisms which cannot be easily seen. Micro-organisms spoil food items when the condition for their growth are appropriate.

What are these appropriate conditions? Like all living beings micro- organisms require air, moisture, right temperature and food to grow and multiply. The situations which provide appropriate conditions for growth of micro-organisms, can be listed as:

- Food having high moisture content.
- Air around the food containing micro-organisms.
- Foods kept for a long time at room temperature.
- Skin of fruits and vegetables getting damaged, thus exposing the food to micro-organisms.
- Foods with low salt, sugar or acid content.

Presence of Enzymes

Enzymes are chemical susbtances found in all plants and animals. Are enzymes harmful to foods? No, enzymes help in ripening of fruits and vegetables. A raw green mango after a few days becomes sweet in taste and yellow in colour due to the enzymes action. What will happen if you keep this yellow, ripe mango for a few more days?

It will become soft, develop black spots and will start smelling bad. This is due to continued action of enzymes. No one likes to eat such as over ripe, spoilt mango. You know that even when the skin of fruits is not cut or damaged, it gets spoilt. This is due to enzyme action.

Principles of Food Preservation

After learning about the causes of food spoilage, it should not be very difficult to list the principles of food preservation. Remember, a good method of food preservation is one that slows down or prevents altogether the action of the agents of spoilage. Also, during the process of food preservation, the food should not be damaged.

In order to achieve this, certain basic methods were applied using the knowledge gained form observation of the effects of natural conditions on different types of foods. For example in earlier days, in very cold weather condition, ice was used to preserve foods.

Thus, very low temperature became an efficient method for preventing food spoilage. Let us now list the principles of food preservation:

- *Removal of Micro-organisms or Inactivating Them*: This is done by removing air, water (moisture), lowering or increasing temperature, increasing the concentration of salt or sugar or acid in foods. If you want to preserve green leafy vegetables, you have to remove the water from the leave so that micro-organisms cannot survive. You do this by drying the green leaves till all the moisture evapourates.

- *Inactivating Enzymes*: Enzymes found in foods can be inactivated by changing their conditions such as temperature and moisture, when you preserve peas, one of the methods of preservations is to put them for a few minutes in boiling water. This method inactivates enzymes and thus, in preserving the food.
- *Removal of Insects, Worms and Rats*: By storing foods in dry, air tight containers the insects, worms or rats are prevented from destroying it.

Methods of Preserving Foods at Home

Foods can be preserved at home by the following methods:

- Dehydration
- Lowering temperature
- Increasing temperature
- Using preservatives.

Let us now discuss each method in some detail.

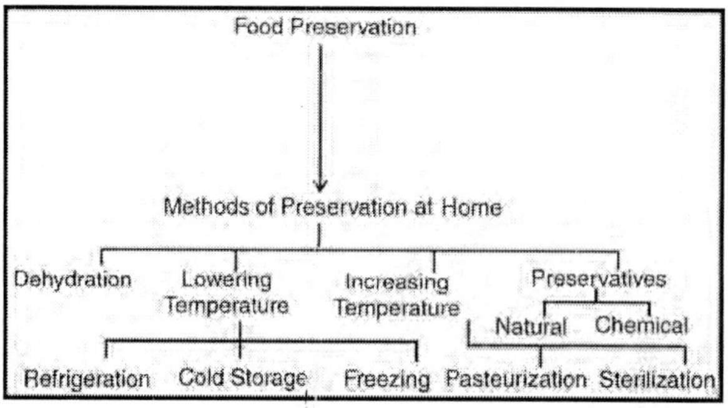

Dehydration

Can you name some dried food items that are stored in your kitchen for a period of one year or more? Are these potato chips, sevia (vermicilli), methi, cauliflower, papad, ginger powder? These are foods which have been preserved by the dehydration method. The word dehydration means removing water or moisture from foods.

The home method of dehydration is sun drying. We will now discuss this method in some more detail. Some foods are dried as they are, eg., green leafy vegetables (methi, pudina, corriander etc.), cauliflower, grapes, amla, onion, raw mango, etc. Some foods are cooked and then dried. For example, potato chips, papad, banana, chips, wadis, etc. The most appropriate weather to dry foods is when the air is dry and there is strong sunshine. Let us understand the basic method of dehydration before we learn to apply it to individual foods:

- Step 1: Clean all tins, plates, etc., to be used to dry and store the food. Dry in sun. Storage tins should have airtight lids.
- Step 2: Wash the vegetables/fruits to be dehydrated. Cut, if required. Remove the stem, seeds, skin. Remove any decaying portions.
- Step 3: Blanch vegetables, i.e., put them in boiling water. Time for blanching varies with hardness of fruit/vegetables. Remove when the food is soft (blanching reduces enzymed activity).
- Step 4: Put vegetables in cold water containing salt and potassium metabisulphite for 5-10 minutes. This prevents blackening of foods. Green leafy vegetables and other dark vegetables should not be put in this solution.
- Step 5: Spread on a clean cloth in the sun. Cover with a thin cloth to avoid dust and flies getting into the food.
- Step 6: When the food is dry (test by looking at hardness), cool to room temperature. Store in an air tight container.

When you want to use dehydrated fruits and vegetables, wash and soak in water for some time. Now let us look at how you can use this method to preserve a specific food items, eg., methi and potato.

Dehydrating Methi

Can you list the steps for drying methi?

- Wash methi and remove the stems.
- Put on a cloth in the sun, cover it.
- Cool to room temperature and store in air tight tins.

Making Potato Chips

- Wash and peel potatoes. Cut in thin round slices.
- Put in boiling water for 3-4 minutes.
- Make a solution in cold water with 4 tsp salt, ¾ tsp potassium metabisulphite (for 4 kg potato).
- Put the blanched potato chips in this solution for 10 minutes.
- Spread each chip separately on a plate in the sun. Cover with a thin cloth.
- When dry, cool and store in air tight containers.

So, even if the basic principle of dehydration remains the same, you have to adapt the method depending on the food you are preserving.

Lowering Temperature

Using low temperature to preserve foods works on the principle that low temperature slows microbial and enzyme action. The food is thus prevented from spoilage. Are you using this method of preservation at home? Yes, if you have a refrigerator you can use it because a refrigerator works on this principle. Foods can be preserved at low temperature by:

- Refrigeration 40°C to 70°C
- Cold storage–10°C to– 40°C
- Freezing–180°C or below.

The duration for which the food can be preserved by using low temperature varies with the type of food and the temperatures. The lower the temperature, longer is the duration for which food can be preserved. Of the three methods, freezing uses the lowest temperature.

Freezing of Peas

- *Step 1*: Select about half a kilogramme of fresh, tender peas and shell them.
- *Step 2*: Take enough water in a stainless steel pan in which the peas can be completely immersed. Add 1 teaspoon of salt for half litre of water, dissolve and bring the solution to boil.
- *Step 3*: Completely immerse the peas in the boiling solution for about 2 minutes.
- *Step 4*: Drain the peas immediately on to a stainless steel sieve and let it cool for 10-15 minutes.
- *Step 5*: Pack the peas in polythene bags, remove the air by pressing and seal the bags.
- *Step 6*: Put the packets of peas into a freezer.

Note: Similarly other vegetables such as cauliflower, beans, carrots etc., can also be frozen.

Using Frozen Vegetables

- Take out the frozen packet from the freezer one and a half hours or two hours before use and let it thaw to room temperature. Put peas in a sieve and keep under tap water for a few minutes. Drain and use.
- Frozen vegetables can be stored up to six months in a freezer.

Precautions while Freezing Fruits and Vegetables

- Packaging material, that is, polythene bags should be strong enough to withstand expansion of food material on freezing.
- The food once brought out of the freezer and up to room temperature should not be refrozen.
- Small packets should be prepared, as food once thawed must be consumed. So there is less chance of the unrequired food material being spoilt. This also helps to avoid refreezing of the unutilized food material.
- Exclude the air carefully and completely from the package before sealing.

- The freezer should not be opened too frequently.
  Thaw: A process by which something frozen is brought to room temperature without applying artificial heat.

Increasing Temperature

By increasing the temperature, enzymes and micro-organisms are destroyed, leaving the food safe from spoilage. Do all organisms get killed by increasing temperature? No, there are some micro-organisms which do not get destroyed at high temperature. If these organisms are not killed, they can spoil food items once the temperature is lowered. There are mainly two methods of preserving foods by using high temperature:

- *Pasteurization*: When you think of pasteurization, which food item comes to your mind? Yes, its milk. We have often heard about pasteurized milk packets. In this method food is heated to a high temperature and then quickly cooled. The micro-organisms are not able to withstand the sudden change in temperature and are destroyed. However, some organisms still survive this method.
- *Sterilization*: What does the word sterilization mean? It means free from any living organism. The high temperature used in this method destroys all the microorganisms in the food. The foods are exposed to high temperature for longer time and in some cases under pressure. When a pressure cooker is used to cook, the food lasts longer because most microorganisms get destroyed. You can also sterilize bottles and other equipments used in preservation.

Using Preservatives

What are preservatives? Any substance that is added to foods to make it last for a longer time is called a preservative. You have learnt that increasing the concentration of salt, sugar or acid in a food prevents its spoilage. Therefore, salt, sugar or acid are substances which act as preservatives. There are two types of preservatives:

- *Natural Preservatives*: Salt, sugar, lemon juice, vinegar, oil and spices are natural preservatives.
- *Chemical Preservatives*: Potassium metabisulphate, citric acid and sodium benzoate are chemical preservatives.

Let us discuss the natural preservatives:

- *Salt*: When you make pickle at home, salt is one of the ingredients used. Did you think that salt is added only for taste? Besides adding to taste, salt has a specific function, i.e., to act as a preservative. If the proportion of salt in pickles is less, it can get spoilt after sometime. How does salt act as a preservative? Increasing the quantity of salt in the food changes its composition. Due to the presence of salt in the food, osmosis takes place. As a result, water comes out of the food. When there is no or less water in the food, the micro-organisms are not able to grow and the food becomes safe. Salt also reduces the activity of enzymes, thus preventing the food from getting spoilt. Salt is used as a preservative in pickles, chatni, sauce, canned food, etc. Salt is rubbed on fish which helps to preserve it.

- *Sugar*: Can you think of some preserved foods where sugar is used as a preservative? Yes, these are jams, jellies, murabbas, squashes. Like in pickle, chatni, etc., sugar is added to these foods not only for taste but also as a preservative. The proportion of sugar has to be correct to protect them from spoiling. How does sugar prevent food spoilage? The sugar dissolves in the water avail able in the food item. This results in less water being available for the growth of micro-organisms. Hence the food becomes safe.
- *Acids*: Can you think of any sour food items used as preservative?

These are lemon juice, vinegar, citric acid, etc. Vinegar is used to preserve onions, tomato ketchup; lemon juice is used in pickles; citric acid is used in squashes. Acids increase the acidic content of food items, thus preventing the activity and growth of micro-organisms.

- *Oils and Spices*: These are used as preservatives in pickles. Can you think of a spice which is commonly used as a preservatives? Yes, mustard powder is one of them. It prevents the growth of micro-organisms, thus preventing spoilage. When pickle is made at home, have you observed that oil is poured to cover the mango, lemon or other vegetables which are being pickled. The oil acts as a protective cover and has two advantages:
    - (i) Prevents contact of micro-organisms with the food, hence they cannot spoil the food.
    - (ii) Prevents contact of air with food, hence the micro-organisms cannot grow and spoil the food.

HOME CANNING FOOD PRESERVATION

The Benefits of Home Canning

Canning food in your own home is a safe and rewarding process that is becoming popular again as food prices soar and people realise they need to pay attention to securing their food supplies. Preserving food with home canning is an excellent way to increase your consumption of local food. Eating locally requires eating foods when they are in season, and canning allows you to capture the bounty of any particular crop in season and extend its availability throughout the year.

You can approach home canning as a hobbyist or a full-time enthusiast who stocks a sizeable percentage of his or her food supply with home preserved food. Whether you want to enjoy a couple fun weekend projects putting up jam or seriously supplement your diet, you will enjoy many personal benefits while being a good steward to the environment and supporting your local economy. And the way things are going with the global food market, you will likely save money as well, especially as time goes on.

How Preserving Food at Home Helps Us

- *Excellent Quality and Taste*: When you use quality produce and perform the canning process correctly, you will create superior products to those for sale at the supermarket. Many recipes for home canned food are delicious and literally the quality is something that money can't buy. You have to make these luscious foods yourself.
- *Control over the Ingredients*: With home canning, you will know exactly where your food is coming from. Ideal sources of produce are your own garden and fruit trees, local organic farms, and any local farm. From any of these sources you will be able to hand select your produce at the peak of ripeness. With home canning you will also reduce your exposure to Bisphenol A that lines the cans of many mass produced food products. Bisphenol A is an endocrine disruptor and people are becoming increasingly aware of its potential harm to humans.
- *Support of the Local Economy*: By directly buying produce from local growers, you are putting money into the hands of local people. Local growers love selling from their own farms or market stands because they are not at the mercy of the big commodity buyers who set prices. This also allows local growers, especially small ones, to remain profitable, which is good for the local economy.
- *Lower Your Carbon Dioxide Footprint*: Great amounts of energy are used to produce and transport the food eaten by society. Highly industrialized agriculture also relies on pesticides, herbicides, and petrochemical fertilizers. All of these things are bad for the environment and degrade the ability of soils

to produce food in the future, which means greater scarcity, lower quality, and higher commodity prices. When you buy local food and can it at home, you are eliminating a huge percentage of the transport costs from burned fuel associated with shipping food across continents. Yes, home canning requires an energy input, but it does not compare to food being trucked halfway across the country to stock a shelf in a store. Reducing the amount of food you eat from distant places reduces the amount of fuel you are causing to be burned. Also when buying local food, try to focus on those growers who use sustainable growing practices that do not poison the environment.

- *Sense of Accomplishment*: Once you begin canning food, you will be thrilled with yourself. You will feel like you did something very meaningful to your existence because you did! For most of human history most people focused a great deal of time and energy on securing their food supplies. We are not suggesting we all go back to digging for roots in the field, but people in general have a deep need to participate in the gathering and preparation of food. Sitting in an SUV for drive-through fast food does not satisfy. It only promotes outrageous energy consumption for low quality products.

Now that you are ready to do some work in the kitchen and participate in food preservation, you need to understand the basics of home canning. The process is a little intimidating at first, but after a couple canning projects, you will feel much more comfortable doing it.

There are safety considerations with home canning, but these are all satisfied by following the directions associated with any particular home canning project. The manufacturers of Mason jars (which are the essential product needed for safe home canning) offer great information on how to can food at home, and many university agriculture departments and the USDA offer very reliable information on this subject as well.

FOOD PRESERVATION WITH HOME

Canning Halts Spoilage

Food preservation in canning jars is accomplished by killing spoilage causing agents with heat, removing air from the food products, and sealing the jars so that air and yeasts, moulds, and bacteria cannot be reintroduced to the food.

Four Causes of Food Spoilage

- Enzymes – Destroyed at 140°F.
- Moulds – Destroyed at 140°F to 190°F.
- Yeasts – Destroyed at 140°F to 190°F.
- Bacteria – Many types of bacteria exist. The toxins produced by some bacteria are also a hazard. Bacteria and associated toxins are destroyed in heat ranges from 190°F to 240°F.

Some bacteria are very tough and resist death even at high temperatures. The toughest bacterium is *Clostridium botulinum,* whose spores cause the deadly botulism. This bacterium is killed at 190°F and its toxic spores are destroyed at 240°F.

This bacterium thrives in low-acid or nonacid foods in the absence of air. Foods in this category include corn, beans, peppers, poultry, fish, and meat. This is the main reason that these types of foods require the higher temperatures achieved during pressure canning.

Boiling canned low-acid or nonacid foods for 10 to 20 minutes before eating them will destroy potential lingering toxins. This added step will give you one more reason to feel safe about eating home canned low-acid or nonacid foods.

Water Bath Canner

- *Equipment*: A large metal enamel kettle with lid and jar rack with the capacity to hold up to 7, quart-sized Mason jars. Widely available at discount stores and hardware stores. Cost: $20 to $25.
- *Uses*: The water bath canner is used to process Mason jars for home preservation of jams, fruits, fruit juices, and pickled vegetables.
- *Safety Considerations*: It is a large kettle of boiling water so be careful to avoid steam burns and splashing hot water.

Tested recipes are widely available from the USDA, numerous University agriculture departments, Mason jar manufacturers, fruit pectin manufacturers, and from friends and family who have recipes that are known to be safe. As you familiarize yourself with the principles of safe home canning, you will be able to judge all recipes for safety and even develop your own.

How to Use Water Bath Can

Please always review the manufacturer's directions for the Mason jars that you are using and pay close attention to the head space and processing times specified by recipes.

- Pick a recipe for the produce that you wish to can. Select only quality produce at or near the peak of ripeness. Prepare the recipe.
- While preparing the food, you will also need to get the Mason jars ready. Wash the jars, bands, and lids in hot soapy water. Only use new lids. Never re-use lids. Jars and bands can be re-used.
- Fill the water bath canner and start to heat it in order to sterilize your jars and lids. Use a large thermometer (a candy thermometer works well) to monitor the temperature. When the water is at least 180°F but less than boiling (212°F) add the jars and lids to the water. Sterilizing bands in unnecessary. Kerr and Ball lids specify that they should not be boiled, so make sure that the water stays just below the boiling point.
- Remove the jars and lids from hot water when the food is ready to be packed in jars.
- Add prepared food to jars. Use the handle of a wooden spoon along the insides of the jars to work out any air bubbles. Leave the specified head space, usually ¼ inch or ½ inch.
- Wipe the edges of jar mouths very carefully. They need to be completely clean. Any food particles or other debris on the mouth edge will interfere with the sealing of the lids.
- Place lids on jars and screw on the bands. Only screw them on hand tight. You don't need to twist hard.
- With a jar lifter, place the Mason jars into the hot water. Make sure that jars are not touching each other or the side of the kettle.
- Bring the water to a boil. Once the water is boiling, you can begin the timer for the processing time specified by the recipe. Adjust the heat source as necessary to keep the water boiling but to prevent it from boiling over.
- Once processing time is complete, shut off heat source, and use a jar lifter to remove jars from the canner. Set the jars on a cloth in a location free of drafts. Do not disturb the jars for 12 to 24 hours. You will likely hear the lids "pop" or "snap" down not long after removal, but the jars need to cool completely to make sure the seal is complete. (Processing times change with your land elevation. Consult charts that come with recipes and/ or equipment.)

Pressure Canner for Home Canning

- *Equipment*: A pressure canner that has a sealed lid and a gauge that measures the pressure created by boiling water and steam. Under pressure, the steam will achieve temperatures of 240 to 250°F. Such high temperatures are necessary to destroy the bacterium *Clostridium botulinum*. Canners for home use typically cost between $80 and $130. Major brand is Presto.
- *Uses*: To process canning jars of fruit, vegetables, meat, fish, and poultry for purposes of preservation. Pressure canning is the only safe method for preserving low-acid vegetables and meats. Note, the pressure canner can also be used like a pressure cooker to prepare meals.
- *Safety Considerations*: Proper use of a pressure canner requires diligent monitoring of the pressure gauge during operation and maintenance of the plugs, gaskets, and metal parts. An actual explosion of the equipment would only occur if the heat was left on and the pressure climbed into the danger zone.

Even so, the plug in the safety valve should blow out before a catastrophic failure of the pressure canner happened. Note that the danger zone for the equipment is several pounds of pressure beyond the pressures necessary for processing foods.

To avoid problems, keep the pressure within the safe zone by watching the gauge and adjusting the heat source. In case of emergency, rapid cooling of the canner can be initiated by running it under cold water.

How to Use Pressure Can

Please follow the manufacturer's directions that accompany your specific pressure canner model. In general:

- The pressure canner will be filled with approximately 3 quarts of water (this amount would vary depending on size of canner).
- The water is brought to a boil and the prepared Mason jars are placed in the canner.
- The lid is placed on the canner, sealed, and locked, but the pressure regulator is *not* put in place yet.
- Once a free flow of steam is initiated through the vent, it will be allowed to vent for 10 minutes. (Time may vary depending on size of canner.) Venting steam exhausts air from the pressure chamber.
- After 10 minutes, the pressure regulator is put over the vent and pressure begins to build inside. When the interior becomes pressurized, the air vent/cover lock will rise and

completely seal the chamber. Then pounds of pressure will start to accumulate and register on the gauge.

- Bring the canner to the pressure specified by the canning recipe and then maintain that pressure by adjusting heat source as necessary. You will find that once pressure has been achieved, the stove burner no longer needs to be on a high setting. Monitor the pressure closely to make sure it does not rise too far beyond desired pressure. Also, do not let the pressure fall below the pressure required by the recipe. It is important for the food within to be kept at the necessary pressure/temperature for the required amount of time.
- Once the food has processed at the required amount of time at the necessary pressure, turn off the heat source. Do not rapid cool the canner because this would cause jars within to break. (Processing times change with your land elevation. Consult charts that come with recipes and/or equipment.)
- Allow canner to cool until air vent/cover lock drops on its own. Then remove pressure regulator and allow canner to set for 10 more inutes.
- At this point you may unlock the lid and open it. Be careful of the steam that comes out because it will be scalding hot.
- With a jar lifter, remove Mason jars and set them on a cloth in a location free of drafts.
- Do not disturb jars for 12 to 24 hours after removal. They will be exceedingly hot. The contents will continue to boil after removal from the canner. As the jars cool, the lids will seal.

General Tips for Home Canning

You will have to attend to many details while preserving food at home, but it gets easier as you become familiar with the process. The following tips will help you successfully complete your home canning project with great results: sealing impossible.

- Always use new lids. Packages of just lids are widely available for this purpose. Jars and bands may be re-used.
- Always wipe completely clean the jar mouth edges before applying the lid. Particles of food on the jar mouth could interfere with sealing.
- Follow canning guidelines. Don't compromise, substitute, or declare something good enough. Follow the directions and your food will be safe and good.
- When pickling foods, make sure to use vinegar with 5% acidity.

Some vinegars only have 4% acidity, but don't use them.

- Allow jars to cool undisturbed for 12 to 24 hours after removing them from the water bath or pressure canner.
- Remove the jar bands and wipe clean the jars and lids before storing. Little bits of food often leak out during processing and you would not want to store the jars with food bits stuck to them. You can put clean jar bands back on for storage if you want to.
- Home canned products have a shelf life of up to 12 months. Label and date your jars as you produce the food. Do not eat food more than 12 months old.
- Select high quality produce at or near the peak of ripeness. You can cut out small blemishes if necessary, but don't use overly damaged foods.

HOME FOOD PRESERVATION

Safe Tomato Tips

Today's tomatoes border the fine line between high and low acid foods. To make sure homecanned tomatoes are safe, it's very important to add acid to tomatoes and tomato products. If acid is not added to each jar of tomatoes or tomato products, bacteria can grow and create an unsafe product. The acid may be added directly to each jar before adding the tomatoes or tomato mixture. A little sugar may be added to offset the taste of the acid, if desired. The sugar will not change the acidity level.

Acid	Effect on Tomatoes	Amount or Tomato Mixtures
Citric Acid	Little change in flavour	½ teaspoon per quart ¼ teaspoon per pint
Bottled Lemon Juice	Easy to use. Can substitute bottled lime juice. Do not use fresh squeezed lemon juice because the acid level is uncertain and there is a chance of contamination	2 tablespoons per quart 1 tablespoon per pint
Vinegar (5% acidity)	Noticeable change in flavour	4 tablespoons per quart 2 tablespoons per pint

Safe Salsa Advice

Most salsa recipes combine onions, peppers and tomatoes with added acid (lemon juice, lime juice or vinegar). The type and amount of ingredients and preparation methods are important considerations in how salsa is canned. If salsa or other tomato-vegetable mixtures are not canned properly, they can support the growth of a potentially harmful bacterium, *Clostridium botulinum*.

To home-can salsa safely, it is extremely important that you follow a tested and approved recipe for home-canning. Food scientists tested recipes to make sure that the amount of acid combined with other ingredients is safe for home-canning, and that the processing times and methods will destroy harmful microorganisms.

The recipe ingredient amounts and processing methods must be followed to the letter. If you enjoy creating your own salsa recipe or tweaking a recipe, plan to freeze it or store it for several weeks in the refrigerator and eat it fresh.

Home-Canned Salsa Guidelines

- Do not reduce the amount of lemon juice, vinegar or tomatoes.
- Do not add extra peppers, onion or garlic but you can reduce the amount of peppers, onion or garlic.
- You can substitute one type of pepper for another.
- Paste tomatoes contribute to a thicker salsa, while slicing tomatoes yield a thinner salsa. Do not drain or squeeze tomatoes to remove the liquid and juices or you will be removing some of the needed acids.
- Red, yellow or white onions may be substituted for each other.
- The amount of dry spices may be altered or deleted.
- For a stronger cilantro flavour, add fresh cilantro just before serving.
- Never add flour or cornstarch to salsa before canning because heat may not penetrate through the jar to destroy harmful microorganisms. Thicken salsas by adding tomato paste or using a paste tomato.

Freeze Peppers

If you have a lot of peppers, store them unwashed in a perforated plastic bag in the refrigerator up to one week. Before using, rinse with cool water. To freeze peppers, choose crisp, tender green, bright red or bright yellow pods. Wash, cut out stem, cut in half and remove seeds.

Peppers may be cut into ½-inch strips or rings. If the peppers will be used in cooked dishes, water-blanch halves for 3 minutes; strips or rings for 2 minutes. Cool promptly, drain and package, leaving ½-inch head space. Seal, label and freeze. If the peppers will be used in uncooked foods, package them raw, leaving no head space. Seal, label and freeze.

Sweet Corn

Sweet corn is an easy vegetable to freeze and produces a tasty, quality product when frozen properly. Harvested corn on the cob is at its optimum quality for 48 hours. When harvesting, do so early in the morning before the heat of the day. Once husked, the ears are blanched in boiling water for 4 minutes, followed by a complete cooling in ice water for about 8 minutes.

Drain and cut the kernels from the cob. An electric knife is a handy tool for cutting off the kernels. Package the corn in freezer containers, leaving ½-inch headspace. Seal and freeze at 0°F or below for best quality. Blanching, followed by chilling in ice water, are critical processes for producing quality frozen corn. The natural enzymes in corn need to be inactivated by blanching to prevent both loss of colour and nutrients, and flavour and texture changes.

Inadequately chilled corn may become mushy due to overcooking the starch. Can you freeze corn on the cob? Yes, it can be done, but with mixed results. Corn lovers are often disappointed with the sometimes mushy, rubbery texture and the cobby taste. It also takes up more space in the freezer. You can enjoy the great taste of summertime sweet corn all year long by following the simple, basic procedures for freezing vegetables.

Pickling: It's Not Just for Cucumbers

Vegetables from asparagus to zucchini can be home preserved by pickling. The key is to select a recipe from an approved source that is specifically designed for the vegetable you are pickling. Follow the directions carefully for a safe, high quality product.

Begin by selecting tender vegetables and plan to pickle within 24 hours of picking. Wash well and drain. Green beans, carrots, and zucchini are raw packed; whereas asparagus is blanched and beets need to be pre-cooked in their skins for 30 minutes. Cider vinegar has a good flavour and aroma, but may darken white or light-coloured vegetables. White distilled vinegar is the preferred choice for pickling.

Follow the recipe recommendations for the ratio of vinegar to water; it does vary by the vegetable. Pickling or canning salt should be used as other salts contain anti-caking materials that may make the brine cloudy. Use fresh whole spices for the best quality and flavour.

Pickled vegetable recipes are developed for pint or ½-pint canning jars. To insure a safe home canned product, water bath process for 5 minutes to 30 minutes as stated in the recipe.

Sauerkraut

A grilled bratwurst topped with sauerkraut, a summertime treat! Sauerkraut can easily be made at home with its basic ingredients cabbage and salt. To make good kraut, begin by selecting disease-free, firm, mature heads of cabbage and begin cleaning and shredding the cabbage within 24 to 48 hours of harvest.

A kraut cutter is the traditional way to shred the cabbage, but a modern- day food processor works well. Canning or pickling salt draws out the cabbage juice so it can ferment. Be sure to use a tested recipe when making sauerkraut as the proportion of salt to cabbage is key to quality kraut.

Using too little salt softens the cabbage and yields a product lacking flavour. Too much salt delays the natural fermentation process.

Sauerkraut tips:

- For every 5 pounds of shredded cabbage, mix in 3 tablespoons of canning salt.
- Select a food-grade plastic pail or an old-fashioned crock in good condition to hold the cabbage. Do not use a metal container.
- Cover the cabbage with a heavy plate, or a salt water brine-filled food grade plastic bag to exclude air.
- Store the container at 68° to 74°F while fermenting. The sauerkraut should be ready in 3 to 4 weeks.
- Sauerkraut may be canned and processed in a boiling water bath or frozen.

Half-gallon Jars

Half-gallon jars are hard to find but they are out there. The only home food preservation foods USDA and manufacturers recommend for half-gallon jars are grape juice or apple juice. Grape juice and apple juice are the only high acid juices safe for these large jars.

Currently, there is no research for safe processing times for other juices or products in half-gallon jars. The density of the product, water content and acid levels are the primary variables that affect safe processing times. At this time, it is not possible to determine a safe formula for other foods in large jars using the boiling water bath canner.

FRUIT PRESERVES

Fruit preserves are fruits, or vegetables, that have been prepared and canned or sealed air-tight for long term storage. The preparation of fruit preserves traditionally involves the use of pectin as a gelling agent, although sugar or honey may be used as well. The ingredients used and how they are prepared will determine the type of preserves; jams, jellies and marmalades are all examples of different styles of fruit preserves that vary based upon the ingredients used. There are various varieties of fruit preserves made globally, and they can be made from sweet or savory ingredients. In North America, the plural form preserves is used, while the singular preserve is used in British and Commonwealth English. Additionally, the name of the type of fruit preserves will also vary depending on the regional variant of English being used.

VARIATIONS

Chutney

A chutney is a pungent relish of Indian origin made of fruit, spices and herbs. Although originally intended to be eaten soon after production, modern chutneys are often made to be sold and so require a preservatives—often sugar and vinegar—to ensure it has a suitable shelf life. Mango chutney, for example, is mangoes reduced with sugar.

Confit

Confit, which is the past participle form of the French verb "confire" or "to preserve", is most often applied to preservation of meats, especially poultry and pork, by cooking them in their own fat or oils and allowing the fats to set. However, the term can also refer to fruit or vegetables which have been seasoned and cooked with honey or sugar until it has reached a jam-like consistency. Savory confits, such as ones made with garlic or tomatoes, may call for a savory oil such as virgin olive oil as the preserving agent.

Conserves

A conserve is a jam made of fruit stewed in sugar. Often the making of conserves can be trickier than making a standard jam, because the balance between cooking, or sometimes steeping in the hot sugar mixture for just enough time to allow the flavour to be extracted from the fruit, and sugar to penetrate the fruit, and cooking too long that fruit will break down and liquefy.

This process can also be achieved by spreading the dry sugar over raw fruit in layers, and leaving for several hours to steep into the fruit then just heating the resulting mixture only to bring to the setting point. As a result of this minimal cooking, some fruits are not particularly suitable for making into conserves, because they require cooking for longer periods to avoid issues such as tough skins. Currants and gooseberries, and a number of plums are among these fruits. Due to this shorter cooking period, not as much pectin will be released from the fruit, and as such, conserves will sometimes be slightly softer set than some jams. An alternate definition holds that conserves are preserves made from a mixture of fruits and/or vegetables. Conserves may also include dried fruit or nuts.

Fruit Butter

Fruit butter, in this context, refers to a process where the whole fruit is forced through a sieve or blended after the heating process:

- "Fruit butters are generally made from larger fruits, such as apples, plums, peaches or grapes. Cook until softened and run through a sieve to give a smooth consistency. After sieving, cook the pulp... add sugar and cook as rapidly as possible with constant stirring.... The finished product should mound up when dropped from a spoon, but should not cut like jelly. Neither should there be any free liquid."

Fruit Curd

Fruit curd is a dessert topping and spread usually made with lemon, lime, orange, or raspberry. The basic ingredients are beaten egg yolks, sugar, fruit juice and zest which are gently cooked together until thick and then allowed to cool, forming a soft, smooth, intensely flavoured spread. Some recipes also include egg whites and/or butter.

Fruit Spread

Fruit spread refers to a jam or preserve with no added sugar.

Jam

Jam contains both fruit juice and pieces of the fruit's flesh, however, some cookbooks define jam as cooked and gelled fruit purees. Properly, the term jam refers to a product made with whole fruit, cut into pieces or crushed. The fruit is heated with water and sugar to activate the pectin in the fruit. The mixture is then put into containers. The following extract from a US cookbook describes the process:

- "Jams are usually made from pulp and juice of one fruit, rather than a combination of several fruits. Berries and other small fruits are most frequently used, though larger fruits such as apricots, peaches, or plums cut into small pieces or crushed are also used for jams. Good jam has a soft even consistency without distinct pieces of fruit, a bright colour, a good fruit flavour and a semi-jellied texture that is easy to spread but has no free liquid."

Jelly

Jelly is a clear or translucent fruit spread made from sweetened fruit juice and set using naturally occurring pectin. Additional pectin may be added where the original fruit does not supply enough, for example with grapes. Jelly can be made from sweet, savory or hot ingredients. It is made by a process similar to that used for making jam, with the additional step of filtering out the fruit pulp after the initial heating. A muslin or stockinette "jelly bag" is traditionally used as a filter, suspended by string over a bowl to allow the straining to occur gently under gravity. It is important not to attempt to force the straining process, for example by squeezing the mass of fruit in the muslin, or the clarity of the resulting jelly will be compromised.

- "Good jelly is clear and sparkling and has a fresh flavour of the fruit from which it is made. It is tender enough to quiver when moved, but holds angles when cut.
- *Extracting Juice*: Pectin is best extracted from the fruit by heat, therefore cook the fruit until soft before straining to obtain the juice.... Pour cooked fruit into a jelly bag which has been wrung out of cold water. Hang up and let drain. When dripping has ceased the bag may be squeezed to remove remaining juice, but this may cause cloudy jelly."

Marmalade

British-style marmalade is a sweet preserve with a bitter tang made from fruit, sugar, water, and a gelling agent. American-style marmalade is sweet, not bitter. In English-speaking usage, "marmalade" almost always refers to a preserve derived from a citrus fruit, most commonly oranges, although onion marmalade is also used as an accompaniment to savoury dishes. The recipe water until soft; indeed marmalade is sometimes described as jam with fruit peel. Such marmalade is most often consumed on toasted bread for breakfast.

The favoured citrus fruit for marmalade production in the UK is the "Seville orange", *Citrus aurantium* var. aurantium, thus called because it was originally imported from Seville in Spain; it is higher in pectin than sweet oranges, and therefore gives a good set. Marmalade can also be made from lemons, limes, grapefruit, strawberries or a combination.

REGIONAL TERMINOLOGY

The term preserves is usually interchangeable with jam. Some cookbooks define preserves as cooked and gelled whole fruit which includes a significant portion of the fruit. The terms jam and jelly are used in different parts of the English-speaking world in different ways. In the United States, both jam and jelly are sometimes popularly referred to as "jelly", whereas in the United Kingdom, Canada, India and Australia, the two terms are more strictly differentiated. In Australia and South Africa, the term jam is more popularly used as a generic term for both jam and jelly. To further confuse the issue, the term jelly is also used in the

UK, South Africa, Australia, India and New Zealand to refer to a gelatin dessert, known in North America as jello, derived from the brand name Jell-O.

PRODUCTION

In general, jam is produced by taking mashed or chopped fruit or vegetable pulp and boiling it with sugar and water. The proportion of sugar and fruit varies just as to the type of fruit and its ripeness, but a rough starting point is equal weights of each. When the mixture reaches a temperature of 104°C, the acid and the pectin in the fruit react with the sugar, and the jam will set on cooling. However, most cooks work by trial and error, bringing the mixture to a "fast rolling boil", watching to see if the seething mass changes texture, and dropping small samples on a plate to see if they run or set. Commercially produced jams are usually produced using one of two methods. The first is the open pan method, which is essentially a larger scale version of the method a home jam maker would use. This gives a traditional flavour, with some caramelization of the sugars.

The second commercial process involves the use of a vacuum vessel, where the jam is placed under a vacuum, which has the effect of reducing its boiling temperature to anywhere between 65-80°C depending on the recipe and the end result desired. The lower boiling temperature enables the water to be driven off as it would be when using the traditional open pan method, but with the added benefit of retaining more of the volatile flavour compounds from the fruit, preventing caramelization of the sugars, and of course reducing the overall energy required to make the product. However, once the desired amount of water has been driven off, the jam still needs to be heated briefly to 95-100 °C to kill off any micro-organisms that may be present; the vacuum pan method does not kill them all.

During the commercial filling of the jam into jars, it is common to use a flame to sterilize the rim of the jar and the lid to destroy any yeasts and molds which may cause spoilage during storage. It is also common practice to inject steam into the head space at the top of the jar immediately prior to the fitting of the lid, in order to create a vacuum. Not only does this vacuum help prevent the growth of spoilage organisms, it also pulls down the tamper evident safety button when lids of this type are employed. How easily a jam sets depends on the pectin content of the fruit.

Some fruits, such as gooseberries, redcurrants, blackcurrants, most citrus fruits, apples, and raspberries, set very well; others, such as strawberries and ripe blackberries, often need to have pectin added. There are commercial pectin products on the market, and most industrially-produced jams use them. Home jam-makers sometimes rely on adding a pectin-rich fruit to a poor setter, for example apple to blackberries. Other tricks include extracting juice from lemons, redcurrants or gooseberries, or making a pectin stock with whole apples or just the cores and skins; once cooled, this "stock" can then be frozen for later use. Making jam at home is a popular handicraft activity, and many take part in this. Homemade jam may be made for personal consumption, or as part of a cottage industry.

SYRUPS FOR PRESERVING FRUITS

Fruits may be canned or frozen in water, juice or a sweet syrup. Adding syrup to canned or frozen fruit helps to retain its flavour, colour and shape. It does not prevent spoilage of these foods. The guidelines for preparing and using syrups offer a new "very light" syrup, which approximates the natural sugar content of many fruits. The sugar content in each of the five syrups is increased by about 10 per cent. Quantities of water and sugar to make enough syrup for a canner load of pints or quarts are provided for each syrup type.

TO MAKE SYRUP

- *Procedure:* Heat water and sugar together. Bring to a boil and pour over raw fruits in jars. For hot packs, bring water and sugar to boil, add fruit, reheat to boil and fill into jars immediately.
- *Other Sweeteners*: Light corn syrups or mild-flavoured honey may be used to replace up to half the table sugar called for in syrups. Commercial unsweetened apple juice, pineapple juice or white grape juice also makes good packing liquids for many fruits. They may be used as-is or diluted with water. Juice can also be extracted from the fruit that is being canned or from fresh apples, pineapples or grapes.

Saccharin-based sweeteners can turn bitter during processing. Aspartame-based sweeteners lose their sweetening power during processing.

Contact the manufacturer of the sweetener for information for preserving foods. The artificial sweeteners are not interchangeable between recipes. Each recipe must be developed and tested for that specific sweetener.

Table. Preparing and Using Syrups for Preserved Fruits.

		Measure of Water and Sugar				
Syrup Type	Aprrox. % Sugar	For 9-Pt.	Load[2] Type[2]	For 7 Qt.	Load	Fruits commonly packed in Syrup
		Cups Water	Cups Sugar	Cups Water	Cups Sugar	
Very	10	6½	3/4	10½	1¼	Approx. natural light sugar levels in most furits and adds the fewest calories
Light	20	5¾	1½	9	24	Very Sweet Fruit
Medium	30	5½	2½	84	20	Sweet apples, sweet cherries, barries and grapes
Heavy	40	5	3½	7½	5½	Tact Apples, apricots, sour cherries, pears and plums
Very	50	4½	4½	6½	9½	Very sour fruti.

Notes:

1 This amount is also adequate for a 4-quart load.

2 Many fruits that are typically packed in heavy syrup are excellent and tasteful products when packed in lighter syrups. It is recommended that lighter syrups be tried, since they contain fewer calories from added sugar.

FRUIT SYRUPS AND HONEYS

Juices from fresh or frozen blueberries, cherries, grapes, raspberries and strawberries are easily made into toppings for use on ice cream, pancakes and pastries. Fruit syrups are made by cooking fruit juice or pulp with sugar to the consistency of syrup.

BERRY SYRUP

- Ingredients:
  - 1¼ cups prepared blackberry, blueberry, raspberry or strawberry juice;
  - 1½ cups sugar;
  - ¼ cup corn syrup;
  - 1 tablespoon bottled lemon juice.
- *Yield:* About 2 half-pint jars.

- *To Prepare Juice:* Select table-ripe berries. Do not use underripe berries. Wash, cap and remove stems. Crush berries and heat to boil. Simmer 1 or 2 minutes until soft, stirring to prevent scorching. Do not overcook; excess boiling will destroy the pectin, flavour and colour.
- *To Extract Juice:* Pour everything into a damp jelly bag or four layers of cheesecloth, and suspend the bag to drain the juice. The clearest jelly or syrup comes from juice that has dripped through a jelly bag without pressing or squeezing.
- *To Make Syrup*: Sterilize canning jars. Combine ingredients in a saucepan. Bring to a rolling boil and boil one minute. Remove from heat and skim off foam. Pour into hot half-pint jars, leaving ¼-inch headspace. Wipe jar rims and adjust lids. Process 10 minutes in a boiling water bath.

GRAPE SYRUP

- Ingredients:
  - 1¼ cups grape purée
  - 1½ cups sugar
  - ¼ cup corn syrup
  - 1 tablespoon bottled lemon juice
- *Yield*: About 2 half-pint jars
- *To Prepare Purée:* Wash and stem ripe grapes. In a large saucepot heat grapes at a low heat setting for 8 to 10 minutes to loosen skins. DO NOT BOIL. Put through a food mill or wide mesh strainer. Discard skins and seeds.
- *To Make Syrup*: Sterilize canning jars. Combine ingredients in a saucepan. Bring to a rolling boil and boil about 1 minute. Remove from heat and skim off foam. Pour into hot half-pint jars, leaving ¼-inch headspace. Wipe jar rims. Adjust lids and process 5 minutes in a boiling water bath.

FRUIT HONEY RECIPES

This sweet fruit product has the consistency of honey, is flavourful and a good way to use all of the fruit being preserved.

GENERAL DIRECTIONS

Save all washed, sound pieces and peelings from fruit used for preserves, pickles, etc. Keep refrigerated until ready to use. Cover with water and slowly cook in a covered saucepan until soft. Then put in a cheesecloth bag and press to remove all juice. Drip the juice through a jelly bag and measure. Place in saucepan and heat. When it boils vigourously, add sugar at the rate of one- half as much sugar as juice. Boil rapidly until consistency of honey then pour into hot jars, leaving ¼-inch headspace. Wipe jar rims and adjust lids. Process 5 minutes in a boiling water bath.

STRAWBERRY HONEY

- 8 cups strawberry juice
- 4 cups sugar

Follow general directions above for making juice. Sterilize canning jars. Wash and cap strawberries. Crush and add 1 cup water to 1 quart berries. Cook slowly for 15 minutes; strain, measure and bring to boil. When it boils vigourously, add sugar. Boil rapidly until the consistency of honey. Pour into hot jars, leaving ¼-inch headspace. Wipe jar rims and adjust lids. Process 5 minutes in a boiling water bath.

PEACH HONEY

- 8 cups peach juice
- 4 cups sugar

Make juice according to general directions. Sterilize canning jars. Measure juice, bring to boil. When it boils vigourously, add sugar. Boil rapidly until the consistency of honey. Pour into hot jars, leaving ¼-inch headspace. Wipe jar rims and adjust lids. Process 5 minutes in a boiling water bath.

PEAR HONEY

- 8 cups pear juice
- 4 cups sugar
- Juice of 1 lemon

Make juice according to general directions. Sterilize canning jars. Measure juice, bring to boil. When it boils vigourously, add sugar and lemon juice. Boil rapidly until the consistency of honey. Pour into hot jars, leaving ¼-inch headspace. Wipe jar rims and adjust lids. Process 5 minutes in a boiling water bath.

BASICS OF JELLY MAKING

- Jellies are usually made by cooking fruit juice with sugar. Jelly should be clear or translucent and firm enough to hold its shape when turned out of the container.
- Conserves are jams made from a mixture of fruits, especially when they include citrus fruits, nuts, raisins or coconut.
- Preserves are made of small, whole fruits or uniform-size pieces of fruits in a clear, thick, slightly jellied syrup.
- Marmalades often contain citrus fruits and are soft fruit jellies containing small pieces of fruit or peel, evenly suspended in the transparent jelly.

COMMON INGREDIENTS

For proper texture, jellied fruit products require the correct combination of fruit, pectin, acid and sugar:

- *Fruit*: Fruit gives each spread its unique flavour and colour. It also supplies the water to dissolve the rest of the necessary ingredients and furnishes some or all of the pectin and acid. Good-quality, flavourful fruits make the best jellied products. Commercially canned or frozen fruit preserved in its own juice may be used to make jellied products, but pectin must be added. If you preserve your own fruit, use ¼ slightly under-ripe and ¾ fully ripe fruit. Preserve the fruit in its own juice and note how much sugar is added to allow for that in the jelly recipe.
- *Pectin:* Pectin is a substance in fruits that forms a gel if it is in the right combination with acid and sugar. All fruits contain some pectin, but some must be combined with fruits high in pectin or with commercial pectin products to obtain gels. Because fully ripened fruit has less pectin, one-fourth of the fruit used in making jellies without added pectin should be under-ripe. The use of commercial pectin simplifies the process, but jelly made without added pectin contains less sugar and tastes fruitier. Follow the manufacturer's directions for using commercial pectin and do not interchange liquid and powdered pectins.
- *Acid:* The proper level of acid is critical to gel formation. If there is too little acid, the gel will never set; if there is too much acid, the gel will lose liquid. For fruits low in acid, add lemon juice or other acid ingredients as directed. Commercial pectin products contain acids that help to ensure gelling.
- *Sugar:* Sugar serves as a preserving agent, contributes flavour and aids in gelling. Granulated white sugar is the usual type of sugar for jelly or jam. Corn syrup and honey may be used to replace part of the sugar in recipes, but too much will mask the fruit flavour and alter the gel structure. Use tested recipes for replacing sugar with honey and corn syrup. Do not try to reduce the amount of sugar in traditional recipes. Too little sugar prevents gelling and may allow yeast and mold growth. Tested recipes must be used to make jellies without added sugar, and these products usually must be stored in the refrigerator or freezer.

PECTIN AND ACID CONTENT OF COMMON FRUITS USED TO MAKE JELLY

- *Group I:* If not overripe, has enough natural pectin and acid for gel formation with only added sugar-Apples (sour), Blackberries (sour), Crabapples Cranberries, Currants, Gooseberries, Grapes (Eastern Concord), Lemons, Loganberries, Plums (not Italian), Quinces
- *Group II:* Low in natural acid or pectin and may need addition of either acid or pectin-Apples (ripe), Blackberries (ripe), Cherries (sour), Chokecherries, Elderberries, Grapefruit, Grape Juice, bottled (Eastern Concord), Grapes (California), Loquats, Oranges
- *Group III:* Always needs added acid, pectin or both-Apricots, Blueberries, Figs, Grapes (Western Concord), Guavas, Peaches, Pears, Plums (Italian), Raspberries, Strawberries

EQUIPMENT AND CONTAINERS

- A large 8-or 10-quart saucepan is recommended because jellies and jams have a tendency to boil over. A heavy metal is best because it allows even heat distribution.
- A jelly bag or suitable cloth is needed when extracting juice for jelly. Firm unbleached muslin or cotton flannel with the napped side turned in, or four thicknesses of closely woven cheesecloth may be used. Jelly bags or cloths should be damp when extracting the juice.
- A jelly, candy, or deep-fat thermometer can be used to determine doneness in jellied products without added pectin.
- A boiling water bath canner is necessary for processing all fruit spreads. A deep cooking pot with a rack may be used for a canner if it's deep enough for one or two inches of boiling water above the tops of jars. Be sure the pot has a close-fitting lid.

PREVENTING SPOILAGE OF JELLIES

Even though sugar helps preserve jellies and jams, molds can grow on the surface of these products. Research now indicates that the mold people usually scrape off the surface of jellies may not be as harmless as it seems. Mycotoxins have been found in some jars of jelly having surface mold growth. Mycotoxins are known to cause cancer in animals; their effects on humans are still being researched. Because of possible mold contamination, paraffin or wax seals are no longer recommended for any sweet spread, including jellies. All jellied products should be processed in a boiling water bath to prevent and close with a treated canning lid and screw band. Place on a rack in a canner filled with boiling water.

The water should cover the jars by at least one inch. Cover the canner. Bring the water back to a boil; boil gently for 5 minutes. Remove the jars to a protected surface and cool, away from drafts, undisturbed for 12 hours.

GENERAL PROCEDURES FOR MAKING JAMS, PRESERVES AND MARMALADES

- Use half-pint canning jars and pretreated lids.
- Check jars and lids. Discard any cracked or chipped jars and any lids with blemished sealing surfaces. Wash in hot, soapy water; rinse. Boil jars for 10 minutes to sterilize. Keep jars hot.
- Wash and rinse all fruits thoroughly before cooking. Do not soak. For best flavour, use fully ripe fruit when making jellied products with added pectin. For recipes without added pectin, use just-ripe fruit. Remove stems, skins and pits from fruit; cut into pieces and crush. For berries, remove stems and blossoms and crush. Seedy berries may be put through a sieve or food mill.
- Combine ingredients and cook in small batches, one recipe at a time, in a large, heavy, 8-to 10-quart saucepot.
- Stir fruit mixture over low heat until sugar dissolves. Then boil rapidly for a clear-finished product. As the fruit mixture begins to thicken, stir frequently to prevent sticking and scorching.
- If not adding pectin, test for doneness using one of the methods. For a softer product, shorten the cooking time; for a firmer product, lengthen it.
- If liquid or powdered pectin is used, follow manufacturer's directions. The method of combining ingredients varies with the form of pectin used. Pectin, acid and doneness tests are not necessary with added pectin. For a softer product, use ¼ to ½ cup more fruit or juice. For a firmer product, use ¼ to ½ cup less fruit or juice.
- Before filling jars, skim off foam that forms from the boiling process. The addition of ¼ teaspoon butter or margarine during cooking helps cut down on the foam formed.
- To fill the jars, pour hot fruit mixture into hot sterilized jars, leaving ¼-inch headspace.
- Process jams, preserves and conserves in a boiling water bath for the length of time specified in the recipe. If no processing instructions are given, process for 5 minutes in sterile jars. If jars have not been sterilized, the filled jars should be processed 10 minutes, but the added 5-minutes

processing time may cause weak gels, especially if using low-pectin fruits.

- Allow to cool undisturbed for 12 hours, then remove screw bands, carefully wipe the outside of the jar with a clean, damp cloth, and store in a dark, dry, cool place. The shorter the storage time, the better the product.

Altitude Adjustments

The processing times given for processing jellied fruit products are for altitudes of 0 to 1000 feet. Most areas in South Carolina will fall within these altitudes. Add 1 minute of processing and sterilizing time for each 1000 feet of additional altitude.

MAKING JELLIES WITHOUT ADDED PECTIN

To Extract Juice

Use only firm fruits naturally high in pectin. Select a mixture of about three-quarters ripe and one-quarter under-ripe fruit. Do not use commercially canned or frozen fruit juices; their pectin content is too low. Wash all fruits thoroughly before cooking. Crush soft fruits or berries; cut firmer fruits into small pieces.

Using the peels and cores adds pectin to the juice during cooking. Put fruit and water in a large saucepan and bring to a boil. Then simmer according to the times or until fruit is soft. Stir to prevent scorching. One pound of fruit should yield at least 1 cup of clear juice. When fruit is tender, strain through a colander, then strain through a double layer of cheesecloth or a jelly bag.

Allow juice to drip through, using a stand or colander to hold the bag. Pressing or squeezing the bag or cloth will result in cloudy jelly.

To Make Jelly

Use no more than 6 to 8 cups of extracted fruit juice at a time.

Double batches do not always gel properly:

- Measure juice and sugar. When a recipe is not available, try using ¾ cups sugar for each 1 cup of juice. Put juice into a large saucepan and bring to a boil.
- Add sugar to juice. Add lemon juice or citric acid if additional acid is required.
- Test for doneness.
- Remove jelly from heat; quickly skim off foam.
- Pour quickly into hot jars, leaving ¼-inch head space. Wipe jar rims, adjust lids and process in a boiling water bath for 5 minutes.

TESTING PECTIN IN THE JUICE

For jellies made without pectin, it is important to know whether there is enough natural pectin to form a gel. There are three ways of determining this.

Cooking Test

Measure S! cup of juice and ¼ cup of sugar into a small saucepan. Heat slowly, stirring constantly until all the sugar is dissolved. Bring the mixture to a boil and boil rapidly until it gives the sheeting test.

Pour the jelly into a clean, hot jelly glass or a small bowl and let it cool. If the cooled mixture is jelly-like, your fruit juice will gel.

Alcohol Test

Add 1 teaspoon of juice to 1 table-spoon of rubbing alcohol. To mix, gently stir or shake the mixture in a closed container so that all the juice comes in contact with the alcohol.

Do Not Taste—the mixture is poisonous. Fruit high in pectin will form a solid jelly-like mass that can be picked up with a fork. If the juice clumps into several small particles, there is not enough pectin for jelly.

Jelmeter Test

The jelmeter is a graduated glass tube that measures the rate at which fruit juices flow through the tube. It gives a rough estimate of the amount of pectin present in the juice and how much sugar should be used.

TESTING ACID IN THE JUICE

There is no home test to determine the amount of acid present. But you can do a simple taste test for tartness by mixing 1 teaspoon lemon juice, 3 table-spoons water and ½ teaspcon sugar. If your fruit juice does not taste as tart as this mixture, it is not tart enough. Add 1 tablespoon lemon juice or 1/8 teaspoon citric acid tc each cup of fruit juice.

DONENESS TEST

The biggest problem in making jelly without added pectin is to know when it is done. It is particularly important to remove the mixture from the heat before it is overcooked, as there is little that can be done to improve an overcooked mixture. Signs of overcooking are a change in colour of the mixture and a taste or odour of caramelized sugar. When cooking jelly remember that it should be boiled rapidly, not simmered.

Temperature Test

This is the most reliable of the doneness tests. First test the accuracy of the jelly or candy thermometer by placing it in boiling water to see if it measures

212 °F. Then place the thermometer in a vertical position into the boiling jelly mixture and read at eye level. The bulb of the thermometer must be completely covered with the jelly but must not touch the bottom of the saucepot. Use a jelly or candy thermometer and boil until mixture reaches 220 °F or 8 °F above the boiling point of water. Most areas in South Carolina would use 220 °F, but at altitudes between 1000 and 2000 feet, boil until the mixture reaches 218 °F.

Sheet or Spoon Test

Dip a cool metal spoon into the boiling jelly mixture. Raise the spoon about 12 inches above the pan. Turn the spoon so the liquid runs off the side. When the mixture first starts to boil, the drops will be light and syrupy. As the syrup continues to boil, the drops will become heavier and will drop off the spoon two at a time. The jelly is done when the syrup forms two drops that flow together and sheet or hang off the edge of the spoon.

Refrigerator/Freezer Test

Pour a small amount of boiling jelly on a plate, and put it in the freezing compartment of a refrigerator for a few minutes. If the mixture gels, it should be done. During the test, the rest of the jelly mixture should be removed from the heat.

JELLIES MADE WITH ADDED PECTIN

Jellies made from powdered or liquid pectin are prepared differently from those made without added pectin. Be sure to follow manufacturer's directions carefully. When commercial pectin is used, it is not necessary to test for pectin, acid or doneness. All-ripe fruit may be used for best flavour.

JELLIED PRODUCTS WITHOUT ADDED SUGAR

Jellied products can be made without adding sugar or by adding less sugar than in a regular recipe. This cannot be done by leaving the sugar out of the regular jelly recipes. Follow the directions on the modified pectin box or in a no-sugar recipe exactly. Alterations in the recipe could result in product failures. These products do not have sugar as their preservative and must be processed or stored as directed.

Some need longer processing in a boiling water bath and some need refrigeration:

- *Special Modified Pectins:* This is a quick, easy way to make lower sugar jellied products that can be stored on the pantry shelf until opened. These pectins are not the same as regular pectin. Look for packages that say "light," "less sugar" or "no sugar needed" in the label. Specific recipes and directions are listed on the package insert. Follow these carefully for the brand of pectin you are using.
- *Regular Pectin with Special Recipes*: These special recipes have been formulated so that no added sugar is needed. However, each package of regular pectin does contain some sugar. Artificial sweetener is often added.
- *Recipes Using Gelatin:* Some recipes use unflavoured gelatin as the thickener for the jelly or jam. Artificial sweetener is often added.
- *Long-Boil Methods*: Boiling fruit pulp for extended periods of time will make a product thicken and resemble a jam, preserve or fruit butter. Artificial sweetener may be added.

REMAKING RUNNY JELLY AND JAM

Remake a trial batch using 1 cup of jelly or jam first. Measure jelly or jam to be remade. Don't remake more than 8 cups at one time.

- *To Remake Cooked Jelly without Added Pectin:* If the fruit juice was not acid enough, add 1½ teaspoons lemon juice per cup jelly before boiling. Heat the jelly to boiling and boil until the jellying point is reached. Remove jelly from heat, skim, pour immediately into sterilized hot containers and seal and process for 5 minutes.
- *To Remake Cooked Jelly or Jam with Powdered Pectin*: For each cup of jelly or jam, measure 2 tablespoons sugar, 1 tablespoon water and 1½ teaspoons of powdered pectin. Mix the pectin and water and bring to a boil, stirring constantly. Add jelly or jam and sugar. Stir thoroughly. Bring to a full rolling boil over high heat, stirring constantly. Boil hard ½ minute. Remove from heat, quickly skim foam off jelly and fill hot, sterile jars, leaving ¼-inch headspace. Adjust new lids and process in a boiling water bath for at least 5 minutes or for time specified in the recipe.
- *To Remake Cooked Jelly or Jam with Liquid Pectin:* For each cup of jelly or jam, measure 3 tablespoons sugar, 1½ teaspoons lemon juice and 1½ teaspoons of liquid fruit pectin. Place jelly or jam in a

saucepan and bring to a boil, stirring constantly. Quickly add the sugar, lemon juice and pectin. Bring to a full rolling boil, stirring constantly. Boil hard for 1 minute. Remove from heat. Quickly skim off foam and fill hot, sterile jars, leaving ¼-inch headspace. Wipe jar rims. Adjust new lids and process in a boiling water bath for 5 minutes.

- *To Remake Uncooked Jelly or Jam with Liquid Pectin*: In a bowl, mix jelly or jam and for each 1 cup of jelly or jam add 3 tablespoons sugar and 1½ teaspoons lemon juice. Stir well until sugar is dissolved. Add 1½ teaspoons liquid pectin per cup of jelly or jam and stir until well blended. Pour into clean containers. Cover with tight lids. Let stand in refrigerator until set. Then store in refrigerator or freezer.
- *To Remake Uncooked Jelly or Jam with Powdered Pectin:* In a bowl, mix jelly or jam and 2 tablespoons sugar for each cup of jelly or jam. Stir well until dissolved. Measure 1 tablespoon water and 1 ½ teaspoons powdered pectin for each cup of jelly or jam. Place in small saucepan and place over low heat, stirring, until the powdered pectin is dissolved. Add to the sugar and fruit mixture and stir until thoroughly blended. Pour into clean containers. Cover with tight lids. Let stand in refrigerator until set. Then store in refrigerator or freezer.

FOOD PASTEURIZATION

PASTEURIZATION OF A APPLE JUICE

Pasteurization is partial sterilization of liquids such as milk, orange juice, wine, and beer, as well as cheese, to destroy disease-causing and other undesirable organisms. The process is named for the French scientist Louis Pasteur, who discovered in the 1860s that undesired fermentation could be prevented in wine and beer by heating it to 135°F (57°C) for a few minutes.

The most important method of preserving apple juice is pasteurization, which involves heating the juice to a given temperature for a length of time that will destroy all organisms that can develop, if juice is put hot into containers that are filled and hermetically sealed. Flash pasteurization is, true to its name, the rapid heating of juice to near the boiling point (greater than 88°C) for 25 to 30 seconds.

Steam or hot water passes the juice between plates or through narrow tubes that are heated. Design of the heat exchanger provides juice flow turbulence and even heating to prevent scorching and burn-on in the unit. There are numerous flash pasteurization heat exchangers available. They are all adaptable to a continuous operation set-up.

Juice can be canned or bottled in cans, glass or plastic. Cans used are enamel or lacquer lined to resist corrosion from the juice. As the cans travel the canning line, they must pass through a can washer, be filled from filling machines and immediately sealed on a can-closing machine.

After closure cans should be positioned or inverted so that the hot fill will be in contact with the lid and thus, pasteurize it. From here, the cans must be removed to a cooling room where they will be cooled to near 38°C to stop the effect of high heat on the contents. If cooled to a temperature lower than 35°C, the labels will tend to detach, the can will not dry and will be susceptible to surface rusting. This necessitates that the cans travel continuously from washing, to filling to cooling to labelling and packing.

Bottling juice requires specialized equipment. Cans can be roughly handled, but bottles are fragile ("bruising" not visible to the eye can cause breakage later) and susceptible to thermal shock. Temperature changes of greater than 7°C should be avoided.

Bottles must be cleaned before filling then heated (steam jets) within 7°C of the fill temperature. The best filler draws the liquid into the bottle by evacuating the bottle, thus reducing oxidation. Bottle closures can be screw caps, crown caps or vacuum caps. The vacuum caps have the advantage of allowing less headspace; if the contents ferment only the cap will blow off rather than the bottle exploding.

Bottles also must be cooled. This can be accomplished in a special cooler that sprays hot water on them and decreases the temperature as the bottles move along. At the end, they emerge close to 38°C, still warm enough to dry.

Newer packaging and processing systems use plastic containers that can be hot filled and rapidly cooled without the danger of thermal shock. In addition, aseptic processing greatly reduces heat-induced flavour changes. Still, glass bottles are the traditional standard and carry a quality image not implicit in cans, plastic bottles or aseptic packs.

Recent concerns about contaminated fresh cider have resulted in United States Federal Regulations that strongly discourage unpasteurized juice and advise pasteurization of all apple juice products, even at small roadside stands and country markets that prepare juice on site. The alternative is a not very appealing warning label on fresh apple juice.

Milk is pasteurized by heating it to about 145°F (63°C) for 30 min. or by the "flash" method of heating to 160°F (71°C) for 15 sec., followed by rapid cooling to below 50°F (10°C), at which temperature it is stored. The harmless lactic acid bacteria survive the process, but if the milk is not kept cold, they multiply rapidly and cause it to turn sour.

PASTEURISATION OF MILK

Science and technology is undoubtedly escalating its claws in every area of nature, and inventions are being made towards advancement of civilization. The world today is not the same as it was decades ago, credit goes to technology growth. Nature has given us myriads of gifts, and technology has made variations in them, apparently for our benefits. There is a big controversy in the West, whether pasteurisation of milk is beneficial or detrimental to human health. Proponents of the process argue that it is to make milk and milk products safe for consumption by razing away injurious bacteria, and to improve keeping quality of raw milk.

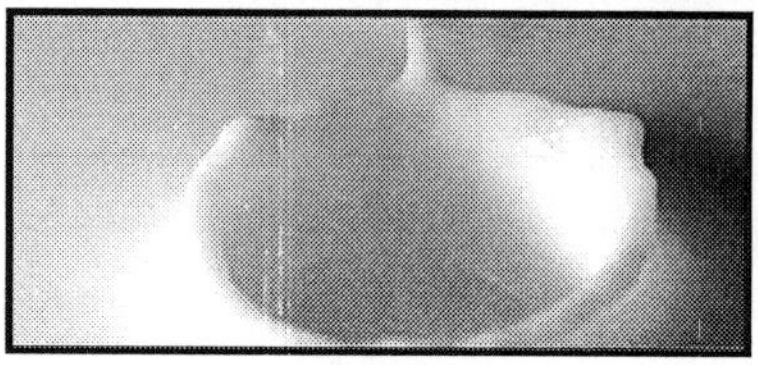

Fig. *Drop of Milk*

Let us briefly know what pasteurization is. It is an artificial process used to destroy dangerous bacteria without substantially changing the composition or flavour of milk. The method also prevents rapid souring of milk. Under this process milk is heated to a temperature between 55 and 70°C for 30 minutes, and then is rapidly cooled and stored at a temperature below 10°C. Sometimes higher temperatures are applied for a shorter period of time.

The temperatures and time are determined by factors necessary to destroy bacteria (pathogens). The process was named after the French chemist Louis Pasteur. Pasteurization has been used to kill bacteria in milk including *Salmonella, Listeria, Campylobacter, E.coli,* and *Bracella.*

The problem is that in addition to the killing of bad bacteria, pasteurization kills good bacteria too. However, researches have been conducted and have proved that pasteurization diminishes the nutritional value of raw milk that is requisite for human health. Some of the effects of pasteu-risation are: the process destroys the enzyme phosphate present in raw milk. Phosphate is required to split and assimilate mineral salts in foods that are in the form of Phytates.

Protein, a valuable nutrient in raw milk, is greatly affected by the process. Its digestibility is reduced by 4% and biological value is reduced by 17%. The effect of the process on vitamins, vital nutrients in raw milk, is that the pasteurization process destroys about 38% of vitamin B complex; and vitamin C is weakened or destroyed.

Studies show that infants who are fed with pasteurized milk might develop scurvy. Not only protein and vitamins, but also mineral contents in raw milk are badly ruined by the process. After the process the calcium content is very much diminished.

The loss of soluble calcium in regards to infant's growth and development is a very important factor. It is not only the concern in children regarding bone formation and teeth, but also in adults about the calcium content in the blood. It also destroys 20% per cent of iodine present in raw milk and causes constipation. After lot of research it is apparently clear that the process of pasteurization deteriorates quality of raw milk. Raw milk is in demand and is desirable by people who are becoming aware about the dangers of pasteurization to a product of daily consumption.

Despite such scientific evidence in favour of raw milk and against pasteurized milk, and the fact that human beings have always lived on raw milk without facing any serious threats to life, an intriguing fact is that sale of raw milk has been made illegal in the US except in a few states.

People can only get pasteurized milk or organic milk. Organic milk is the milk that comes from the cows that are raised on organic food, no growth hormones or antibiotics are used and cattle graze on grass which hasn't been sprayed with pesticides. However, organic milk is around two and a half times the price of pasteurized milk, which becomes difficult for everyone to afford. However, milk is such an important component in daily life, that despite so much of controversy about pasteurization and no good alternative for raw milk, people don't have choices but to have pasteurised milk in the US. The problem is not of the West anymore, but is rapidly transferring to countries like India too.

This is the issue created by technology and need to be raised in India before pasteurized milk becomes the choice of the Government of India. Pasteurization destroys most disease producing organisms and limits fermentation in milk, beer, and other liquids by partial or complete sterilization. Pasteurization does not destroy organisms that grow slowly or produce spores.

While pasteurization destroys many microorganisms in milk, improper handling after pasteurization can recontaminate milk. Many dairy farms use a home-pasteurizing machine to pasteurize small amounts of milk for personal use. Raw milk can also be pasteurized on the stovetop.

Microwaving raw milk is not an effective means of pasteurization because of uneven heat distribution. Ultra-high temperature (UHT) processing destroys organisms more effectively and the milk is essentially sterilized and can be stored at room temperature for up to 8 weeks without any change in flavour.

Milk, a natural liquid food, is one of our most nutritionally complete foods, adding high-quality protein, fat, milk sugar, essential minerals, and vitamins to our diet. However, milk contains bacteria that—when improperly handled— may create conditions where bacteria can multiply. Most of the bacteria in fresh milk from a healthy animal are either harmless or beneficial. But, rapid changes in the health of an animal, or the milk handler, or contaminants from polluted water, dirt, manure, vermin, air, cuts, and wounds can make raw milk potentially dangerous.

How do Microorganisms Enter the Milk Supply?

Our environment contains an abundance of micro-organisms that find their way to the hair, udder, and teats of dairy cows and can move up the teat canal. Some of these germs cause an inflammatory disease of the udder known as mastitis while others enter the milk without causing any disease symptoms in the animal.

In addition, organisms can enter the milk supply during the milking process when equipment used in milking, transporting, and storing the raw the potential to transmit pathogenic (disease-causing) organisms to humans.

The nutritional components that make milk and milk products an important part of the human diet also support the growth of the organisms. Drinking raw milk causes foodborne illness, and dairy producers selling or giving raw milk to friends and relatives are putting them at risk.

What are Common Pathogens in Milk?

Illnesses from contaminated milk and milk products have occurred worldwide since cows have been milked. In the 1900s it was discovered that milk can transmit tuberculosis, brucellosis, diphtheria, scarlet fever, and Q-fever (a mild disease characterized by high fever, chills, and muscular pains) to humans. Fortunately, the threat of these diseases and the incidence of outbreaks involving milk and milk products has been greatly reduced over the decades due to improved sanitary milk production practices and pasteurization.

Salmonella

Salmonellosis is the most common disease transmitted in raw milk. This organism is shed in the faces of cattle and picked up on the animals' hair or teats. Many strains of *Salmonella* can cause foodborne illness in humans, and all strains exhibit the same symptoms such as gastroenteritis (vomiting and diarrhoea).

Pasteurization destroys the *Salmonella* organism, and although pasteurized milk, powdered milk, and cheese have been implicated in salmonellosis outbreaks, in these cases, the pasteurized milk was contaminated during further processing.

Listeria Monocytogenes

This widespread organism is found principally in soil. Listeriosis in humans may cause serious illness, and is especially dangerous to pregnant women, causing stillbirths or infant death soon after birth. Pasteurization inactivates *Listeria monocytogenes.*

Yersinia Enterocolitica

This common organism has been found in many foods of animal origin including milk, cheese, and red. *Yersinia,* found in streams, lakes, and wells, spreads from the water to warm-blooded animals. The most common symptom of yersinosis is gastroenteritis and mimics the symptoms of appendicitis. *Yersinia enterocolitica* is destroyed by pasteurization.

Campylobacter Jejuni

This organism, isolated in raw milk and meat, can cause mastitis in dairy cattle. It has also been isolated in the faces of many species including dogs, cats, rodents, cattle, sheep, swine, and poultry. Symptoms include vomiting, cramps, bloody diarrhoea, mild enteritis, or severe enterocolitis. Individuals who have recovered from the disease may suffer a relapse. *Campylobacter jejuni* is destroyed by pasteurization.

Staphylococcus Aureus

It is a common cause of mastitis in dairy cattle and can enter the milk supply from sores on the teats of cows or from the hands and nasal discharges of dairy farmers and workers. The *Staphylococcus* organism produces an enterotoxin (toxins causing vomiting and diarrhea) in raw milk when it is held at temperatures above 50°F. Sufficient amounts of enterotoxin in foods can cause illness. The incidence of staphylococcal intoxication has been greatly reduced by pasteurization.

Escherichia Coli 0157: H7

Recent studies show that young dairy cattle are host to *E.coli* and fecal contamination is a likely source of *E.coli* in raw milk. It can cause hemorrhagic colitis and hemolytic uremic syndrome in humans. Milk should be stored at temperatures below 40°F to inhibit the growth of *Escherichia coli.*

Temperature abuse during holding and shipping can cause significant growth of the organism. Pasteurization destroys this organism. Pasteurization, named for Louis Pasteur who developed the process for other foods, is a moderate but exact heat treatment of milk. Pasteurization kills bacteria that produce disease and retards spoilage in milk.

What are the Requirements for Safe Handling of Milk?

The requirements for proper pasteurization and handling of milk are:

- A potable water supply and proper dispensing system must be available to avoid contamination. A pure hot and cold water supply for the animals' health, and for proper cleaning of the animals, milk handlers and utensils. Regular inspection and maintenance of the system is necessary.
- Clean and healthy animals, clean hands, and clean utensils are essential. The animals' hair should be clipped regularly around the flanks and udder to keep it from collecting dirt. Milkers should wash their hands and the udder with clean water or use an approved germicidal solution before milking. *Milk from diseased animals or those under antibiotic treatment may not be used.* All equipment and utensils should be cleaned immediately after use. Stainless steel utensils are preferred since they are durable and easy to clean.
- Rapid cooling, cold storage, proper pasteurization, and clean cold storage of pasteurized are necessary for the prevention of foodborne illness. Milk must be promptly cooled to 40°F (4°C) or less and stored in a closed container before and after pasteurization to maintain the quality and flavour of the milk. Care should be taken not to transfer barnyard dirt from the bottom or sides of the storage container to the countertop or to utensils in the pasteurization and storage areas. Do not mix fresh milk with previously cooked milk unless you plan to pasteurize the entire batch immediately.

How Do I Pasteurize Milk?

Milk must be heated, with agitation, in such a way that every particle of the milk, including the foam, receives a minimum heat treatment of 150°F (66°C) continuously for 30 minutes or 161°F (72°C) for 15 seconds. The temperature should be monitored with an accurate metal or protected glass thermometer.

Commercial operations commonly use a high temperature, short-time process in which the milk is heated to 170°F (77°C) for 15 seconds and then cooled immediately to below 40°F (4°C) to increase storage life without any noticeable flavour change in the milk. Pasteurization of fluid milk has very specific requirements for time and temperature as listed in the chart.

Table: Temperature-Time Requirements for Pasteurization of Fluid Milk

Temperature	*Time*
• 150°F (66°C) (vat pasteurization)	30 minutes
• 191°F (89°C)	1 second
• 212°F (100°C)	0.01 second

While pasteurization destroys many microorganisms in milk supplies, improper handling after pasteurization can recontaminate milk.

Home Pasteurization of Milk

Many dairy farms have a home-pasteurizing machine to pasteurize small amounts of milk for personal use. When they are operated according to manufacturers' directions, proper pasteurization will require little attention. A good compromise for home pasteurization is to heat the milk to 165°F (74°C) in a double boiler and to hold it at this temperature for 15 seconds while stirring constantly.

Then cool it immediately while stirring to 145°F (63°C) by setting the top of the double boiler in cold water. Add ice to the cooling water to cool the milk further, stirring occasionally until the temperature of the milk falls below 40°F (4°C). Store the cooled milk in clean, covered containers and keep it at a temperature below 40°F (4°C) until used.

This is the preferred method over the 30-minute/150°F (63°C) method because if at any time during the 30-minute period the temperature drops below 150°F (63°C), the milk must be reheated for 30 consecutive minutes.

Another method is using jars for 30 minutes in a waterbath canner, again, provided care is taken to maintain the temperature at 150°F (63°C), and the milk is promptly cooled to 40°F (4°C) or less.

All stirring devices, thermometers, or any other utensil that comes in contact with the milk must remain in the milk for the entire process—do not remove them at any time during the process—to prevent contamination. Many dairy farms have a home-pasteurizing machine to pasteurize small amounts of milk for personal use. When they are operated according to manufacturers' directions, proper pasteurization will require little attention.

Microwaving raw milk is not an effective means of pasteurization because of the oven's uneven heat. Proper pasteurization and handling will greatly increase the storage life of milk and will inactivate certain enzymes responsible for spoilage. However, pasteurized milk has not received sufficient heat treatment to improve baking qualities in recipes calling for scalded milk.

PASTEURIZATION OF JUICE

Juice makers have classically marketed juice in two extremely different forms—completely unpasteurized/"raw" juice and ultra-pasteurized/sterile juice. The makers of raw juice have recently come under scrutiny due to safety concerns and many feel they are going to have to change their production methods in order to maintain public trust. However, these makers do not wish to ultra-pasteurize their juice because of possible changes to the flavour.

There is another option. The method by which milk has been pasteurized for decades can be considered a "middle ground" between raw and ultra- pasteurized. The flavour of milk is affected by pasteurization much more strongly than fruit juices tend to be.

Therefore, methods had to be found which made the product safe, yet still palatable to the customer. This section attempts to describe this "middle ground" form of pasteurization and provide information on the equipment required.

The process of "pasteurization" envisioned by Louis Pasteur was aimed at the destruction of all bacteria, molds, spores, etc. Pasteur discovered that the destruction of bacteria can be performed by exposing them to a certain minimum temperature for a certain minimum time—the higher the temperature, the shorter the time required.

Most of Pasteur's early experiments involved using boiling water to maintain temperature. This process killed all bacteria. Eventually, lower temperatures for longer times were determined to have similar effects. Pasteur's experiments with milk eventually proved that heating to 145°F for 30 minutes destroyed 99.9% of the bacteria (known as a 3-log kill), which was enough to make a product safe.

Long after Pasteur, micro-biologists have been able to create a "curve" of different time/temperature combinations that will sufficiently reduce a given bacteria population. These curves are different for every organism.

Note: We use the phrase "100% kill" a few times in this chapter. There really is no such thing as a 100% kill of any micro-organism... ever. Some incredibly small population will always survive. When we say 100%, we really mean 99.999% or 99.9999% (5-log or 6-log) kill. A 5-log kill of pathogens is often considered the goal of any pasteurization process. Today, many of the products available for sale are "pasteurized" using Pasteur's information. This does not mean 100% of bacteria are gone—bacteria still exist in these products, but in very low concentrations. These products are refrigerated to keep the growth of the remaining bacteria very low.

They also have a predetermined shelf-life after which bacteria concentrations rise to unacceptable levels. This is the practice for milk in the US. The term "pasteurized" can therefore be used to refer to products with reduced bacteria. Products with no bacteria are referred to as "sterile" or "ultra- pasteurized".

The general term "pasteurization" used in the dairy and beverage business is sometimes mis-understood. Knowing that some bacteria still exist, many people think of it as the process of destroying all the bacteria "that can make you sick". This is not necessarily the only goal.

Pathogenic bacteria (those that make you sick) such as *E. coli, Lysteria, Salmonella,* and others are much more easily killed off than people may think. Making milk "safe" to drink requires much lower pasteurization temperatures than are used in the industry. There are other bacteria in milk that are not necessarily very harmful to humans, but produce the acids that sour the milk and make it undrinkable.

These bacteria are called lactophilic because they consume the lactose in milk and produce lactic acid. The time/temperature required to for a 3-log kill of these lactophilic bacteria conveniently results in a 100% kill of most of the pathogenic bacteria. Therefore, the process required to simply make a product safe may not be identical to those finally decided on for the product.

Some products are actually "sterilized" before they are sold to the public. Most of the fruit juice sold on store shelves is produced this way. These products have relatively unlimited shelf life without refrigeration. However, the time/temperature combination required to kill 100% of bacteria also over how much flavour degredation actually occurs and since this is solely a subjective opinion on the part of the consumer, no definitive data is available.

The current trend toward "natural" products has led some manufacturers to produce un-pasteurized products. These makers are relying on low bacterial counts in the raw juice and then refrigerating the product to retard growth.

Makers of "natural" juice products are currently stuck in the quandary described above—pasteurize and possibly give up some of the flavours that make their products unique or risk leaving unwanted bacteria in their product.

ACCEPTED METHODS OF PASTEURIZATION

The following methods of pasteurization are in common use across the country and are accepted by the US public health agencies.

- Product passes through the "hold tube". The length/volume of the hold tube is specifically designed so that the time required for the product to reach the end is 15 seconds or more. This is why the controlled flow rate is so important—if the flow rate is allowed to increase beyond the expected rate, then the product would spend less than the required 15 seconds in the hold tube.
- At the end of the hold tube, a sensor measures the temperature of the product. If the temperature is at or above the required temperature, then the product is considered pasteurized and is permitted to pass on further in the process. If the product is not up to temperature, then a divert valve returns the product to the balance tank.
- Pasteurized product is then sent through the "other" side of the regenerative heater. The heat from the pasteurized product is transferred to the incoming raw product. Efficiency of a regenerative system such as this can exceed 90% so that the exiting pasteurized product is only slightly warmer than the incoming raw product.
- In most situations, the product passes through a final heat exchanger which cools it to a final storage temperature (40°F or lower). The cooling media is typically chilled water (34°F) or food-grade glycol (28°F).

Public Health Controls

In order to ensure that the process of pasteurization occurs as expected, the government requires that certain public health controls be installed on all dairy product pasteurizers. Whether or not these controls will be required on juice system is still unknown:

- Controlled, sealable timing system.
- Sealable "Safety Thermal Limit Recorder" (STLR) to record temperature and divert under-temperature product.
- Certified mercury thermometer at end of hold tube for visual check of temperature or Digital Reference Thermometer accurate to 0.1°F with dual, 1000 ohm platinum sensors.
- Approved Flow Diversion Valves system with dual divert valves and return lines. Position sensors verify the position of the valves at all times.
- Regen system differential pressure switch.
- USDA Approved equipment for all pumps, valves, and other equipment.

Associated Costs

The question on everyone's mind is "How much is this going to cost?" The cost of a short-time pasteurizer can vary considerably with the required capacity.

However, some costs are extremely variable while others are relatively fixed. The table below classifies the required equipment:

Fixed Costs	Highly Variable Costs	Somewhat Variable Costs
Controllers/ Equipment	Heat Exchanger	Flow Diversion Instruments
Public Health Controls	Hold Tube	Balance Tank Timing System Valves Interconnecting Piping Mounting Skid (if used)

Fully Legal Systems vs "Heat Treat" Systems

A major question at the current time is whether or not the government is going to require full "dairy-type" controls on pasteurizers for apple and fruit juices. If fully legal controls are not required, the same functionality can be obtained via less expensive controls. In some cases, equipment can be used that is fully "sanitary", but not currently "approved" for use with milk. Since such a system has no formal definition, we are currently dubbing it a "Heat-Treat" system. The difference in price between a "dairy" type pasteurizer and a fully-functional, but non-approved heat-treat system could be quite substantial. At this time, we cannot predict if the regulatory agencies will permit the use of the word "pasteurized" on products pasteurized on non-approved system.

We are aware of apple cider producers who are using this designation on non-approved systems without any trouble from the inspection agencies. There appears to be no labelling law which directly dictates the use of the word "pasteurized", but it is recommended that anyone considering the use of a system such as this should check with their local authorities before making any decisions.

These prices are *estimates* only, but are in the "ballpark". As the prices demonstrate, the additional cost of "fully legal" controls become less significant as the size of the system increases. However, for smaller systems, the cost of the legal controls can increase the cost of the system substantially.

GPM	Fully Legal	Heat Treat
10	$45,000	$30,000
50	$90,000	$75,000
100	$110,000	$95,000

Some producers are already being pressured by their larger customers (especially large supermarket chains) to provide pasteurized product. If the likelihood of government regulations decreases, smaller producers may wish to reduce capital investment via the use of "heat treat" systems to satisfy their customer's immediate demands. They may risk, however, being forced to upgrade these systems at a later date. The answers to these questions will only be answered when the regulatory agencies finally decide whether or not to enforce dairy-style controls on juice bottling operations.

Juice Stabilization

Despite the many pathways to deterioration, there are a number of effective preservation methods that have evolved to combat spoilage. A principle tenet of food preservation is to maintain the quality and nutritional attributes while preventing spoilage.

In general, the fresher the juice, the higher the quality, so the standard of excellence is often freshly prepared, unprocessed juice. As indicated, this is a very transitory product having a limited shelf life of hours or days even under the best of circumstances.

Thermal Processing

The acid nature of most juices permits pasteurization, defined as the use of temperatures near 100°C to effect destruction of spoilage organisms. Although spores conceivably can survive at a pH less than 4.6, outgrowth is unlikely. In contrast, at a pH greater than 4.6, spore heat resistance dictates a process temperature of greater than 115°C for an extended time. Hence pH reduction by acid addition to turn low acid or marginal pH juices into high acid products is widely practiced.

A potentially effective process for fresh juice involves heating clean, well-sorted whole fruit for up to 1 minute at 80°C. This greatly reduces surface contamination without influencing the underlying flesh that, if juiced in a sanitary manner, has the sensory quality of fresh juice. A great deal of research is underway combining surface heat with other decontamination practices. Whether these treatments will qualify as producing "fresh" juice for labelling purposes remains to be seen.

Canning

Standard canning procedures specify filling cans or jars with hot juice (~70 to 80°C), sealing and processing at 100 to 105°C for up to 10 minutes and retort, since slow heating and cooling would ruin the quality.

Instead, a continuous rotary retort provides rapid heating and cooling as a result of the juice being stirred inside the can by the headspace bubble movement during rotation . Another rapid system is the spin cooker/cooler where the spinning action provides good internal and external surface contact.

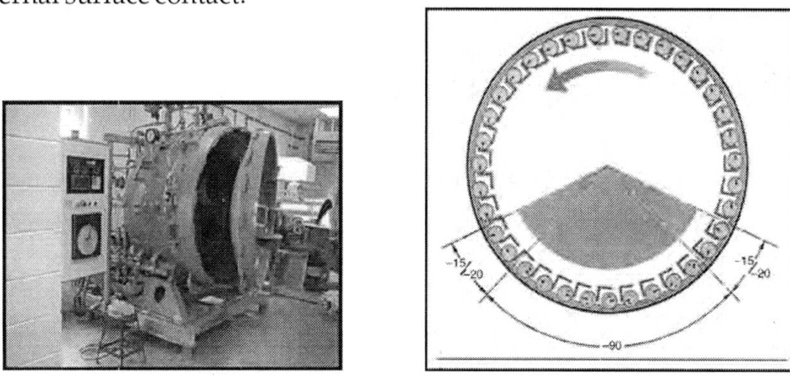

Fig. *Rotary Retort and Schematic ~2 to 5 rpm Rotation Provides in-container Mixing*

Hot Fill

It is fairly easy to hot fill pack juices by rapidly heating the juice in a heat exchanger and filling containers with the hot juice measuring around 95°C followed by sealing and inverting, thus pasteurizing the container.

Reasonably rapid cooling is accomplished by rotary or spin action. This is known as flash pasteurization and can be achieved almost instantaneously. However, once in a container, cooling cannot be as rapid. The major quality problem is scorching, due to holding the juice hot, either before or after filling.

Many types of heat exchangers are used. The simplest is a coil submerged in boiling water with the juice flow adjusted to the desired pasteurization temperature. For pulp-containing juices or those likely to leave a film on the heating surface, a swept surface unit can continuously heat a juice stream.

Fig. *Pilot Aseptic Line. Swept Surface Heat Exchanger on Right*

Fig. *Plate Heat Exchanger*

A plate heat exchanger with a regeneration section by which the cool entering product is preheated by the exiting hot product stream can be quite energy efficient, although the cooled stream must then be handled, filled and sealed in a sterile environment.

Hot fill has the additional advantages of driving air from the juice and ensuring a partial vacuum in the sealed container as vapour condenses upon cooling. Of course, deaeration and use of an inert gas during packaging are also useful.

Sanitation is quite critical, since there are acid resistant moulds such as B*ysochalmous fulva* and *Talarmyces flavus* with unusually high temperature tolerance that require temperatures close to 100°C for up to 60 seconds for adequate pasteurization. Such a process could be excessive for some delicate- flavoured juices, thus requiring either gentler processes or exceptionally sanitary preparation. These moulds are not too common, but once established in a processing facility, they are difficult to eliminate. ❒

Chapter - 5

Food Processing

This book is designed to give food technologists an understanding of the engineering principles involved in the processing of food products. They may not have to design process equipment in detail but they should understand how the equipment operates.

With an understanding of the basic principles of process engineering, they will be able to develop new food processes and modify existing ones. Food technologists must also be able to make the food process clearly understood by design engineers and by the suppliers of the equipment used.

Only a thorough understanding of the basic sciences applied in the food industry-chemistry, biology and engineering-can prepare the student for working in the complex food industry of today. This book discusses the basic engineering principles and shows how they are important in, and applicable to, every food industry and every food process.

For the food process engineering student, this book will serve as a useful introduction to more specialized studies.

METHOD OF STUDYING FOOD PROCESS ENGINEERING

As an introduction to food process engineering, this book describes the scientific principles on which food processing is based and gives some examples of the application of these principles in several food industries. After understanding some of the basic theory, students should study more detailed information about the individual industries and apply the basic principles to their processes.

For example, after studying heat transfer in this book, the student could seek information on heat transfer in the canning and freezing industries.

To supplement the relatively few books on food process engineering, other sources of information are used, for example:

- Specialist descriptions of particular food industries. These in general are written from a descriptive point of view and deal only briefly with engineering.
- Textbooks in chemical and biological process engineering. These are studies of processing operations but they seldom have any direct reference to food processing. However, the basic unit operations apply equally to all process industries, including the food industry.
- Engineering handbooks. These contain considerable data including some information on the properties of food materials.
- Periodicals. In these can often be found the most up-to-date information on specialized equipment and processes, and increased basic knowledge of the unit operations.

HIGH PRESSURE PROCESSING TECHNIQUE

High Pressure Processing (HPP) preserves a food's natural flavour, nutrients, and other sensory properties while extending the shelf life of foods through the inactivation of microorganisms. The uniform application of this non-thermal food processing technology also provides the food industry with new products and new product development opportunities that can fully exploit the functional properties of food ingredients such as hydrocolloids, proteins, etc.

Some of the successful food applications include dressings, sauces, salsas, packaged meats, seafood, cut fruit, purees, juices, chilled ready-to-serve desserts, soups, yogurt, neutraceuticals, pharmaceuticals and other food products. The many advantages of using high pressure processing (HPP) in food production have been known for over a century. However, the technology and equipment required to efficiently and reliability generate the extreme pressures (up to 600 MPa/87,000 psi) used in HPP have only recently become commerciably viable.

Food preservation using high pressure is a promising technique in food industry as it offers numerous opportunities for developing new foods with extended shelf life, high nutritional value and excellent organoleptic characteristics. High pressure is an alternative to thermal processing. The resistance of microorganisms to pressure varies considerably depending on the pressure range applied, temperature and treatment duration, and type of microorganism. Generally, Gram-positive bacteria are more resistant to pressure than Gram-negative bacteria, moulds and yeasts; the most resistant are bacterial spores. The nature of the food is also important, as it may contain substances which protect the microorganism from high pressure.

This chapter presents results of studies involving the effect of high pressure on survival of some pathogenic bacteria—*Listeria monocytogenes, Aeromonas hydrophila* and *Enterococcus hirae*—in artificially contaminated cooked ham, ripening hard cheese and fruit juices. The results indicate that in samples of investigated foods the number of these microorganisms decreased proportionally to the pressure used and the duration of treatment, and the effect of these two factors was statistically significant (level of probability, *P* d″ 0.001). *Enterococcus hirae* is much more resistant to high pressure treatment than *L. monocytogenes* and *A. hydrophila*. Mathematical methods were applied, for accurate prediction of the effects of high pressure on microorganisms.

The usefulness of high pressure treatment for inactivation of microorganisms and shelf life extention of meat products was also evaluated. The results obtained show that high pressure treatment extends the shelf life of cooked pork ham and raw smoked pork loin up to 8 weeks, ensuring good micro-biological and sensory quality of the products. Food products are an excellent environment for growth of pathogenic microorganisms, which may cause food-borne diseases.

Quality and shelflife of food products depend greatly on the properties of microorganisms contaminating the food. Despite the introduction of food standards obligatory in EU countries, epidemiologists believe that 75 per cent of food-borne diseases are caused by bacteria.

For this reason, the control of microorganisms is an important aspect of food quality and safety. Many methods of food preservation are used for ensuring microbiological safety, among which high pressure processing (HPP) seems a very promising technique for food industry, as it offers numerous opportunities for developing new shelf life stable foods with extended shelf- life, high nutritional value and excellent organoleptic characteristics— minimally processed but safe for consumers. High pressure is an alternative to thermal processing. The resistance of microorganisms to pressure varies considerably depending on the pressure range applied, temperature and treatment duration, and type of microorganism. As a result of technical progress and government support, the first high pressure processed food products appeared in Japan in the early 1990s.

In Europe, high pressure processing (HPP) of foods was rather at the stage of research or pilot production in the last decade. EU legislation included HPP foods in the "novel food" category. EC Novel Food regulation has introduced a statutory pre-market approval system for novel foods across the whole of the European Union. Recently, rapid progress of HPP toward commercial exploitation has been achieved, but still the process requires close collaboration between researchers, food and equipment manufacturers, as well as proper financial support. In Poland, research on the application of high pressure for food preservation was initiated in 1992 by the High Pressure Research Centre (now Institute of High Pressure Physics) of the Polish Academy of Sciences in collaboration with others Institutes.

The research programmes, sponsored by the State Committee for Scientific Research and by EU funds, were devoted to high pressure processing of fruit products, fruit and vegetable juices, milk and meat products. This chapter presents some of the results concerning the effect of high pressure on the survival of *Listeria monocytogenes, Aeromonas hydrophila* and *Enterococcus hirae* in artificially contaminated food products. This microorganisms could be a source of food-borne diseases.

NEED OF HIGH PRESSURE PROCESSING

High Pressure Processing (HPP) is a method of food processing wherein the food is subjected to elevated pressures (pressures up to 87,000 pounds per square inch or approximately 6000 atmospheres) with or without the addition of heat to achieve microbial inactivation or to alter the food attributes in order to achieve consumer-desired qualities. Pressure is effective in inactivating most of the vegetative bacteria at pressures above 400 MPa. HPP retains food quality, maintains natural freshness, and extends microbiological shelf life. HPP can be used to process both liquid and solid (water-containing) foods.

The process is also called as high hydrostatic pressure processing (HHP) and ultra high-pressure processing (UHP) in the literature. High pressure processing causes minimal changes in the fresh characteristics of foods by eliminating thermal degradation. Compared to thermal processing, HPP results in foods with fresher taste, better appearance, texture and nutrition. High pressure processing can be conducted at ambient or refrigerated temperatures, thereby eliminating thermally induced cooked off-flavours. The technology is especially beneficial for heat sensitive products.

FUNCTION OF HPP

Most processed foods today are heat processed to kill bacteria. Heat oftentimes diminishes the quality of a product. High pressure processing provides an alternative means of killing bacteria which can cause spoilage or food-borne disease without a loss of sensory quality or nutrients. In a typical HPP process, the product is packaged in a flexible container (pouch or plastic bottle) and is loaded into a high pressure chamber filled with a pressure transmitting (hydraulic) fluid.

The hydraulic fluid in the chamber is pressurized with a pump and this pressure is transmitted through the package into the food itself. Pressure is applied for a specific time, usually 3-5 minutes. The processed product is then removed and stored/distributed in the conventional manner. Because of the uniform manner in which the pressure is transmitted (in all directions simultaneously), food retains its shape, even at extreme pressures. And because no heat is needed, the sensory characteristics of the food are retained without compromising microbial safety.

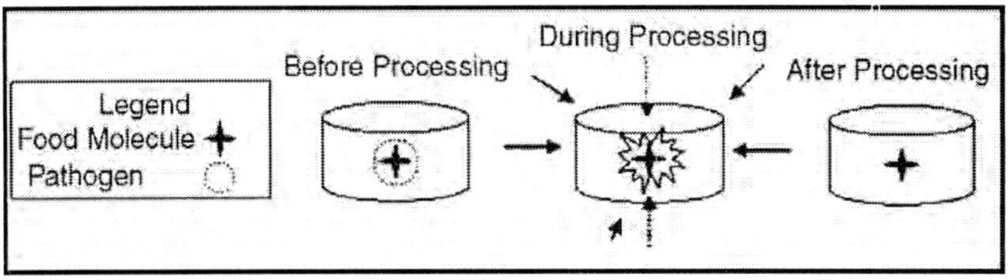

Fig. *High Pressure Processing utilizes ultra-high pressures to destroy pathogens without the application of heat that can damage the taste, texture, and nutritional value of the food*

HPP AT A GLANCE

- High Pressure Processing (HPP) is based on the Le Chatelier principle which states that actions that have a net volume increase will be retarded and actions that have a net volume decrease will be enhanced.
- HPP utilizes isostatic or hydrostatic pressure which is equal from every direction.
- During HPP, foods are subjected to pressures up to 100,000 psi. which destroy pathagenic microor-ganisms by interrupting their cellular functions.
- Within a living bacteria cell, many pressure sensitive processes such as protein function, enzyme action, and cellular membrane function are impacted by high pressure resulting in the inability of the bacteria to survive. Small macromolecules that are responsible for flavour, odour, and nutrition are typically not changed by pressure.

- HPP is gaining in popularity within the food industry because of its capacity to inactivate pathogenic microorganisms with minimal to no heat treatment, resulting in the almost complete retention of nutritional and sensory characteristics of fresh food without sacrificing shelf life.
- One of the unique advantages of HPP is that pressure transmission is instantaneous and uniform, is not controlled by product size and is effective throughout the entirety of the food item.
- As well, HPP offers several advantages over traditional thermal processing including: reduced process times; minimal heat damage problems; retention of freshness, flavour, texture, and colour; and no vitamin C loss.

Like any other processing method, HPP cannot be universally applied for processing all types of foods. At the moment, HPP is being used in the United States, Europe and Japan on a select variety of high value foods either to extend shelf life or to improve food safety. Some products that are being commercially produced using HPP are cooked ready-to-eat meats, avocado products (guacamole), tomato salsa, applesauce, orange juice and oysters.

HPP cannot yet be used to make shelf-stable versions of low-acid products such as vegetables, milk or soups because of the inability of this process to destroy spores. However, it can be used to extend the refrigerated shelf life of these products and to eliminate the risk of various food-borne pathogens such as *Escherichia coli, Salmonella* and *Listeria*. Acid foods are particularly good candidates for HPP technology.

Another limitation is that the food must contain water and not have internal air pockets. Food materials containing entrapped air such as strawberries or marshmallows would be crushed under high pressure treatment, and dry solids apart from caking do not have sufficient moisture to make HPP effective for microbial destruction.

During HPP processing, pressure is uniformly applied around and throughout the food product. For example, a grape placed between fingers can be easily squeezed and broken; this is because the pressure is not applied evenly from all sides simultaneously. On the other hand, if the same grape is squeezed from all sides simultaneously, it will not be crushed. This can be demonstrated by placing a grape inside soda bottle filled with water. By squeezing the bottle, you pressurize the water inside as well as the grape. Yet the grape is not damaged, no matter how hard you squeeze. In the same way, foods processed by high pressure will not be damaged by the applied pressure.

SHELF LIFE OF HPP PROCESSED PRODUCT

In general, HPP can provide shelf lives similar to thermal pasteurization. Pressure pasteurization kills vegetative bacteria and, unless the product is acidic, it requires refrigerated storage. For foods where thermal pasteurization is not an option (due to flavour, texture or colour changes) HPP can extend the shelf-life by 2-3 fold over a non-pasteurized counterpart, and improve food safety. As commercial products are developed, shelf life can be established based on microbiological and sensory testing.

High pressure processed products are commercially available in the United States, European and Japanese retail markets. Examples of high- pressure processed products commercially available in the US include fruit smoothies, guacamole, ready meals with meat and vegetables, oysters, ham, chicken strips, fruit juices, and salsa. Low acid shelf-stable products such as soups are not commercially available yet because of the limitations in killing spores with HPP. This is a topic of current research.

It has been generally known that high pressure has very little effect on low molecular weight compounds such as flavour compounds, vitamins and pigments compared to thermal processes. Accordingly, the quality of HPP pasteurized food is very similar to that of fresh food products and the quality degradation is influenced more by subsequent storage and distribution rather than the pressure treatment. Pressure also provides unique opportunity to create and control novel food textures in protein based foods.

In some cases, pressure can be used to form protein gels and increase viscosity without using heat. HPP products currently marketed worldwide are primarily distributed refrigerated. In some cases this is necessary for safety (to prevent the growth of spores in low acid foods). For acid foods, refrigeration is not a necessity for microbial stability, but is employed to preserve flavour quality for extended periods of time.

HIGH-PRESSURE FOOD PROCESSING OF RICE AND STARCH FOODS

The use of pressure (P) in addition to temperature (T) has been accepted in the field of food science and technology over the past 15 years, and research and development are now under way in the food industry, universities, and government institutes. Several commercial products are now on the market that are prepared using high-pressure techniques. This section describes the principle of high-pressure treatment and the effects of high pressure on foods, with emphasis on the high-pressure effects on starches. Finally, recent successes of the Echigo Seika Company in the application of high-pressure techniques to rice and rice products are discussed.

Principle and Method

High pressure means high hydrostatic pressure generated by the compression of water. A pressure of 100 MPa or higher (usually lower than 1,000 MPa) is used under temperatures below 100 °C. A unit of pressure is expressed in kg cm–2, bar, or pounds in–2, but now the international Pascal unit is commonly used. Therefore, 1,000 bar or 1,000 kg cm–2 almost equals 100 MPa. Food, which is contained in a plastic bag and sealed by carefully removing air, is placed in a pressure vessel filled with water and high pressure is then generated in the vessel by a pressure pump.

Pressurization of Food

An egg is not crushed by compression at 600 MPa, but the egg white and yolk are coagulated. The colour of egg yolk of a pressurized egg is naturally yellow, whereas a boiled egg changes to a faded yellow. The colour difference is attributed to changes associated with pressurization: pressure affects only noncovalent bonding and coagulates proteins without splitting covalent bonds, thus keeping the colour and smell intact. High pressure induces protein denaturation in the same way as high temperature. Meat protein is also denatured by pressure treatment at 400 MPa, preserving the properties of raw meats. An example of prawns or shrimp is interesting: although a boiled prawn turns red and the meat coagulates, the appearance of a pressurized prawn is the same as that of raw shrimp, but the meat coagulates after pressurization at 400 MPa for 10 min.

High pressure also has an effect on starches: a thick suspension of rice starch forms a ball by standing against its own weight after pressurization at 700 MPa, indicating that starches are gelatinized by the pressure treatment.

Versatile Utility of High Pressure

A high-pressure treatment generally coagulates protein, thereby inactivating the enzymes, gelatinizing the starches, and killing microorganisms. Thus, the use of high pressure promises to be a versatile process in food science and technology. Pressure produces a new texture in meats and starch-based foods, while keeping the original nutrients, flavour, and colour.

HIGH-PRESSURE EFFECTS ON PURE STARCHES

High-pressure-induced Gelatinization of Starch

Effect of Pressure on Amylase Digestibility of Starches. The starches of potato, maize, and wheat are gelatinized by pressure treatment at warm conditions of 45–50°C. The pressurization produces unique properties that are different from those of heat-gelatinization: heat-treatment destroys starch granules, resulting in a transparent solution, but a pressure-treatment swells the granules while maintaining the granular structure. Nevertheless, amylolytic enzymes such as α-, β-, and glc-amylases digest the pressurized starches well, being similar to the phenomenon in which the pressure-treatment of proteins increases protease digestibility. The pressure-induced gelatinization of starches exhibits a sigmoid curve, suggesting that a two-state transition is involved, as in heat-induced gelatinization.

Effect of Pressurization Time on Amylase Digestibility of Starches. To attain full amylase digestibility of starches, pressurization under warm conditions for 2 to 6 h is necessary. Interestingly, pressurization of starches for a longer time makes amylase digestion difficult: the amylase digestibility of starches decreased by 20–50 per cent after pressurization for 17 h compared with the maximum digestibility obtained after pressurization for 2 to 6 h.

These observations suggest that pressure induces gelatinization of starches, similar to heating, but prolonged pressurization produces a new stable structure of starches, which is not susceptible to attack by amylase. *Birefringence of Starches after Pressurization.* The birefringence of starches is lost as increasing pressure is applied. Wheat starch is sensitive to pressure and birefringence is lost at 200 MPa. In the pressurization of starches, the number of granules exhibiting complete birefringence decreases without increasing the incomplete birefringent granules. This loss of birefringence shows that the crystalline structure is destroyed by high pressure as well as by high temperature and that the high-pressure-induced gelatinization of starches follows a two-state transition without an intermediate state of destruction.

Physical Properties of Pressurized Starches

When a 50 per cent water suspension of starches is pressurized at 100 to 500 MPa and at 45°C for 1 h and air-dried, followed by analyses of their physical properties, the results are as follows. According to X-ray crystal analysis, the crystalline structure of potato, waxy maize, and maize starches decreases with an increase in pressure, although the crystalline structure of potato starch does not change up to 500 MPa. The decrease

shelf life. HPP can also more than double the shelf life of products using alternative preservation methods.

Fig. High Pressure Processed Foods.

High pressure processing is a science-based post-lethality intervention step for ready-to-eat meats. HPP is not merely a surface treatment, but effective throughout the product package, whatever its size or shape. This is especially important to those meat processors producing sliced deli meats, where the risk of re-contamination with harmful pathogens, particularly *Listeria monocytogenes*, may be greatest. The Food Safety and Inspection Service published its Interim Final Rule in June 2003, which directs meat processors to declare the food safety protocols they use to control *L. monocytogenes*: High-pressure processing (HPP) gives consumers safe packaged fruit and vegetable products with fresh, just-prepared characteristics without additives or preservatives.

The products add great consumer value by retaining the sensory qualities, texture, colour and nutritional content of the fresh-picked product with HPP, have almost unlimited opportunities to createexceptional value-added products. Many consumers were introduced to high-pressure processing with their first taste of all-natural refrigerated guacamole, soon followed by ripe avocado halves with up to 30-day shelf life. Avure's technology has expanded the universe of avocado products. This was only the beginning. Now, innovative food processors are merchandizing fresh, great-tasting products to supermarkets, club stores, food service distributors and major chain users. Salsa, pre-chopped onions, organic juices, flavourful fruit smoothies, colourful applesauce— these are just a few of the premium food items that only HPP makes possible.

High pressure processing inactivates *Salmonella, E. coli* and *Listeria monocytogenes* in fruit and vegetable products. Processors can use HPP in their HACCP programme to achieve the FDA requirement of 5-log reduction of pathogens in fresh juice. Consumers want foods that taste good and that are good for them. HPP makes this possibleby retaining more of the taste, texture and vitamins that consumers want in fruits and vegetable products. High-pressure processing (HPP) leaves juice not only safe, but also with a fresh, just-squeezed appearance and flavour, natural texture and nutrition, without any need for additives or preservatives. The extended refrigerated shelf life achieved by HPP increases distribution opportunities, reducesreturns and sensitivity to cool chain abuse, and allows more efficientproduction scheduling.

Fig. *Juice and Beverages*

A treatment at very high pressure, up to 600 MPa (87,000 psi) lasting less than a minute, results in the inactivation of spoilage organisms, including yeast and mould, and harmful pathogens, as well as the reduction of enzymatic activity. High pressure processing (HPP) gives manufacturers of ready-to- use wet salads and dips the tools to provide safer and more natural products with extended quality and shelf life. HPP offers natural, wholesome products without the need for heat or chemicals.

Fig. *Deli Salads.*

With the assistance of the high-pressure processing technology, some segments of the industry are also able to optimize organoleptical properties of their products because of the positive effects on food components such as hydrocolloids and proteins. The results are improved viscosity, mouth feel and the reduction of syneresis.

HYGIENE COOL MEASURES IN FOOD PROCESSING

Hygiene in food processing started with the introduction of general measures, including cleaning and disinfection, prevention of re-contamination and treatment of food products to kill any microbial pathogens present. Heat treatment was introduced into food processing even before the underlying causes of foodborne illness were known. It was Nicholas Appert in France and Peter Durand in England who introduced canning of food and the use of thermal processing around 1800.

However, neither Appert nor Durand understood why thermally processed foods did not spoil and remained safe to eat. Then, Louis Pasteur showed that certain bacteria were either associated with food spoilage or caused specific diseases. Based on Pasteur's findings, commercial heat treatment of wine was first used in 1867 to destroy any undesirable microorganisms, and the process was described as "pasteurization". This process was also recommended by Escherich to decontaminate milk.

In the course of time, it became clear that the effects of certain antimicrobial treatments were predictable. Two historical examples were the setting of performance criteria for destroying spores of *Clostridium botulinum* in low- acid, canned foods by Esty and Meyer and the process criteria for *Coxiëlla burnetii* in milk pasteurization, as determined by Enright *et al.* Further research resulted in predictions relating to many other processes, such as acidification, drying and the use of curing agents in meat products, on both pathogenic and spoilage organisms.

Such knowledge ushered in a new era in safe food production. This era is characterized by the division of hygiene measures into specific practices that are controllable and other general measures, the effects of which are largely unpredictable at present.

General Hygiene Practices

One of the first safety systems developed by the food industry was that involving the application of Good Manufacturing Practices (GMP), as a supplement to end-product testing. GMP covers all aspects of production, from starting materials, premises and equipment to the training of staff, and the WHO has established detailed guidelines.

GMP also provide a framework for hygienic food production, which is often referred to as Good Hygienic Practice (GHP). The establishment of GHP is the outcome of long practical experience and major components of the system are:

- *Design of Premises and Equipment*: This includes the location and layout of the premises to avoid hygiene hazards and facilitate safe food production. Food processing and handling equipment should always be designed with hygiene in mind, including ease of cleaning.
- *Control of the Production Process*: Control measures are applied throughout the supply chain and cover factors such as raw materials, packaging and process water, as well as the product itself. Key aspects include management and supervision of the process as a whole, as well as appropriate recording systems.
- *Plant Maintenance and Cleaning*: Both processing equipment and the fabric of the building should be maintained in good order. Suitable programmes need to be developed for plant cleaning and disinfection, and their effectiveness monitored routinely.

Systems are also needed for pest control and management of waste.

- *Personal Hygiene*: Staff are required to maintain high standards of personal hygiene in relation to wearing of protective clothing, hand washing and general behaviour. Visitors must also be strictly controlled in these respects. The health status of personnel should be monitored regularly and any illness or injuries recorded.
- *Transportation*: Requirements should be established for the use and maintenance of transport vehicles, including their cleaning and disinfection. Vehicle usage should be managed and supervised.
- *Product Information and Consumer Awareness*: It is important that the final product is suitably labelled and that the consumer is provided with all relevant information on product handling and storage, including a "use-by" date. Labelling should also indicate the batch and origin of the product, so that full traceability is possible.
- *Staff Training*: In relation to food hygiene and safety, all personnel should receive appropriate training and be made fully aware of their individual responsibilities. Such training should be repeated and updated as required.

The GHP concept is largely subjective and its benefits tend to be qualitative rather than quantitative. It has no direct relationship to the safety status of the product, but its application is considered to be a necessary preventive measure in producing safe food.

Those hygiene measures that have a predictable outcome and are subject to control can be incorporated in the Hazard Analysis Critical Control Point (HACCP) concept. This concept seeks, among other things, to avoid reliance on microbiological testing of the end-product as a means of controlling food safety. Such testing may fail to distinguish between safe and unsafe batches of food and is both time-consuming and relatively costly. However, effective application of the HACCP concept depends upon GHP being used.

SEPARATION IN FOOD PROCESSING

Biological raw materials are usually mixtures, and to prepare foodstuffs it may be necessary to separate some of the components of the mixtures. One method, by which this separation can be carried out, is by the introduction of a new phase to the system and allowing the components of the original raw material to distribute themselves between the phases.

For example, freshly dug vegetables have another phase, water, added to remove unwanted earth; a mixture of alcohol and water is heated to produce another phase, vapour, which is richer in alcohol than the mixture. By choosing the conditions, one phase is enriched whilst the other is depleted in some component or components.

The maximum separation is reached at the equilibrium distribution of the components, but in practice separation may fall short of this as equilibrium is not attained. The components are distributed between the phases in accordance with equilibrium distribution coefficients which give the relative concentrations in each phase when equilibrium has been reached. The two phases can then be separated by simple physical methods such as gravity settling.

This process of contact, redistribution, and separation gives the name contact equilibrium separations. Successive stages can be used to enhance the separation. An example is in the extraction of edible oil from soya beans. Beans containing oil are crushed, and then mixed with a solvent in which the oil, but not the other components of the beans, is soluble. Initially, the oil will be distributed between the beans and the solvent, but after efficient crushing and mixing the oil will be dissolved in the solvent. In the separation, some solvent and oil will be retained by the mass of beans; these will constitute one stream and the bulk of the solvent and oil the other. This process of contacting the two streams, of crushed beans and solvent, makes up one contact stage. To extract more oil from the beans, further contact stages can be provided by mixing the extracted beans with a fresh stream of solvent.

For economy and convenience, the solvent and oil stream from another extraction is often used instead of fresh solvent. So two streams, one containing beans and the other starting off as pure solvent, can move counter current to each other through a series of contact stages with progressive contacting followed by draining. In each stage of the process in which the streams come into contact, the material being transferred is distributed in equilibrium between the two streams. By removing the streams from the contact stage and contacting each with material of different composition, new equilibrium conditions are established and so separation can proceed.

In order to effect the desired separation of oil from beans, the process itself has introduced a further separation problem—the separation of the oil from the solvent. However, the solvent is chosen so that this subsequent separation is simple, for example, by distillation. In some cases, such as washing, further separation of dissolved material from wash water may not be necessary and one stream may be rejected as waste. In other cases, such as distillation, the two streams are generated from the mixture of original components by vapourization of part of the mixture.

The two features that are common to all equilibrium contact processes are the attainment of, or approach to, equilibrium and the provision of contact stages. Equilibrium is reached when a component is so distributed between the two streams that there is no tendency for its concentration in either stream to change. Attainment of equilibrium may take appreciable time, and only if this time is available will effective equilibrium be reached. The opportunity to reach equilibrium is provided in each stage, and so with one or more stages the concentration of the transferred component changes progressively from one stream to the other, providing the desired separation.

Some examples of contact equilibrium separation processes are:

- Gas absorption.
- Extraction and washing.
- Distillation.
- Crystallization.
- Membrane separations.

For the analysis of these processes, there are two major sets of quantitative relationships: the equilibrium conditions which determine how the components are distributed between the phases, and the material flow balances which follow the progression of the components stage by stage.

CONCENTRATIONS

The driving force, which produces equilibrium distributions, is considered to be proportional at any time to the difference between the actual concentration and equilibrium concentration of the component being separated. Thus, concentrations in contact equilibrium separation processes are linked with the general driving force concept.

Consider a case in which initially all of the molecules of some component *A* of a gas mixture are confined by a partition in one region of a system. The partition is then removed. Random movement among the gas molecules will, in time, distribute component *A* through the mixture. The greater the concentration of *A* in the partitioned region, the more rapidly will diffusion occur across the boundary once the partition is removed. The relative proportions of the components in a mixture or a solution are expressed in terms of the concentrations. Any convenient units may be used for concentration, such as $g\ g^{-1}$, $g\ kg^{-1}$, $mg\ g^{-1}$, percentages, parts per million, and so on.

Because the gas laws are based on numbers of molecules, it is often convenient to express concentrations in terms of the relative numbers of molecules of the components. The mole fraction of a component in a mixture is the proportion of the number of molecules of the component present to the total number of the molecules of all the components.

Gas/Liquid Equilibria

Molecules of the components in a liquid mixture or solution have a tendency to escape from the liquid surface into the gas above the solution. The escaping tendency sets up a pressure above the surface of the liquid owing to the resultant concentration of the escaped molecules. This pressure is called the vapour pressure of the liquid.

The magnitude of the vapour pressure depends upon the liquid composition and upon the temperature. For a solution or a mixture, the various components in the liquid each exert their own partial vapour pressures. When the liquid contains various components it has been found that, in many cases, the partial vapour pressure of any component is proportional to the mole fraction of that component in the liquid.

Solid/Liquid Equilibra

Liquids have a capacity to dissolve solids up to an extent, which is determined by the solubility of the particular solid material in that liquid. Solubility is a function of temperature and, in most cases, solubility increases with rising temperature. A solubility curve can be drawn to show this relationship, based on the equilibrium concentration in solution measured in convenient units, for example gkg^{-1}, as a function of temperature. Such a curve is illustrated in Fig. for sodium nitrite in water. There are some relatively rare systems in which solubility decreases with temperature, and they provide what is termed a reversed solubility curve. The equilibrium solution, which is ultimately reached between solute and solvent, is called a saturated solution, implying that no further solute can be taken into solution at that particular temperature.

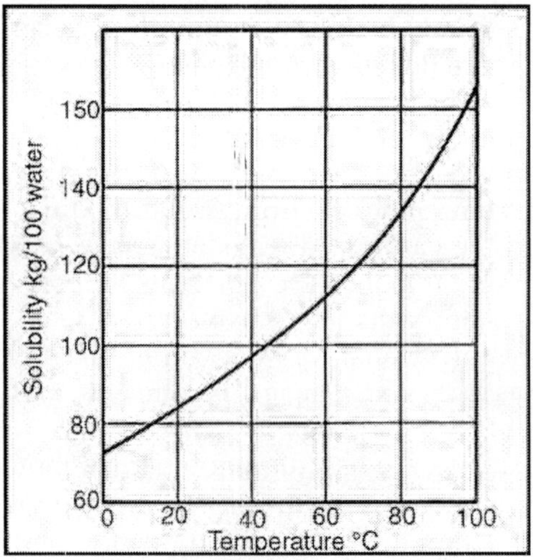

Fig. *Solubility of Sodium Nitrite in Water*

An unsaturated solution plus solid solute is not in equilibrium, as the solvent can dissolve more of the solid. When a saturated solution is heated, if it has a normal solubility curve the solution then has a capacity to take up further solute material, and so it becomes unsaturated. Conversely, when a saturated solution is cooled it becomes super saturated, and at equilibrium that solute which is in excess of the solubility level at the particular temperature will come out of solution, normally as crystals. However, this may not occur quickly and in the interim the solution is spoken of as super saturated and it is said to be in a metastable state.

EQUILIBRIUM-CONCENTRATION RELATIONSHIPS

A contact equilibrium-separation process is designed to reduce the concentration of a component in one phase, or flowing stream in a continuing process, and increase it in another. Conventionally, and just to distinguish one stream from another, one is called the overflow and the other the underflow. The terms referred originally to a system of two immiscible liquids, one lighter (the overflow) and the other heavier (the underflow) than the other, and between which the particular component was transferred. When there are several stages, the overflow and underflow streams then move off in opposite directions in a counter flow system.

Following standard chemical engineering nomenclature, the concentration of the component of interest in the lighter stream, that is the stream with the lower density, is denoted by y. For example, in a gas absorption system, the light stream would be the gas; in a distillation column, it would be the vapour stream; in a liquid-extraction system, it would be the liquid overflow. The concentration of the component in the heavier stream is denoted by x. Thus we have two streams; in one the concentration of the component is y and in the other, the heavier stream, it is x.

In the simple case of multistage oil extraction with a solvent, equilibrium is generally attained in each stage. The concentration of the oil is the same in the liquid solution spilling over or draining off in the overflow as it is in the liquid in the underflow containing the solids, so that in this case $y = x$ and the equilibrium/concentration diagram is a straight line. In gas absorption, such relationships as Henry's Law relate the concentration in the light gas phase to that in the heavy liquid phase and so enable the equilibrium diagram to be plotted.

In crystallization, the equilibrium concentration corresponds to the solubility of the solute at the particular temperature. Across a membrane there is some equilibrium distribution of the particular component of interest. If the concentration in one stream is known, the equilibrium diagram allows us to read off the corresponding concentration in the other stream if equilibrium has been attained.

The attainment of equilibrium takes time and this has to be taken into account when considering contact stages. The usual type of rate equation applies, in which the rate is given by the driving force divided by a resistance term. The driving force is the extent of the departure from equilibrium and generally is measured by concentration differences. Resistances have been classified in different ways but they are generally assumed to be concentrated at the phase boundary.

In many practical cases, allowance can be made for non-attained equilibrium by assuming an efficiency for each stage, in effect a percentage of equilibrium actually attained.

Gas Absorption

Gas absorption/desorption is a process in which a gaseous mixture is brought into contact with a liquid and during this contact a component is transferred between the gas stream and the liquid stream.

The gas may be bubbled through the liquid, or it may pass over streams of the liquid, arranged to provide a large surface through which the mass transfer can occur. The liquid film in this latter case can flow down the sides of columns or over packing, or it can cascade from one tray to another with the liquid falling and the gas rising in the counter flow.

The gas, or components of it, either dissolves in the liquid (absorption) or extracts a volatile component from the liquid (desorption). An example of the first type is found in hydrogenation of oils, in which the hydrogen gas is bubbled through the oil with which it reacts.

Generally, there is a catalyst present also to promote the reaction. The hydrogen is absorbed into the oil, reacting with the unsaturated bonds in the oil to harden it. Another example of gas absorption is in the carbonation of beverages. Carbon dioxide under pressure is dissolved in the liquid beverage, so that when the pressure is subsequently released on opening the container, effervescence occurs.

An example of desorption is found in the steam stripping of fats and oils in which steam is brought into contact with the liquid fat or oil, and undesired components of the fat or oil pass out with the steam.

This is used in the deodorizing of natural oils before blending them into food products such as margarine, and in the stripping of unwanted flavours from cream before it is made into butter. The equilibrium conditions arise from the balance of concentrations of the gas or the volatile flavour, between the gas and the liquid streams.

In the gas absorption process, sufficient time must be allowed for equilibrium to be attained so that the greatest possible transfer can occur and, also, opportunity must be provided for contacts between the streams to occur under favourable conditions.

Stage Equilibrium Gas Absorption

The performance of counter current stage contact gas absorption equipment can be calculated if the operating and equilibrium conditions are known. The liquid stream and the gas stream are brought into contact in each stage and it is assumed that sufficient time is allowed for equilibrium to be reached. In cases where sufficient time is not available for equilibration, the rate equations have to be introduced and this complicates the analysis.

However, in many cases of practical importance in the food industry, either the time is sufficient to reach equilibrium, or else the calculation can be carried out on the assumption that it is and a stage efficiency term, a fractional attainment of equilibrium, introduced to allow for the conditions actually attained. Appropriate efficiency values can sometimes be found from published information, or sought experimentally.

After the streams in a contact stage have come to equilibrium, they are separated and then pass in opposite directions to the adjacent stages. The separation of the gas and the liquid does not generally present great difficulty and some form of cyclone separator is often used.

In order to calculate the equipment performance, operating conditions must be known or found from the mass balances.

Very often the known factors are:

- Gas and liquid rates of flow.
- Inlet conditions of gas and liquid.
- One of the outlet conditions.
- Equilibrium relationships.

Gas Absorption Equipment

Gas absorption equipment is designed to achieve the greatest practicable interfacial area between the gas and the liquid streams, so that liquid sprays and gas-bubbling devices are often employed. In many cases, a vertical array of trays is so arranged that the liquid descends over a series of perforated trays, or flows down over ceramic packing that fills a tower.

For the hydrogenation of oils, absorption is followed by reaction of the hydrogen with the oil, and a nickel catalyst is used to speed up the reactions. Also, pressure is applied to increase gas concentrations and therefore speed up the reaction rates. Practical problems are concerned with arranging distribution of the catalyst, as well as of oil and hydrogen. Some designs spray oil and catalyst into hydrogen, others bubble hydrogen through a continuous oil phase in which catalyst particles are suspended. For the stripping of volatile flavours and taints in deodorizing equipment, the steam phase is in general the continuous one and the liquid is sprayed into this and then separated. In one design of cream deodorizing plant, cream is sprayed into an atmosphere of steam and the two streams then pass on to the next stages, or the steam may be condensed and fresh steam used in the next stage.

Extraction and Washing

It is often convenient to use a liquid in order to carry out a separation process. The liquid is thoroughly mixed with the solids or other liquid from which the component is to be removed and then the two streams are separated.

In the case of solids, the separation of the two streams is generally by simple gravity settling. Sometimes it is the solution in the introduced liquid that is the product required, such as in the extraction of coffee from coffee beans with water. In other cases, the washed solid may be the product as in the washing of butter. The term washing is generally used where an unwanted constituent is removed in a stream of water. Extraction is also an essential stage in the sugar industry when soluble sucrose is removed by water extraction from sugarcane or beet. Washing occurs so frequently as to need no specific examples. To separate liquid streams, the liquids must be immiscible, such as oil and water. Liquid-liquid extraction is the name used when both streams in the extraction are liquid. Examples of extraction are found in the edible oil industry in which oil is extracted from natural products such as peanuts, soya beans, rapeseeds, sunflower seeds and so on. Liquid- liquid extraction is used in the extraction of fatty acids.

Washing

Washing is almost identical to extraction, the main distinction being one of the emphasis in that in washing the inert material is the required product, and the solvent used is water which is cheap and readily available. Various washing situations are encountered and can be analysed. That to be considered is one in which a solid precipitate, the product, retains water which also contains residues of the mother liquor so that on drying without washing these residues will remain with the product.

The washing is designed to remove them, and examples are butter and casein and cheese washing in the dairy industry. Calculations on counter current washing can be carried out using the same methods as discussed under extraction, working from the operating and equilibrium conditions. In washing, fresh water is often used for each stage and the calculations for this are also straightforward.

Extraction and Washing Equipment

The first stage in an extraction process is generally mechanical grinding, in which the raw material is shredded, ground or pressed into suitably small pieces or flakes to give a large contact area for the extraction. In some instances, for example in sugarcane processing and in the extraction of vegetable oils, a substantial proportion of the desired products can be removed directly by expression at this stage and then the remaining solids are passed to the extraction plant. Fluid solvents are easy to pump and so overflows are often easier to handle than underflows and sometimes the solids may be left and solvent from successive stages brought to them.

This is the case in the conventional extraction battery. In this a number of tanks, each suitable both for mixing and for settling, are arranged in a row or a ring. The solids remain in the one mixer-settler and the solvent is moved progressively round the ring of tanks, the number, *n*, often being about 12. At any time, two of the tanks are out of operation, one being emptied and the other being filled.

In the remaining (n - 2), tanks extraction is proceeding with the extracting liquid solvent, usually water, being passed through the tanks in sequence, the "oldest" (most highly extracted) tank receiving the fresh liquid and the "youngest" (newly filled with fresh raw material) tank receiving the most concentrated liquid. After leaving this "youngest" tank, the concentrated liquid passes from the extraction battery to the next stage of the process. After a suitable interval, the connections are altered so that the tank which has just been filled becomes the new "youngest" tank.

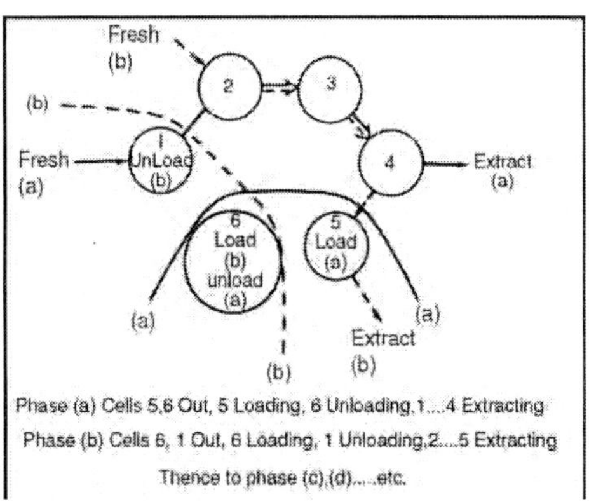

Fig. *Extraction Battery*

In the same way and for the same reasons as with counter flow heat exchangers, this counter current (or counter flow) extraction system provides the maximum mean driving force, the log mean concentration difference in this case, contrasting with the log mean temperature difference in the heat exchanger. This ensures that the equipment is used efficiently.

Washing is generally carried out in equipment that allows flushing of fresh water over the material to be washed. In some cases, the washing is carried out in a series of stages. Although water is cheap, in many cases very large quantities are used for washing so that attention paid to more efficient washing methods may well be worthwhile. Much mechanical ingenuity has been expended upon equipment for washing and many types of washers are described in the literature.

Crystallization

Crystallization is an example of a separation process in which mass is transferred from a liquid solution, whose composition is generally mixed, to a pure solid crystal. Soluble components are removed from solution by adjusting the conditions so that the solution becomes supersaturated and excess solute crystallizes out in a pure form. This is generally accomplished by lowering the temperature, or by concentration of the solution, in each case to form a supersaturated solution from which crystallization can occur. The equilibrium is established between the crystals and the surrounding solution, the mother liquor.

The manufacture of sucrose, from sugarcane or sugar beet, is an important example of crystallization in food technology. Crystallization is also used in the manufacture of other sugars, such as glucose and lactose, in the manufacture of food additives, such as salt, and in the processing of foodstuffs, such as ice cream. In the manufacture of sucrose from cane, water is added and the sugar is pressed out from the residual cane as a solution. This solution is purified and then concentrated to allow the sucrose to crystallize out from the solution.

Crystallization Equilibrium

Once crystallization is concluded, equilibrium is set up between the crystals of pure solute and the residual mother liquor, the balance being determined by the solubility (concentration) and the temperature. The driving force making the crystals grow is the concentration excess (supersaturation) of the solution above the equilibrium (saturation) level. The resistances to growth are the resistance to mass transfer within the solution and the energy needed at the crystal surface for incoming molecules to orient themselves to the crystal lattice.

❒

Index

I

L

M

N

O

P

R

S

T

V

Y

❑❑❑